THE CHILD CARE ACTS

2nd edition

AUSTRALIA
Law Book Co.
Sydney

CANADA and USA
Carswell
Toronto

HONG KONG
Sweet & Maxwell Asia

NEW ZEALAND
Brookers
Wellington

SINGAPORE and MALAYSIA
Sweet & Maxwell Asia
Singapore and Kuala Lumpur

THE CHILD CARE ACTS

2nd edition

Paul Ward

B.C.L. (N.U.I.), LL.M. (Lond.), BL

THOMSON ROUND HALL
2005

Published in 2005 by
Round Hall Ltd
43 Fitzwilliam Place
Dublin 2
Ireland

Typeset by
Gough Typesetting Services,
Dublin

Printed by
MPG Books, Cornwall

ISBN 1-85800–288–5

A catalogue record for this book
is available from the British Library

For Esmé, Theo and Phoebe

Contents

Contents

Foreword

For over 80 years, the Children's Act 1908 was the governing legislation concerning the welfare of children in this State. It was not until the enactment of the Child Care Act 1991 that the repeal of the 1908 Act was brought about. Indeed, the 1991 Act itself took no less than eight years between its initiation and ultimate implementation. These facts speak for themselves and require no comment from me as to where children's welfare has figured in the State's order of priorities.

Although the 1991 Act represented a significant improvement in child protection legislation, it was sadly deficient in a number of respects. Whilst it imposed a duty on Health Boards to promote the welfare of children in their areas who were not receiving adequate care and protection, it provided little by way of powers, and less by the way of resources, to enable them to do so. In particular, it made no provision in respect of secure placements for disturbed children in need of such care. That legislative void fell to be filled, in part at least, by the High Court, in reliance upon its inherent jurisdiction to protect the welfare of children.

The recognition of such a jurisdiction by the High Court (and its affirmation by the Supreme Court) gave rise throughout the latter part of the 1990s to many cases brought before that court in an effort to seek appropriate accommodation for such children. Some of these cases were initiated by Health Boards, but many were brought at the instance of parents of such children or at the suggestion of District Court judges who found themselves utterly frustrated at their inability to take any effective action to protect such children.

Unhappy and tragic personal histories were unfolded to the High Court on an almost daily basis during that time. Many of the children involved required to be placed in secure therapeutic accommodation but none was available for them. The executive branch of Government formulated policies to address these accommodation difficulties. They involved the building or refurbishment of premises and the provision of appropriate backup services. Over time it became clear that the Executive was not implementing these policies within the timescales it had set itself. Ultimately, the High Court was asked to intervene and did so. As a result of orders made by that court, appropriate facilities to cater for children within the greater Dublin area were both built and put into operation. A similar application was made later on to deal with the situation outside the capital. The same type of order was made but on this occasion was appealed to the Supreme Court. By a majority decision, the Supreme Court discharged the order, but by then the premises were so far advanced in construction that they were ultimately completed.

That decision of the Supreme Court, together with one given a few months previously, raised major questions as to the justicability of socio-economic rights and the effective remedies, if any, available in respect of their breach. Questions of this type have of course created much jurisprudence in other constitutional democracies throughout the world. It is not within the compass of this work, still less this foreword, to analyse or comment further on these issues. No doubt they will be played out again before the courts in due course. Suffice it to say that the approach of the Irish Supreme Court to the issues is in marked contrast to a more vibrant attitude adopted by its equivalent in many other countries.

The lacunae in the 1991 Act were addressed significantly in the Children Act of 2001. This Act empowers courts to order the secure detention of children who need special care and attention. Mercifully, therefore, there is no longer any necessity to reply upon any inherent jurisdiction in the court. It remains to be seen, however, whether appropriate facilities will be available to accommodate children who are the subject of such an order.

This book is in its second edition. The first was published in 1997, shortly after the provisions of the 1991 Act had been brought into effect. Since then a good deal of jurisprudence has developed on the 1991 Act, and the 2001 Act has of course brought about very substantial amendments by the insertion of a number of new parts into it. The author is to be congratulated for once again providing a comprehensive commentary on the legislation through a section-by-section analysis of it.

The present work is every bit as useful to practitioners and academics alike as its predecessor was. The gratitude of the legal profession and the judiciary is due to Mr. Ward for his endeavours, which have resulted in this very worthwhile publication.

Judge Peter Kelly,
The High Court,
July, 2005

Preface

The first edition of this short text was published in 1997. It attempted to analyse the operation and interpretation of the 1991 Act by reference to much of the then relevant and available case law from this and our neighbouring jurisdiction across the Irish Sea. A cursory glance through the text on the more important sections of the Act evidences significant developments in child care law since the first edition. The Act survived a constitutional challenge in *A and B v Eastern Health Board* [1998] 1 I.R. 464, was the subject of extensive analysis and interpretation by Barr J. in *MQ v Gleeson* [1998] 4 I.R. 85, curtailed in its usage in *North Western Health Board v H.W. and C.W.*, [2001] 3 I.R. 622 and, one might say, generously interpreted in *Western Health Board v K.M.* [2002] 2 I.R. 493. Other decisions have clarified the respective roles and authority of the courts and health boards in such cases as *Eastern Health Board v McDonnell* [1999] 1 I.R. 174. In addition, the deficiencies in the 1991 Act were highlighted in *DG v Ireland* (2002) 35 E.H.R.R. 33. These domestic judicial interpretations aside, there have been significant legislative developments with the enactment of the Children Act 2001 and the provision now for special care orders.

Another important legislative development are provisions relating to the giving of evidence by children and the rules relating to the admission of hearsay evidence in the Children Act 1997. I have identified a number of important English decisions on evidential issues in care proceedings. There have also been extensive ministerial regulations introduced on foot of the introduction of the Children Act 2001.

An attempt has been made to trawl other common law jurisdictions for relevant case on the interpretation and operation of similar legislation. In particular, our neighbouring jurisdiction of England and Wales has been relatively bountiful in producing case law on various child care law issues and their resolution. I also encountered some helpful decisions from other common law jurisdictions. By far the most revealing research arose from an examination of the ECHR case law on child care proceedings. With the implementation of the European Convention on Human Rights Act 2003 now complete, this case law signifies that the decision making process involved in care proceedings will be carefully scrutinised for a breach of the European Convention on Human Rights and Fundamental Freedoms. Since the submission of the manuscript, the Health Act 2004 has been introduced, which dissolves the Eastern Region Health Authority, the area health boards in the Eastern Region and the health boards. The functions formerly carried out by the health boards are now vested in the "Health Service Executive" or the "Executive". Every effort has been made to amend the text accordingly, but

any reference in the text to a "health board" should read the "Health Service
Executive" or "Executive".

The production of this second edition has been slow, indeed very slow.
First up, Round Hall Thompson must be thanked for their patience. So too
my wife, Niamh, who has endured the progress of this writing, and special
mention is due to little Phoebe, whose arrival before Christmas provided the
necessary spur to complete the task. A final mention is owed Judge Peter
Kelly to whom I am obliged for his thoughts on this work, and indeed who is
largely responsible for the major legislative changes in child care law.

The law in this area is stated as of March 2005, and the usual responsibility
for errors and mistakes lies with the author.

Paul Ward
Faculty of Law
University College Dublin

Table of Cases

IRELAND

UK

EUROPEAN CASES

OTHER

Table of Legislation

STATUTES—ENGLAND

CONVENTIONS

STATUTORY INSTRUMENTS

RULES

CHILD CARE ACT 1991

(No. 17 of 1991)

ARRANGEMENT OF SECTIONS

PART I

PRELIMINARY

SECT.
1. Short title and commencement.
2. Interpretation.

PART II

PROMOTION OF WELFARE OF CHILDREN

3. Functions of [Health Service Executive].
4. Voluntary care.
5. Accommodation for homeless children.
6. Provision of adoption service.
7. Child care advisory committees.
8. Review of services.
9. Provision of services by voluntary bodies and other persons.
10. Assistance for voluntary bodies and other persons.
11. Research.

PART III

PROTECTION OF CHILDREN IN EMERGENCIES

12. Power of Garda Síochána to take a child to safety.
13. Emergency care order.
14. Notification to be given by [Health Service Executive].
15. Provision of accommodation for purposes of *Part III*.

PART IV

CARE PROCEEDINGS

16. Duty of [Health Service Executive] to institute proceedings.
17. Interim care order.
18. Care order.
19. Supervision order.
20. Proceedings under Guardianship of Infants Act, 1964, Judicial Separation and Family Law Reform Act, 1989, etc.
21. Effect of appeal from orders.
22. Variation or discharge of orders etc.
23. Powers of court in case of invalidity of orders.

PART VI

CHILDREN IN THE CARE OF HEALTH BOARDS

PART VII

SUPERVISION OF PRE-SCHOOL SERVICES

PART VIII

CHILDREN'S RESIDENTIAL CENTRES

PART I X

ADMINISTRATION

70. Charges for certain services.
71. Prosecution of offences.
72. Functions of chief executive officer.
73. Expenses.

PART X

MISCELLANEOUS AND SUPPLEMENTARY

74. Sale etc. of solvents.
75. Amendment of section 17 of the School Attendance Act, 1926.
76. Amendment of section 15 of the Guardianship of Infants Act, 1964.
77. Amendment of section 16 of the Guardianship of Infants Act, 1964.
78. Maintenance—saver in relation to members of Defence Forces.
79. Repeals.

SCHEDULE

ENACTMENTS REPEALED

An Act to provide for the Care and Protection of Children and for related matters.   [10*th July*, 1991]

INTRODUCTION AND GENERAL NOTE

The Child Care Act 1991 ("the 1991 Act") took some eight years to initiate, pass and implement. The remaining provisions of the Act were brought into effect on December 18, 1996. The 1991 Act replaced a piece of legislation over 80 years in existence, the Children Act 1908. The 1991 Act has been amended significantly by the Children Act 2001 which empowers the courts to order the secure detention of children who are in need of special care and attention. Section 16 of the Children Act 2001 inserts new Pts IVA and IVB after s.23 of the 1991 Act. Section 77 of the 2001 Act confers an important power on a court before which a child charged with an offence appears. The court may adjourn and indeed dismiss such a charge and direct the Health Board to investigate the child's welfare needs by convening a family welfare conference. The outcome of such a direction can result in a supervision, care or special care order. This provision appears to reverse the decision in *DPP (Murphy) v PT* [1999] 3 I.R. 254, [1998] 1 I.L.R.M. 344 which held that where a child was the subject of fit person order and was also before the court charged with offences, the court had no jurisdiction to postpone the hearing of the criminal charges while an investigation was directed to be conducted by the Health Service Executive into the child's circumstances. Section 267 of the 2001 Act now provides that the maximum duration for an interim care order under s.17(2) is 28 days. The other significant legislative effect in relation to the 1991 Act is the introduction of the Children Act 1997, Pt III of which clarifies the law on evidence in proceedings relating to children. The significance of the 1997 and 2001 Acts are discussed in the context in which they arise.

There have been important High and Supreme Court decisions on the interpretation of the 1991 Act, such as *A and B v Eastern Health Board* [1998] 1 I.R. 464, *MQ v Gleeson* [1998] 4 I.R. 85, *Eastern Health Board v McDonnell* [1999] 1 I.R. 174, *Western Health Board v KM* [2002] 2 I.R. 493, *North Western Health Board v HW and CW* [2001] 3 I.R. 622 and *East Coast Area Health Board v M(M) v P(M)*, unreported, High

Court, February 5, 2002. There have been also a number of significant child care decisions in England from both the House of Lords and Court of Appeal since 1997 and further afield in the European Court of Human Rights in recent years, particularly that of *DG v Ireland* (2002) 35 E.H.R.R. 33 relating to the secure detention of minors. The relevance of these decisions is noted in the appropriate context in which they arise.

The constitutionality of the 1991 Act was challenged in *A and B v Eastern Health Board* [1998] 1 I.R. 464 (the 'C' case). Geoghegan J. upheld the validity of the 1991 Act in rejecting the contention that it was constitutionally impermissible for the District Court under s.17(4) to give a direction that the child 'C' undergo a termination of pregnancy. Geoghegan J. was satisfied that a termination of pregnancy was, in the circumstances of the case, a medical procedure constituting both medical and psychiatric treatment for the purposes of s.13(7)(*a*)(iii). By contrast, however, Hardiman J. in *North Western Health Board v HW* [2001] 3 I.R. 622, at 744 noted that it would be inappropriate to utilise an interim care order and direct a child undergo a P.K.U. test against the wishes of the parents where there are no grounds for seeking a care order under the 1991 Act. To use the 1991 Act in this fashion could call into question its constitutionality validity.

The main purpose of the Act is to provide a means by which the welfare and protection of children can be safeguarded. In extreme circumstances, the 1991 Act authorises the interference with familial relations whereby a child can be removed from the care, custody and authority of his parents and delivered into the care of a State agency, namely the Health Service Executive. Interference with fundamental constitutional rights, the rights of the family under Art.41, is made legally permissible by Art.42.5 of the Constitution, which authorises the State to intervene on behalf of children where parents have failed for physical or moral reasons in their duty towards their children. The Supreme Court in *North Western Health Board v HW* [2001] 3 I.R. 622 reaffirmed the constitutional autonomy of parents in determining a child's welfare but also noted that children possess constitutional rights, both as members of a family protected by Art.41 and as individuals as protected by Art.40.3. The fundamental justification for interfering with the autonomy of parents is the vindication of the child's constitutional rights. This vindication, as noted by Murphy and Hardiman JJ. at 730–731 and 758–759, respectively, in the above case, can be achieved by invoking either Art.42.5 or Art.40.3 of the Constitution.

In this regard, the application for any order under the Act requires the court to consider the welfare of the child as the first and paramount consideration, as well as the wishes of the child, and to also have regard to the rights of parents under the Constitution, and otherwise. This express statutory obligation safeguards the rights of all concerned. In addition, the Health Service Executives is likewise obliged to consider the above rights in relation to parents and children in the exercise of any of their functions under the Act. Barr J. noted in *MQ v Gleeson* [1998] 4 I.R. 85 that before a decision to institute care proceedings is made, an investigation must be conducted by the Health Board to assess whether allegations warranting care proceedings exist. Such an investigation must afford the alleged abuser of a child all the requirements of natural and constitutional justice.

It should be stressed that the involuntary taking of a child into care by the Health Service Executive is a measure of last resort. Denham J. succinctly put it in *North Western Health Board v HW* [2001] 3 I.R. 622 at 722: "Responsibility for children rests with their parents except in exceptional circumstances". Lord Clyde has expressed similar sentiments and caution in the important decision of *Lancashire C.C. v B* [2000] 2 A.C. 147 at 157 and [2000] 1 F.L.R. 583 at 593 stating: "… that the intervention by the State into matters of family life may often call for immense caution and restraint.

The policy of the Act is to secure the welfare of children. But that policy recognises that that object will very often be best served by retaining the child in the custody of his or her parents and that very considerable harm may be done by an intervention, however well-intentioned".

In addition the European Court of Human Rights has repeatedly stated and most recently in *Scozzari and Giunta v Italy* (2002) 35 E.H.R.R. 12: "... it is an interference of a very serious order to split up a family. Such a step must be supported by sufficiently sound and weighty considerations in the interests of the child ..." (citing *Olsson v Sweden (No.1)* (1989) 11 E.H.R.R. 259 at para.72).

The preferable way to proceed in matters relating to a child's welfare under the 1991 Act is by way of co-operation with the parents. Where a child does require the care services of the Health Service Executive, a voluntary placing into the Health Service Executive's care by the parents should be pursued under s.4.

Of particular note is the definition of child, which relates to all persons under the age of 18 who are not married.

The Act provides for a general statutory obligation to promote the welfare of children, which is imposed upon the Health Service Executive.

The means by which the Health Service Executive fulfils this obligation is clearly defined under the Act. Whilst the Health Service Executive enjoys a degree of discretion in the promotion of children's welfare, the exercise of certain functions, particularly those relating to care proceedings, are subject to the judicial process which prescribes criteria and conditions for the exercise and performance of functions by the Health Service Executive.

The welfare of the child is secured by the interaction of the State's administrative agencies (Health Service Executive) and the judiciary. Neither can operate effectively without the others participation and this interaction best secures a child's welfare whereby the judiciary oversees and approves the Health Service Executive's plans for a child. The role of the judiciary should not be underestimated in this regard, who in certain proceedings, determine what measures may be taken concerning the child's care. The judicial role in care proceedings safeguards the rights, constitutional and otherwise, of both the child and his parents. It is only where a care order is granted that the Health Service Executive is conferred with discretion in determining a child's welfare but this is subject to the overall judicial control of the courts. In addition, care orders are subject to appeal or to an application for directions made in relation to a care order or indeed the variation or discharge of same. The interaction between the courts and Health Service Executive is aptly demonstrated by *Eastern Health Board v McDonnell* [1999] 1 I.R. 174, where McCracken J. upheld the detailed directions imposed upon the Health Board for the future care of the child. Notwithstanding the fact that the Health Board had parent-like authority over the child as conferred by s.18, McCracken J. held the District Court retained overall control of children in the care of the Health Board. McCracken J.'s approach was approved by McGuinness J. in *North Western Health Board v KM* [2002] 2 I.R. 493. Further, the rights of the child are also protected by enabling a child to be represented and have a guardian *ad litem* appointed as well as having his wishes considered in any application under the Act.

There are three main aspects to the Act. The first major aspect relates to care proceedings and the requirements for maintaining children in care. The second aspect of the Act relates to the regulation of crèche and other child-minding services described under the Act as "pre-school services". The last aspect to the Act concerns solvent abuse by children which s.74 deals with.

The 1991 Act as amended by the Children Act 2001 now comprises 12 Parts.

Part I concerns commencement and definitions relating to the Act.

Part II deals with the obligation imposed upon the Health Service Executive to promote the welfare of children, the primary, but not the only, method of which being voluntary care. Part II also deals with the general duties of the Health Service Executive which include the provision of accommodation for homeless children, the provision of adoption services and establishment of child care advisory committees. There is also an obligation to review services provided by the Health Service Executive. Voluntary bodies to which the Health Service Executive may give assistance may also provide services. There is also provision for research to be conducted.

Part III deals with the emergency protection of children whereby children can be brought into care by a member of the gardaí with or without a warrant and order to that effect.

Part IV deals with care proceedings and the orders available to secure the welfare of children.

Parts IVA and B, inserted by s.16 of the Children Act 2001, deal with the jurisdiction of the court to order the civil detention of children who are in need of special care and attention. The Health Service Executive is in turn statutorily empowered to care for and maintain such children in special care units. Part II of the Children Act 2001 also provides for the establishment of a "family welfare conference" which must first be convened by the Health Service Executive prior to applying for a special care order.

Part V concerns the jurisdiction of the courts and procedures to be followed in applications under the Act.

Part VI deals with the obligations upon the Health Service Executive who have children in their care and the typ of care that the Health Service Executive may provide. Part VIII, in this regard, provides for regulations governing children's residential centres.

Part VII deals with crèches and other child-minding services (pre-school service).

Part IX concerns administration and Pt X deals with certain miscellaneous and supplemental provisions.

Citation

Child Care Act 1991

Commencement

The whole Act did not come into force on signature by the President. The taking effect of the provisions of the Act are dependent upon the making of Ministerial orders which the Minister may fix. The various statutory instruments and commencement orders bringing into force the provisions of the Act are set out in the Note to s.1 below.

Statutory Instruments

Child Care Act 1991 (Commencement) Order 1991 (S.I. No.292 of 1991)

Child Care Act 1991 (Commencement) Order 1992 (S.I. No.123 of 1992)

Child Care Act 1991 (Children's Residential Centres) (Superannuation) Order 1992 (S.I. No.124 of 1992)

Child Care Act 1991 (Children's Residential Centres) (Superannuation) (No. 2) Order 1992 (S.I. No.125 of 1992)

Child Care Act 1991 (Commencement) (No.2) Order 1992 (S.I. No.264 of 1992)

Child Care Act 1991 (Commencement) (No.3) Order 1992 (S.I. No.349 of 1992)

Child Care Act 1991 (Commencement) Order 1995 (S.I. No.258 of 1995)

Child Care (Placement of Children in Residential Care) Regulations 1995 (S.I. No.259 of 1995)

Child Care (Placement of Children in Foster Care) Regulations 1995 (S.I. No.260 of 1995)

Child Care (Placement of Children with Relatives) Regulations 1995 (S.I. No.261

of 1995)
Child Care (Standards in Children's Residential Centres) Regulations 1996 (S.I. No.397 of 1996)
Child Care (Pre-school Services) Regulations 1996 (S.I. 398 of 1996)
Child Care Act 1991 (Commencement) Order 1996 (S.I. No.399 of 1996)
District Court Rules 1997 (S.I. No.93 of 1997)
Child Care Act 1991 (Pre-School Services) (Amendment) Regulations 1997 (S.I. No.268 of 1997)
Health and Children (Delegation of Ministerial Function) (No.2) Order, 2000 (S.I. No.33 of 2000)
Child Care Act 1991 (Commencement) Order 2004 (S.I. No.547 of 2004)
Child Care Act 1991 (Commencement) (No.2) Order 2004 (S.I. No.548 of 2004)
Children (Family Welfare Conference) Regulations 2004 (S.I. No.549 of 2004)
Child Care (Special Care) Regulations 2004 (S.I. No.550 of 2004)

Parliamentary Debates

382 *Dáil Debates* Cols 138–191 (Second Stage)
384 *Dáil Debates* Cols 437–468 and 504–543 (Second Stage)
392 *Dáil Debates* Cols 1161–1249 (Committee Stage)
403 *Dáil Debates* Cols 1724–1767, 1911–1968, 2005–2057, 2082–2138, 2212–2274, 2274–2277, 2319–2350 and 2399–2473 (Report Stage)
403 *Dáil Debates* Cols 2567–2652 (Report Stage resumed and Final Stages)
410 *Dáil Debates* Cols 420–464 (From the Seanad)
517 *Dáil Debates* Cols 32–37, 56–57, 95–136, 469–500, 693–728, 770–808 (Second Stage, Children Act 2001)
518 *Dáil Debates* Cols 18–32 (Second Stage, Children Act 2001)
538 *Dáil Debates* Cols 28–48, 84–130 (Fourth and Final Stages, Children Act 2001)
127 *Seanad Debates* Cols 1568–1605, 2039–2083 and 2084–2118 (Second Stage)
129 *Seanad Debates* Cols 489–545, 607–682 and 806–837 (Committee Stage)
129 *Seanad Debates* Cols 837–858 (Report and Final Stages)
167 *Seanad Debates* Cols 480–525
167 *Seanad Debates* 751–799 (Committee and Remaining Stages, Children Act 2001)

Acts referred to

Adoption Act 1952	1952, No. 25
Adoption Act 1964	1964, No. 2
Adoption Acts, 1952 to 1988	
Children Act 1908	8 Edw. 7, c. 67
Children Act 1934	1934, No. 15
Children Act 1941	1941, No. 12
Children (Amendment) Act 1957	1957, No. 28
Children (Employment Abroad) Act 1913	3 & 4 Geo. 5, c. 7
Courts Act 1964	1964, No. 11
Courts Act 1971	1971, No. 36
Defence Act 1954	1954, No. 11
Guardianship of Infants Act 1964	1964, No. 7
Health Act 1953	1953, No. 26
Health Act 1970	1970, No. 1
Health Acts, 1947 to 1986	
Health (Amendment) Act 1987	1987, No. 3

Interpretation Act 1937	1937, No. 38
Judicial Separation and Family Law Reform Act 1989	1989, No. 6
Local Government (Superannuation) Act 1980	1980, No. 8
Mental Treatment Acts, 1945 to 1966	
Misuse of Drugs Acts, 1977 and 1984	
Prevention of Cruelty to Children Act 1904	4 Edw. 7, c. 15
Petty Sessions (Ireland) Act 1851	14 & 15 Vict., c. 93.9
Public Offices Fees Act 1879	42 & 43 Vict., c. 58
School Attendance Act 1926	1926, No. 17

Be it enacted by the Oireachtas as follows:

PART I

PRELIMINARY

Short title and commencement

1.—(1) This Act may be cited as the Child Care Act, 1991.

(2) This Act shall come into operation on such day or days as, by order or orders made by the Minister under this section, may be fixed either generally or with reference to any particular purpose or provision, and different days may be so fixed for different purposes and different provisions.

DEFINITIONS

"the Minister": s.2.

NOTE

An amendment to the title of the Act was proposed in the first tabled amendment at second stage by Deputy Yates (see 392 *Dáil Debates* Col.1161) who received support from Deputies Fennell (see 392 *Dáil Debates* Col.1163) and Sherlock (see 392 *Dáil Debates* Col.1164) for the title to read "The Child Care and Welfare Act". The Minister for State refused to accept the amendment on the basis that the "integrity" and "identity" of the bill ought not to be affected by the insertion of the word "welfare" which has a broad and profound meaning in relation to children (see 392 *Dáil Debates* Col.1165).

Section 1(2) reserves to the Minister a discretion as to when to implement the legislative provisions. No section of the Act can come into effect without a Ministerial order. This provision caused severe criticism and comment at second stage in the Dáil. An amendment proposed by Deputy Sherlock that, on the passing of the Bill, the Act would be brought into effect within 12 months (see 392 *Dáil Debates* Col.1166) received cross Party support from the opposition (see 392 *Dáil Debates* Col.1168, Deputy Howlin; Col.1168, Deputy Yates; Col.1170, Deputy Fennell; Col.1170, Deputy Garland). This amendment was, however, ruled out of order as constituting a charge to the Exchequer.

The Act was signed into law on July 10 1991 and at the date of publication of this volume has been brought completely into effect with the exception of s.79 and Schedule (for the purpose of repealing s.119 of the Children Act 1908 and s.31(2) of the Adoption Act). The dates of commencement of the various provisions are illustrated in the following Table:

Section	Date commenced	Statutory Instrument
Part I (ss. 1 and 2), ss. 71 and 74	December 1, 1991	S.I. No. 292 of 1991
Sections 9, 10, 79 (for purpose of repealing of s.65 (2) of the Health Act, 1953)	June 1, 1992	S.I. No. 123 of 1992
Section 66	June 1, 1992	S.I. No. 125 of 1992
Sections 5, 6 (1), (2) and (5), 11, 69, 72 and 73	October 1, 1992	S.I. No. 264 of 1992
Sections 3, 7 and 8	December 1, 1992	S.I. No. 349 of 1992
Sections 4, 6 (3) and (4), 12 to 48, 68, 70, 75 to 78, 79 and Schedule (for certain purposes only).	October 31, 1995	S.I. No. 258 of 1995
Sections 49 to 65 and 67	December 18, 1996	S.I. No. 399 of 1996
Section 79 and Schedule, for purpose of all non com- menced repeals in Schedule, with the exception of repeal of s.119 of the Children Act 1908 and s.31(2) of the Adoption Act 1952	September 23, 2004	S.I. No. 347 of 2004

Interpretation

2.—(1) In this Act, except where the context otherwise requires—
"area", in relation to a [the Health Service Executive], means functional area;
"child" means a person under the age of 18 years other than a person who is or has been married;
"functions" includes powers and duties;
[...];
"the Minister" means the Minister for Health;
"parents" includes a surviving parent and, in the case of a child who has been adopted under the Adoption Acts, 1952 to 1988, or, where the child has been adopted outside the State, whose adoption is recognised by virtue of the law for the time being in force in the State, means the adopter or adopters or the surviving adopter;
"prescribed" means prescribed by regulations made by the Minister.
　(2) In this Act—
　　(a) a reference to a Part, section or Schedule is to a Part, section or Schedule of this Act unless it is indicated that a reference to some other enactment is intended;
　　(b) a reference to a subsection, paragraph or subparagraph is to the subsection, paragraph or subparagraph of the provision in which the reference occurs, unless it is indicated that reference to some other provision is intended;
　　(c) a reference to any other enactment shall, unless the context otherwise requires, be construed as a reference to that enactment as amended or extended by or under any other enactment, including this Act.

AMENDMENT

Definition of "area" amended and definition of "health board" deleted by s.75 and Schedule 7 of the Health Act 2004, No.42 of 2004, with effect from January 1, 2005 (S.I. No.887 of 2004).

NOTE

This is the definition section for the Act. The terms set out here are discussed, where relevant, in the context of the sections where they arise. Of general note here is the definition of child, which is a person under the age of 18 other than a person who is or has been married. Section 31 of the Family Law Act 1995 renders void any marriage entered into by a person under the age of 18, unless an exemption from this requirement is granted. Both the judgment of Kenny J. in *Ryan v Attorney General* [1965] I.R. 294 and Art.41 of the Constitution lend considerable weight to the argument that the citizen possesses, as a personal right, the constitutional right to marry. In theory a child could avoid being the subject of a care order by marrying but this would require applying for an exemption under s.33(2)(*d*) of the Family Law Act 1995. An applicant must establish that the exemption is justified by serious reasons and that it is in the interests of the parties to the intended marriage. Such an application is held in camera (s.33(2)(*b*) of the Family Law Act 1995) and most commonly heard in the Circuit Court. In light of the definition of "child" for the purposes of the 1991 Act the courts should be vigilant about marriage age exemption applications.

Of further note is the fact that a child is defined by age rather than by nationality, domicile or residence. *Re B* (*A Child*) (*Care Proceedings: Diplomatic Immunity*) [2003] 2 W.L.R. 168, [2003] 1 F.L.R. 341 dealt with the issue of whether a child of a parent who was a member of a diplomatic staff was immune from the provisions of the English Children Act 1989. The Children Act 1989 in s.105 defines a child as a person under the age of 18. The *Re B* case may be of relevance if the issue were to arise in this jurisdiction. The child in question was the subject of an interim care order having been observed at school manifesting severe, significant and non-accidental injuries from repeated beatings to the arms and legs. The child's father was a driver employed by the embassy in question and was part of the administrative and technical staff for the purposes of Art.37(2) of the Vienna Convention. As such he enjoyed the same immunities and privileges as a diplomatic agent save in relation to civil or administrative action which relate to acts performed outside the course of his duties. Further, the inviolability of private premises conferred by Art.30(1) could not be interpreted so as to confer immunity in respect of the consequences of acts committed therein. The child in question enjoyed diplomatic immunity from arrest and detention by virtue of Art.29. In this regard, the interim care order did not violate this immunity as the parents retained joint parental authority with the local authority over the child who was placed with foster parents. Dame Butler-Sloss, however, did acknowledge that difficulties of enforcing the order might arise in the event that the interim care order was breached. A child of a diplomatic agent would be absolutely immune from the provisions of the child care legislation.

Section 8(5) of the Immigration Act 1996 as amended by s.11(1)(*c*)(v) of the Immigration Act 1999 makes applicable the Child Care Act 1991 to an unaccompanied minor arriving at the State's frontiers with the intention of seeking refugee status. The Health Service Executive is obliged to facilitate an application for such a declaration for refugee status.

Most of the important definitions, such as "functions" and "parents" are discussed in the Note to s.3.

PART II

PROMOTION OF WELFARE OF CHILDREN

Functions of [Health Service Executive]

3.—(1) It shall be a function of [the Health Service Executive] to promote the welfare of children [...] who are not receiving adequate care and protection.

(2) In the performance of this function, [the Health Service Executive] shall—

    (*a*) take such steps as it considers requisite to identify children who are not receiving adequate care and protection and co-ordinate information from all relevant sources relating to children [...];

    (*b*) having regard to the rights and duties of parents, whether under the Constitution or otherwise—

        (i) regard the welfare of the child as the first and paramount consideration, and

        (ii) in so far as is practicable, give due consideration, having regard to his age and understanding, to the wishes of the child; and

    (*c*) have regard to the principle that it is generally in the best interests of a child to be brought up in his own family.

(3) [The Health Service Executive] shall, in addition to any other function assigned to it under this Act or any other enactment, provide child care and family support services, and may provide and maintain premises and make such other provision as it considers necessary or desirable for such purposes, subject to any general directions given by the Minister under *section 69.*

[(4) The provisions of the Health Acts 1947 to 2004 shall apply in relation to the functions of the Health Service Executive and its employees under this Act and the powers of the Minister under those Acts shall have effect accordingly as if those Acts and this Act were one Act.]

AMENDMENT

    Subsections (1), (2), (2)(*a*) and (3) amended, and subs.(4) substituted, by s.75 and Schedule 7 of the Health Act 2004, No.42 of 2004, with effect from January 1, 2005 (S.I. No.887 of 2004).

DEFINITIONS

    "area": s.2.
    "child": s.2.
    "function": s.2.
    "health board": s.2.
    "parents": s.2.
    "the Minister": s.2.

COMMENCEMENT

    Child Care Act, 1991 (Commencement) (No.3) Order, 1992 (S.I. No. 349 of 1992) which took effect as of December 1, 1992.

Section 3(1) imposes upon the Health Service Executive a positive statutory function (duty) to promote the welfare of children in its functional area. Of interest in s.3(1) is the omission of the term "residing". Thus a child need not be residing or ordinarily residing within the Health Service Executive's functional area but merely be in the area of the Health Service Executive.

The omission of the term "residing" or "ordinarily resident" avoids the difficulties the English Courts have encountered with s.17 of the Children Act 1989 (see *R. (On The Application Of S) v Wandsworth L.B.C.* [2002] 1 F.L.R. 469; *R. v Kent C.C. Ex p. S* [2000] 1 F.L.R. 155 and *R. v Lambeth L.B.C. Ex p. Caddell* [1998] 1 F.L.R. 253 which interpreted the phase "within its area" as being satisfied where the individual was simply physically present in the relevant local authority catchment area.

The need to impose a duty, to promote the welfare of children, is emphasised by *The State (D and D) v Groarke* [1990] 1 I.R. 303 where a unanimous Supreme Court held that the Health Board was not legally designated a "fit person" for the purposes of s.24 of the Children Act 1908, which enabled the Health Board to take children into care. Chief Justice Finlay held that s.66(2) of the Health Act 1970 could not be interpreted so as to confer upon the Health Board the authority to take into care all children as opposed to those children over the age of six who are attending national school. As a consequence of the decision, the Children Act 1989 was enacted, s.1 of which provides that the Health Service Executive is prospectively and retrospectively deemed to be a "fit person" conferred with the appropriate functions.

Section 3(1) has been considered in the important case of *MQ v Gleeson* [1998] 4 I.R. 85 which identifies the nature and extent of the function (duty) imposed upon the Health Board where the welfare of a child is considered to be at risk. The case also outlines the Health Board's rights in such circumstances. The Health Board's duty is neither conditional upon specific children being identified nor upon a present or current risk to their welfare existing. The Health Board is obliged to protect children who are as yet unascertained from a potential future risk, provided it is based upon present knowledge of that future risk. In *MQ*, the applicant, against whom allegations of child sexual abuse had been made, enrolled on a social studies course run by the City of Dublin Vocational Education Committee. The applicant intended to qualify as a social worker and work with children. The course involved a practical three-week work placement with children. The Eastern Health Board became aware of the applicant's enrolment and recommended that he be removed from the course. Barr J. held that the duty imposed upon the Health Board related not just to at risk children who were identified or identifiable but also to children who were as yet unascertained who may be subject to a specific potential risk which is known to the Health Board or reasonably suspected may occur later. Present knowledge or a reasonable suspicion of potential harm was sufficient to oblige the Health Board to exercise its functions under s.3. The potential future harm was either to the children with whom the applicant would work with on his three-week work placement or those with whom he could work with after qualification. The Health Board's duty in this regard was to protect children at risk from the applicant. In particular the Health Board was obliged to form an opinion on his suitability for childcare work and to communicate a request that he be removed from the course.

These specific duties, however, are conditional upon the Health Board first conducting a reasonable investigation into each allegation of abuse. Once a significant doubt arises from the investigation, the Health Board is obliged to act to protect children from the risk in the fashion outlined. In serious cases, the investigation should afford the alleged abuser an opportunity of responding to the specific complaint made except where such would jeopardise an abused complainant child. The obligation to afford the alleged abuser a right of reply would also arise where it was proposed to disclose the investigation results to a third party. Interestingly Barr J. also noted that the same obligation would arise where care proceedings were proposed.

MQ v Gleeson [1998] 4 I.R. 85 further holds that the Health Board is obliged to keep records of all allegations of abuse, irrespective of whether such are substantiated. The record should identify the weight the Health Board attaches to each allegation and also contain factors favourable to the alleged abuser. Where allegations are positively false, the Health Board is obliged to clearly record the allegation as false and must not identify the alleged abuser.

MQ v Gleeson [1998] 4 I.R. 85 also holds that the Health Board has a right to disclose to a third party information about an alleged abuser. This right, however, is subject to the Health Board affording the alleged abuser the opportunity to be informed of the complaints and the right to respond. Barr J. noted that the alleged abuser should be interviewed, provided with notice of and information concerning the complaints and the opportunity to respond. The Health Board should also conduct a follow up investigation arising from the alleged abuser's response. Most importantly the Health Board should not form any opinion on the substance of the complaints leading to disclosure of the Health Board's opinion or other positive action without first conducting an investigation in accordance with constitutional and natural justice. The Court of Appeal decision in *Re V and W (Minors) (Disclosure)* [1999] 1 W.L.R. 299, [1999] 1 F.L.R. 267 held that a local authority was not under a duty to inform other local authorities of a finding that an individual had sexually abused children in care proceedings. Such a finding is considered confidential and the discretion to disclose the information should not be exercised unless it was helpful to the administration of justice, the prosecution of offences or needed by the police or other agency in assisting investigations.

Section 3(1) has also been considered in the *Eastern Health Board v EA* [2000] 1 I.R. 430, in which Laffoy J. held that the applicant was statutorily obliged to conduct an inquiry under Art.40.4.2 of the Constitution. The case concerned an attempted illegal adoption by the respondents of a newly-born baby. The decision of the natural mother to give custody of her child to the respondent's constituted a risk to the child's welfare necessitating the Health Board to institute proceedings.

The primary function or duty of the Health Service Executive is to promote the welfare of children in its area who are not receiving adequate care and protection (s.3(1)). This function is performed by obliging the Health Service Executive, first, to identify children who are not receiving adequate care and protection and, secondly, to co-ordinate information from all relevant sources relating to children in its area. It should be noted that the statutory obligation is couched in general subjective terms whereby the Health Service Executive in performing the function need only take such steps as it considers requisite. A similar provision in the English Children Act 1989 was considered by the House of Lords in *R. (On The Application Of G.) v Barnet L.B.C.* [2003] 3 W.L.R. 1194, [2004] 1 All E.R. 97. The general duty to promote the welfare of children did not extend to providing the applicant mother and her three children, two of whom were autistic, with accommodation appropriate to the needs of the autistic children.

The House of Lords further ruled that the duty imposed on local authorities was not specific to each individual child in need but rather, that the local authority was obliged to provide a range of services to discharge the general duty imposed.

In relation to the duty to co-ordinate information relating to children, the Health Service Executive may be obliged to make full disclosure of all reports of a child formerly maintained in care by the Health Service Executive. In *MG v UK* (2003) 36 E.H.R.R. 3 the UK was found in breach of Art.8 (respect for family life) of the European

Convention on Human Rights for failing to disclose the entire social service records of the applicant. The ECHR found that the social service records contained information relevant to the applicant's formative years and thus related to his private and family life. The lack of both a statutory right to access the information and to appeal a refusal to divulge the information were relevant to the court's finding. The same difficulty may not arise in light of the Freedom of Information Act 1997 and the Freedom of Information (Amendment) Act 2003.

In performing the primary function of promoting the welfare of children (for example by initiating care or supervision order proceedings) the Health Service Executive can affect the rights of the family as protected under Art.41 and Art.42 of the Constitution (see Casey, *Constitutional Law in Ireland* (3rd ed., Sweet & Maxwell, Dublin, 2000), chap.17)) and the European Convention on the Protection of Human Rights and Fundamental Freedoms. To lessen the conflict s.3 requires the Health Service Executive to have regard to the rights and duties of parents under the Constitution or otherwise (s.3(*b*)) when considering the welfare of the child, which is the first and paramount consideration (s.3 (*b*)(i)). As evident from the *Buchberger v Austria* (2003) 37 E.H.R.R. 13 decision, the principles of natural and constitutional justice must be respected. In this case the mother was not informed of new evidence, which was submitted to an appellate court resulting in the placing of children in care. The failure to inform the applicant mother constituted a breach of Arts 6 and 8 of the Convention. In addition, care proceedings must be prosecuted in a timely fashion by the relevant Health Service Executive as delay can amount to a denial of a fair trial as falling foul of the "reasonable time" requirement stipulated under the European Convention of Human Rights (see *EP v Italy* (2001) 31 E.H.R.R. 17 and *H v UK* (1988) 10 E.H.R.R. 95).

In considering the child's welfare regard is also to be had to the child's wishes where practicable (s.3(*b*)(ii)). Section 3(*c*) further ensures that the rights of the family, and more specifically parents, are respected by the Health Service Executive observing the principle that being brought up within the family serves the best interest of the child. This principle is clearly evident from a number of important and influential sources. The Supreme Court has stressed this point in *North Western Health Board v HW* [2001] 3 I.R. 622 and Lord Clyde has expressed similar sentiments and caution in the important decision of *Lancashire C.C. v B* [2000] 2 A.C. 147 at 157, [2000] 1 F.L.R. 583. In addition the European Court of Human Rights has repeatedly stated and most recently in *Scozzari and Giunta v Italy* (2002) 35 E.H.R.R. 12: "… it is an interference of a very serious order to split up a family. Such a step must be supported by sufficiently sound and weighty considerations in the interests of the child …" (citing *Olsson v Sweden* (*No.1*) (1989) 11 E.H.R.R. 259 at para.72).

These provisions clearly acknowledge the well-established constitutional rights of the child, of parents and of the family as well as the State's obligation as default parent. The significance of these express obligations to regard the rights and duties of the child, parents and the family should not be underestimated. The Health Service Executive's obligation can be a difficult and delicate one to perform. By fulfilling the express statutory obligation and thereby attempting to safeguard the child's constitutional right, the Health Service Executive may infringe not alone the constitutional rights of the child but also that of parents and the family. The Supreme Court in *North Western Health Board v HW* [2001] 3 I.R. 622 considered the complexity of the interaction of the child's rights as an individual and as a member of the family with the rights of the family and in particular the decision-making autonomy of parents where the State intended to rely upon Art.42.5 as default parent to vindicate the constitutional right of the child. The Supreme Court endorsed the constitutional principle that a child's welfare is best secured within the family and that parents possess parental supremacy in decisions concerning a child's welfare. The State through the aegis of the Health Service Executive, is relegated to a subordinate role save in exceptional circumstances justifiable only by the provisions of Art.42.5 of the Constitution. Here the court refused an order authorising the conducting of a P.K.U. test on a child against the wishes of the parents. The Supreme Court stated obiter that the use of the Child Care Act to conduct such a test would be inappropriate and would call into question its constitutional validity.

It would appear from both *North Western Health Board v HW* [2001] 3 I.R. 622 and *MQ v Gleeson* [1998] 4 I.R. 85 that before the Health Service Executive performs its functions (duties) under the Child Care Act 1991, it would first have to satisfy itself that there has been a parental failure in accordance with Art.42.5 of the Constitution. An investigation in accordance with natural and constitutional justice must be conducted by the Health Service Executive, the result of which warrants the institution of care proceedings.

A specified, and mandatory, function of the Health Service Executive is the obligation to provide child care and family support services. In contrast, the Health Service Executive has both a discretion in the provision and maintenance of premises and how best to achieve this purpose (s.3(3)).

Since the passing of the Child Care Act there have been a number of legislative developments which impact on child care legislation.

Section 8(5) of the Immigration Act 1996 (as amended by s.11(1)(c)(v) of the Immigration Act 1999) obliges the Health Service Executive to appoint an officer to make an application for refugee status in relation to an unaccompanied child who arrives at the frontiers of the State. An immigration officer is obliged to inform the Health Service Executive of the arrival of such a child.

Section 53 of the Children Act 2001 enables the gardaí to liase with the Health Service Executive where a child under the age of 12 which if committed by a person over 12 would have been an offence, is brought to his parent or guardian in circumstances where the gardaí reasonably believe the child is not receiving adequate care or protection. In those circumstances the gardaí are obliged to inform the Health Service Executive of the area where the child normally resides of the child's name, address, age and reasons for coming to the attention of the gardaí. Where the circumstances warrant a removal of the child for the purposes of s.12 of the 1991 Act the gardaí may remove the child to a place of safety which removal is deemed to be a removal for the purposes of s.12.

Section 254(4) of the Children Act 2001 confers a power of arrest without warrant where there is a risk to the child's safety, health or well-being. An arrest in these circumstances is deemed to be a removal in accordance with s.12. Where the child is delivered to the Health Service Executive in these circumstances and the Health Service Executive considers that the child requires care and protection which he is unlikely to receive, the Health Service Executive is obliged to apply for a care or supervision order under Pt IV.

Under s.59 of the Children Act 2001 the Health Service Executive may exercise any of its powers under the Act where a child is in garda custody on suspicion of having committed an offence. The Health Service Executive's authority is first dependent upon the member in charge of the station having reasonable cause to believe the child is in need of care or protection. Where this is the case, the Health Service Executive is obliged to send a representative to the station to ascertain the child's need for care or protection. The representative is entitled to be present during the questioning of the child.

The Mental Health Act 2001 confers a discretion on the Health Service Executive to apply to the District Court for authorisation to detain a child in an approved centre where the child is suffering from a mental disorder (defined in s.2 of the Mental Health Act 2001) and the child requires attention which he or she is unlikely to receive unless an order is made under s.25(1) of the Mental Health Act 2001. The application may be made *ex parte* where the urgency of the matter so requires (s.25(7)) and the order may have conditions attached (s.25(8)). An application for directions concerning the care and custody of the child may be brought between the application for the order and its determination (s.25(8)). An application under s.25(1) cannot be brought until the child is first examined by a consultant psychiatrist who must not be a relative of the child (s.25(2)). Where the parent, guardian or person acting *in loco parentis* refuse consent to such an examination or the individuals whose consent is required cannot be found after reasonable enquiries have been made, the Health Service Executive may make an application to court without first obtaining a psychiatric examination (s.25(3)(*a*) and (*b*)). The court, may however, direct a psychiatric examination (s.25(4)) where none has been conducted and the psychiatrist is obliged to report to the court (s.25(5)). Where the court is satisfied that the child is suffering from a mental disorder, an order for a maximum period of 21 days may be made detaining the child in an approved centre for the purpose of receiving treatment (s.25(6)). Before the expiry of the 21-day period, an application may be brought to extend the period of detention for a period not exceeding three months (s.25(9)) and thereafter for renewable periods not exceeding six months (s.25(10)). No order extending the detention can be without a consultant psychiatrists examination and report on the child which satisfies the court that the child continues to suffer from a mental disorder (s.25(11)). Neither psycho-surgery nor electro-convulsive therapy can be performed or administered without court approval (s.25(12) and (13)). Applications under s.25 of the 2001 Act are governed by ss.21, 22, 24– 35, 37 and 47 of the 1991 Act.

The Health Service Executive has emergency powers of placement and detention under s.23 of the Mental Health Act 2001 in circumstances where the parent, guardian or person acting *in loco parentis* attempt to remove a child who is a voluntary patient receiving treatment in an approved centre. Where a consultant psychiatrist, registered medical practitioner or registered nurse is of the opinion the child suffers from a mental disorder, the Health Service Executive can take custody of the child (s.23(2)) but must make an application under s.25(2) within three days to the next available sitting or specially arranged sitting of the District Court. The application is facilitated by the application of s.13(4) of the 1991 Act which provides jurisdictional flexibility for the making of such applications. During this time the Health Service Executive has lawful custody of the child.

Subsection (1)

Sets out the general statutory duty or function of the Health Service Executive which is the obligation to promote the welfare of children who are not receiving adequate care and protection. This provides for a potential conflict with the constitutional rights of the family as set out in Art.41 and 42 and the personal rights of the individual members of the family as protected under Art.40.3. The right of the State to interfere in the primacy of the rights enjoyed by children and parents is justified by Art.42.5 where the parents have failed for physical or moral reasons in their duty towards their children (*Re Art.26 and the Adoption (No.2) Bill, 1987* [1989] I.R. 656 and *North Western Health Board v HW* [2001] 3 I.R. 622). The performance of the duty in s.3 is protected against constitutional attack by the Health Service Executive regarding the constitutional rights of the individuals concerned.

Function: The term "function" as defined in s.2 includes "powers and duties". *MQ v Gleeson* [1998] 4 I.R. 85 details the nature and extent of the Health Service Executive's primary statutory function in promoting the welfare of children. The statutory function includes an obligation to investigate, record, report and conduct a fair hearing where allegations of child abuse arise. Arising from this process the Health Service Executive may also communicate to a third party the results of an investigation. Any statutory function has important public law, tort and European fundamental human rights implications.

In administrative or public law terms a failure on the part of the Health Service Executive to fulfil or perform a statutory duty or power may be investigated and enforced by way of judicial review (see de Blacam, *Judicial Review* (Butterworths) and generally Hogan and Morgan, *Administrative Law in Ireland* (3rd ed., Sweet & Maxwell, Dublin, 1998), chaps 9, 12 and 13). Breach of a statutory function in this regard is properly remedied by way of judicial review which "will ensure the actual performance of the duties" (*Paul Stephens v The Eastern Health Board*, unreported, July 27, 1994, Geoghegan J. at 18. See also *X (A Minor) v Bedfordshire C.C.* [1995] 3 All E.R. 353).

Whether damages for breach of statutory duty can be recovered is ultimately a question of interpretation of the statute in question (see de Blacam, *Judicial Review* (Butterworths), Hogan and Morgan, *Administrative Law in Ireland* (2nd ed., Sweet & Maxwell, Dublin, 1991), chap.15 and McMahon & Binchy, *Irish Law of Torts* (3rd ed., Butterworths, 2000), chaps 21 and 44). In *Paul Stephens v The Eastern Health Board*, unreported, High Court, July 27, 1994, Geoghegan J. dismissed an application for damages for a failure on the part of the Health Service Executive to provide suitable accommodation for the applicant, the judge being of the view that: "no breach of any of the provisions of the Child Care Act 1991, gives rise to an action for damages for breach of statutory duty" (at 18). A similar approach was adopted in *X (A Minor) v Bedfordshire C.C.* [1995] 3 All E.R. 353; *M (A Minor) v Newsham London B.C.* [1995] 3 All E.R. 353 and *E (A Minor) v Dorset C.C.* [1995] 3 All E.R. 353 where the right to pursue a private law right to damages on foot of a breach of statutory duty was denied. In the former case the House of Lords found that the duty imposed upon the local authorities in relation to the welfare of children was so general and unspecific that it conferred a wide scope to exercise subjective judgment that the legislation could not be interpreted as conferring a private law right to damages for breach of statutory duty.

Whilst recovery of damages on foot of a public law right may be difficult, liability in tort for the negligent exercise of a statutory duty may arise. In *Ward v McMaster* [1988] I.R. 337 the Supreme Court held that a duty to take reasonable care arose from the public duty of the County Council under statute. While damages were recovered in *Ward* it is questionable whether a monetary award would be made for a claim for breach of duty owed based upon the Child Care Act 1991. The *House of Lords in X (A Minor) v Bedfordshire C.C.* [1995] 3 All E.R. 353 held (Bingham M.R. dissenting) that in the absence of a breach of statutory duty no private law duty in negligence would be imposed upon a local authority in the negligent exercise of its functions under the Children Act 1989. Alternatively a monetary award of damages may not be seen as an appropriate remedy.

Since the *Ward, M (A Minor)* and *X (A Minor)* decisions there have been significant developments in this area. The Supreme Court in *Glencar Explorations plc v Mayo C.C.* [2002] 1 I.R. 112, [2002] 1 I.L.R.M. 481 adopted the House of Lords approach in *Caparo Industries v Dickman* [1990] 2 A.C. 605 to the application of the duty of care in negligence and rejected the approach adopted by the former Supreme Court in *Ward*. The *Caparo* decision rejected the long-standing two-stage test advocated by Lord Wilberforce in *Anns v Merton L.B.C.* [1978] A.C. 728. The *Caparo* three-stage test requires the establishment of proximity of relationship between the parties, reasonable foreseeability that the defendant's negligence will cause damage to the plaintiff and that it is fair, just and reasonable to impose a duty of care. How the application of the *Glencar* test will develop remains to be seen. But the approach of the Chief Justice does provide some guidance on how a court will assess a claim for damages linked to a breach of statutory duty. In *Glencar*, a case concerning the defendant's negligent exercise of statutory powers, the Chief Justice first considered whether there was sufficient proximity between the parties. Keane C.J. approached the matter by considering for whose benefit the exercise of the statutory power was intended. Here the exercise of the statutory power in question was for the benefit of the community in general rather than the plaintiff in particular notwithstanding the fact that the defendant was fully aware of the consequences to the plaintiff in exercising the power in question.

In England the House of Lords have considered the negligent exercise of statutory duty under the Children Act 1989 by adopting the *Caparo* three-stage test approach but essentially determining this on the fair, just and reasonable aspect to the test. In *M (A Minor)* [1995] 3 All E.R. 353 and *X (A Minor)* (above) the House of Lords held that, assuming that the exercise of the statutory function by the local authority (the decision to take the child into care in the *M* case and the failure to do so in the *X* case) was not unjusticiable, it was neither just nor reasonable to impose a duty of care on the local authority. In so concluding, the House of Lords advanced a number of policy reasons as to why no duty should be owed. The multi-disciplinary involvement in the decision-making process concerning care proceedings and the delicate nature of those decisions were important factors militating against the imposition of a duty of care. These policy factors were relied upon by the Court of Appeal in *H v Norfolk C.C.* [1997] 1 F.L.R. 384 to strike out the plaintiff's claim which was based exclusively in negligence. The plaintiff in *H v Norfolk C.C.* [1997] 1 F.L.R. 384 alleged he had been physically and sexually abused by the foster father the defendant had placed him with. The action in negligence against the local authority centred on the failure to supervise the foster placement, investigate the reports of abuse and remove him from foster care. The Court of Appeal held that it was not fair, just and reasonable to impose upon the local authority a duty of care to the plaintiff in circumstances where the social worker and local authority were exercising statutory functions. The correctness of this decision was undermined by the House of Lords in *Barrett v Enfield L.B.C.* [1999] 3 All E.R. 193 and overruled in *S v Gloucestershire C.C.* [2000] 3 All E.R. 346, [2001] 2 W.L.R. 909, [2000] 1 F.L.R. 825, in which the Court of Appeal held that a foster child who was sexually abused by a foster parent in circumstances where the defendant local authority failed to properly investigate and discover the suspicion or allegation of sexual abuse was an arguable case in negligence. The Court of Appeal refused to strike out *S's* action but did so in *L v Tower Hamlets L.B.C.* [2000] 3 All E.R. 346, [2001] 2 W.L.R. 909, [2000] 1 F.L.R. 825 where the defendant local authority was found to have conducted a rigorous and detailed assessment of the foster parents in question so that an action in negligence could not possibly succeed. The child, L, had been sexually abused by a foster father.

In *C v Flintshire C.C.* [2001] 2 F.L.R. 33 the plaintiff recovered £70,000 in damages against the local authority who had admitted negligence in twice placing the plaintiff in residential care where she was subjected to bullying from other children and assault and sexual abuse at the hands her care workers.

While the Health Service Executive may not be liable in negligence in deciding whether to take a child into care, liability may arise as a result of the negligent management of a child whilst in the care of the Health Service Executive. In *Barrett v Enfield L.B.C.* [1999] 3 All E.R. 193, the House of Lords revisited the issue of liability for the negligent exercise of a statutory duty. The plaintiff was taken into care at the age of 10 months until the age of 17 and placed nine times in both foster and residential care. He alleged the local authority has been negligent in placing him with unsuitable foster families, separating him from his half sister, failing to have him adopted and failing to re-unite him with his mother. As a consequence the plaintiff suffered psychiatric harm, was unemployed and had alcohol problems. The House of Lords reversed the Court of Appeal decision to strike out the plaintiff's claim which relied

The Child Care Acts

upon *X (A Minor)* v *Bedfordshire C.C.* [1995] 3 All E.R. 353. The House of Lords distinguished the *X (A Minor)* decision and the policy factors supporting it as that case concerned the decision whether to take children into care or not. The Barrett decision by contrast involved allegations of negligence after the child had been taken into care. Similarly in *W* v *Essex C.C.* [1998] 3 All E.R. 111, [1998] 3 W.L.R. 534, [1998] 2 F.L.R. 278, the Court of Appeal refused to strike out a claim brought by four children who were sexually abused by a foster child placed with their family by the defendant. The children's action, based both in negligence and negligent misstatement, arose in circumstances where their parents had expressly requested from the defendant that a child sexual abuser would not be placed with them as a foster child. Here the parents expressly asked whether the particular foster child was a sexual abuser to which a deliberate and incorrect reply was given. More recently the decision in *L & P* v *Reading B.C.* [2001] 1 W.L.R. 1575, [2001] 2 F.L.R. 50 involved a negligence action by the first plaintiff, L, against both the local authority and police for the negligent conducting of a sexual abuse investigation and reporting of same by both a social worker and a police officer. L was unnecessarily taken into care on foot of an unfounded allegation of sexual abuse by her father. The social worker and a police officer had negligently conducted interviews with L from which they erroneously concluded that L had been sexually abused by her father, P. The police sought to strike out the child's negligence action which the Court of Appeal rejected. The court held that the child plaintiff had an arguable case in negligence, misfeasance of public office and conspiracy. The court also noted that the case had implications for a breach of Art.8 (interference with the right to family life) of the European Convention on Human Rights and Fundamental Freedoms.

In addition to local authorities potentially being liable to children in relation to whom they exercise statutory functions, recent English cases identify that a duty may be owed to third parties. In *L & P* v *Reading B.C.* [2001] 1 W.L.R. 1575, [2001] 2 F.L.R. 50 P, the father of a child was entitled to maintain his action against both the local authority and police where his child was erroneously taken into care on foot of false allegations of sexual abuse. The case centred on the failure to properly investigate and report the allegations of sexual abuse. Also in *W* v *Essex C.C.* [1998] 3 All E.R. 111, [1998] 3 W.L.R. 534, [1998] 2 F.L.R. 278, the parents of four children suffered post traumatic stress disorder on learning that each of their children had been sexually abused by a foster child they had agreed to accommodate on the specific understanding that the foster placement would not involve a child suspected of child sexual abuse. The House of Lords here allowed the parent's "nervous shock" action to proceed to trial notwithstanding the fact that the case, on the basis of existing authority (*White* v *Chief Constable of the South Yorkshire Police* [1999] 1 All E.R. 1 and *Page* v *Smith* [1995] 2 All E.R. 576), appeared unsustainable. There is a detectable change in judicial attitude concerning these types of case. Owing to the Osman decision (*Osman* v *UK* (2000) 29 E.H.R.R. 245) the English courts have been reluctant to strike out negligence actions justified on public policy grounds. The Barrett decision in particular now stresses the public policy desirability of such actions proceeding to trial. The primary reason identified by Lord Hutton was that "wrongs should be remedied" (citing Lord Browne-Wilkinson in *X (Minors)* v *Bedfordshire C.C.* [1995] 3 All E.R. 353 at 380). In light of the extensive nature of the Health Service Executive's statutory duty identified in *MQ* v *Gleeson* [1998] 4 I.R. 85 the above English decisions may be of significance were the issue to arise here.

The Court of Appeal has recently considered the liability of local authorities for negligence in the exercise of statutory duty where children are unnecessarily taken into care. *JD* v *East Berkshire Community Health, MAR* v *Dewsbury Health Care NHS Trust* and *RK* v *Oldham NHS Trust* [2003] 4 All E.R. 796, [2004] 2 W.L.R. 58, [2003]

2 F.L.R. 116 (*JD*, *MAR* and *RK* respectively) held that a duty of care was owed to children negligently taken into care but that no duty was owed to the parents arising from the local authority's negligence. *JD* concerned a claim by the plaintiff mother where her child was erroneously placed on the "At Risk Register" for a period of three months owing to fears of the defendant local authority that the mother was incapable of caring for her child. The unfounded fears arose from a misdiagnosis that the mother was suffering from Muchausen Syndrome by Proxy. The Court of Appeal held that in light of the *Barrett* decision, *X (Minors) v Bedfordshire C.C.*[1995] 3 All E.R. 353 was restricted to the exercise of a decision as to whether or not to take a child into care and nothing more. In addition there had been two New Zealand decisions, which have determined whether a duty of care was owed by local authorities. In *Attorney General v Price Gardner* [1998] 1 N.Z.L.R. 262 the New Zealand Court of Appeal rejected the *X (Minors) v Bedfordshire* policy factor in denying the operation of a duty of care to the children. The *Attorney General v Price Gardner* decision concerned a plaintiff who was abused by adopters. The New Zealand Court held that the plaintiff was owed a duty of care. In another more recent decision, *B v Attorney General* [2003] U.K.P.C. 61, unreported, Privy Council, July 16, 2003, the New Zealand Court of Appeal had held that two daughters could maintain an action against the defendant where a clinical psychologist negligently investigated allegations of sexual abuse by the father. The father's action, however, was struck out as the court held that no duty of care was owed to him. The reasoning being that as the father was the alleged perpetrator, the psychologist owed the daughters a duty to investigate the matter to ensure their welfare and that in those circumstances it would not be consistent to owe the father a duty of care. The New Zealand Court could not distinguish the earlier *Price Gardner* decision and the Privy Council saw no reason to disturb the reasoning. A similar result arose in *S v Attorney General* [2002] N.Z.F.L.R. 295 where the plaintiff successfully sued the Department of Social Welfare for the sexual, physical and emotional abuse he suffered at the hands of foster parents some 30 yeas earlier. In denying the father a duty of care, the Court of Appeal in *JD* relied upon the ECHR decision of *TP and KM v UK* (2002) 34 E.H.R.R. 2, which noted that the negligent taking into care of children did not in itself constitute a breach of the right to respect for family life. In that regard no duty of care was owed to a parent. Similarly in *RK* the defendant negligently misdiagnosed the plaintiffs' daughter as having suffered a non-accidental injury when in fact the daughter suffered from a brittle bone condition. The parents were separated from their daughter for a period of six months but the Court of Appeal refused to impose a duty of care on the defendants in favour of the parents. In *MAR*, however, the child did succeed in her action against the local authority arising from a misdiagnosis resulting in the child being separated from her father for a period of 10 days. The child suffered from skin discoloration which the doctor assumed to have arisen from sexual abuse perpetrated by the father. In holding that a duty of care was owed to the child, the Court of Appeal rejected an argument that the defendant should benefit from an immunity akin to "witness immunity" decided in *Darker v Chief Constable for West Midlands* [2001] A.C. 435. The Court of Appeal noted that it was a thin line between the concepts of investigating and preparing for the giving of evidence as a witness but as other professionals owed a duty of care to their clients, professionals in the child care services likewise should owe a duty of care to child whom they assess.

The negligent exercise of statutory duty may have European Human Rights implications. The *X (A Minor) v Bedfordshire C.C.* [1995] 3 All E.R. 353 and *M (Minor) v Newham L.B.C.* [1994] 4 All E.R. 602 cases resulted in successful applications before the European Court of Human Rights. In *Z v UK* (2002) 34 E.H.R.R. 3 (*X (Minors) v Bedfordshire C.C.*) the ECHR held that the children's right to freedom from inhuman and degrading treatment, as protected by Art.3 of the Convention had been violated.

For over four years the children had suffered grave neglect at the hands of their parents. The local authority was aware of the children's' plight but failed to take them into care for four and half years and only did so after the mother specifically requested such action. The ECHR also found that there had been a breach of Art.13 in that there was neither a domestic remedy to determine their allegation of inhuman and degrading treatment nor the ability to obtain an enforceable award of compensation for the damage suffered (see also *DP and JC v UK* (2003) 36 E.H.R.R. 14). Similarly in *E v UK* (2003) 36 E.H.R.R. 31, [2003] 1 F.L.R. 348 the four applicants succeeded in their violation of Art.3 claim where the social services failed to investigate allegations of sexual and physical abuse. In *TP and KM v UK* (2002) 34 E.H.R.R. 2 (*M v Newham L.B.C.*) the local authority conducted an interview with the child which revealed that the child had been sexually abused not by the mother's current partner but by a former partner who co-incidentally shared the same first name as the mother's current partner. The child was taken into care and returned to the mother a year later when the mother's lawyers received the video and transcript of the interview which identified that there was no risk to the child. The ECHR held, in the context of Art.8 and the right to respect for family life, that there was a positive obligation to furnish to the parent concerned the material upon which it was proposed to take the child into care. This was the case even in the absence of an express request by the parent for the material. Further any issue as to whether to disclose the material should have been promptly submitted to a court for its determination. These failures constituted a deprivation of the mother's right to adequate involvement in the decision-making process concerning her daughter amounting to a failure to respect both the mother's and the daughter's right to respect for family life.

The Health Service Executive in carrying out its function under s.3 may be vicariously liable, in appropriate circumstances, for the negligent acts, omissions or statements of its servants and agents. In the *M* case (above) the House of Lords refused to impose a common law duty of care upon the local authorities in question for the alleged negligence of the respective servants and agents. In *M* (above) the child, who had been sexually abused, was unnecessarily brought into care on the advice of a social worker and a psychiatrist as a result of their failure to take an accurate case history from the child's mother. *M* was distinguished in the case of *E v Dorset C.C.* [1995] 3 All E.R. 353 where the House of Lords held that there was a case for damages for negligent advice concerning the special educational needs of the plaintiffs. That position has now been clarified by *Phelps v Hillingdon L.B.C.* [1999] 1 All E.R. 421, [1999] 1 W.L.R. 500 and *Barrett v Enfield L.B.C.* [1999] 3 All E.R. 193 in the latter of which Lord Browne-Wilkinson clarified his earlier remarks in *E v Dorset C.C.* to the extent that the vicarious liability of a statutory body for the negligence of another person providing a service essentially depends upon determining for whom the health care professional is providing the service. In *Phelps* the psychology service examined children with learning difficulties but the service was established to advise the local authority on how to exercise its educational responsibilities rather than a service akin to a hospital which is accessible to the public. In that respect the psychologist was held not to owe a duty of care to the child.

Lister v Hesley Hall Ltd [2001] 2 All E.R. 769, [2001] 2 W.L.R. 1311, [2001] 2 F.L.R. 307 considered the issue of vicarious liability within the child care context. Here a local authority boarded out boys with emotional and behavioural difficulties to a boarding house managed by the defendant company. The defendant company employed a married couple as warden and housekeeper to care for the boys. The husband sexually abused the plaintiffs over a three-year period. The House of Lords held that the defendant company could be vicariously liable for the unlawful and unauthorised acts of sexual abuse committed by the warden husband. Central to the court's ruling was the fact that the warden not alone had access or opportunity to abuse the children but more importantly the school was responsible for the care of the children and the warden was entrusted to discharge that function. The House of Lords in so concluding overruled the earlier Court of Appeal decision in *Trotman v North Yorkshire C.C.* [1999] L.G.R. 584 where a deputy headmaster of a school for mentally handicapped children sexually abused a child on a trip to Spain. The House of Lords also applied and endorsed the Canadian Supreme Court decisions in *Bazley v Curry* (1999) 174 D.L.R. (4th) 45 and *Jacobi v Griffiths* (1999) 174 D.L.R. (4th) 71, the former of which imposed liability on the defendant non-profit child-care service for sexual abuse committed by a paedophile employed by them despite having vetted the abuser and being unaware of his abusive history. In the latter decision the defendant was held not to be vicariously liable for abuse due to the fact that the abuse occurred in the abuser's home. The Canadian Supreme Court reasoning centres on two fundamental policy reasons of providing a just remedy for the harm inflicted and providing deterrence against future harm. The issue of liability rests upon the sufficiency of the connection between the wrongful act and the conduct authorised by the employer. In particular five factors were identified as to whether the connection was sufficient which were: the opportunities the enterprise afforded to the employee to abuse his power; the extent to which the wrongful act may have furthered the employer's aims and hence more likely to be committed by the employee; the extent to which the wrongful act was related to friction or confrontation or intimacy inherent in the employer's enterprise; the extent of power conferred on the employee in relation to the victim; and the vulnerability of the potential victim through wrongful exercise of the employee's power. Both the English and Canadian decisions have been adopted in the New Zealand decision of *S v Attorney General* [2002] NZF.L.R. 295. More recently the Supreme Court of Canada has considered the basis for imposing liability in negligence on both the State and a school board. In *KLB v British Columbia* [2003] 2 S.C.R. 403 the respondent State was held liable for their direct negligence in failing to properly monitor and supervise foster parents. The plaintiffs had been subjected to abuse, including sexual abuse, in two foster homes but the State was not held vicariously liable for the injury suffered. The Canadian Supreme Court also noted that a fiduciary relationship existed between the State and the children but in the circumstances no breach of that duty arose in the case and further a breach of a non-delegable duty of care did not arise (see also *MB v British Columbia* [2003] 2 S.C.R. 459). In *EDG v Hammer* [2003] 2 S.C.R. 477 a school board of trustees were likewise not held vicariously liable for the unknown sexual abuse committed by the school janitor. Similar claims for liability for beach of non-delegable duty of care and breach of fiduciary duty were rejected. The Australian approach to these issues contrasts with the above. In *New South Wales v Lepore, Samin v Queensland* and *Rich v Queensland* (2003) 77 A.L.J.R. 558, the High Court of Australia emphasised that ordinarily a non-delegable duty of care did not arise on behalf of a school authority for the deliberate physical and sexual abuse of students by teachers even where such occurred on school grounds and within school hours. Only where the school authority was at fault could liability arise, otherwise the school authority would be absolutely liable for any injury sustained irrespective of how such was caused, be it intentional or accidental. Ordinarily a school authority could not be vicariously liable for the predatory abuse of a student by a teacher. Where the responsibilities of the teacher, however, placed him in a position of power and intimacy that his conduct could be regarded as so closely connected with his responsibilities as to be in the course of employment, the school authority could be held liable. The provision of care alone by the teacher would be insufficient to attract liability for the school authority.

In *Delahunty v South Eastern Health Board* [2003] 4 I.R. 361, O'Higgins J. did not have to address the issue of the Health Service Executive's vicarious liability for the sexual assault committed by a housemaster employed by the second defendant orphanage as the matter against the Health Service Executive was struck out by the agreement of the parties. O'Higgins J., did, however, tacitly support the test laid down by the House of Lords in *Lister* but on an application of that test found no vicarious liability on behalf of the orphanage as the employee here had no particular duty to the plaintiff who was a mere visitor to the orphanage as opposed to being a resident of the home. In addition, the third defendant, the Minister for Education and Science, was neither vicariously liable for the plaintiff's assault nor did the Minister owe a non-delegable duty to the plaintiff on the basis that he had no control over the life of the plaintiff. Similarly an argument that there had been a breach of statutory duty by the Minister under the Children Act 1941 was rejected on the basis that Minister did not exercise management functions over the orphanage. Further O'Higgins J. rejected the argument that the Minister owed an indemnity of contribution to the orphanage arising from the State's constitutional obligation under Art.42.5. The orphanage in question was found liable in negligence for failing to investigate earlier reports of abuse of children.

The 1991 Act sets the parameters of the powers and duties of the Health Service Executive. The Health Service Executive can and must operate within the powers and duties conferred. In exceptional circumstances the Health Service Executive may be called upon to perform a function which does not fall within the statutory powers or duties conferred but is constitutionally authorised in order to discharge the State's duty to vindicate the constitutional rights of children. The 1991 Act did not originally confer jurisdiction upon the courts to order the secure detention of children whose health and welfare required such. This absence of jurisdiction resulted in applications to the High Court seeking declarations that the children concerned, in vindication of their constitutional rights, required the State to civilly detain the children to ensure their welfare. The reported and unreported judgments include: *MF v Superintendent Ballymun Garda Station* [1991] 1 I.R. 189; *FN v The Minister for Education* [1995] 1 I.R. 409, [1995] 1 I.L.R.M 297; *DT v Eastern Health Board*, unreported, High Court, March 14, 1995; *GL v Minister for Justice*, unreported, HC, March 24, 1995; *DD v The Eastern Health Board*, unreported, High Court, May 3, 1995; *PS v Eastern Health Board*, unreported, High Court, July 27, 1995; *Comerford v Minister for Education* [1997] 2 I.L.R.M 234; *DG v The Eastern Health Board* [1997] 3 I.R. 511, [1998] 1 I.L.R.M 241; *DB v Minister for Justice* [1999] 1 I.R. 29, [1999] 1 I.L.R.M 93; *DH v Minister for Justice*, unreported, High Court, May 23, 2000, *TD v Minister for Education* [2001] 4 I.R. 259.

These cases are considered in more detail in Pt IVA which was introduced by s.16 of the Children Act 2001 the effect of which authorises the District Court to make special care orders authorising the secure detention of children whose welfare so requires it.

Welfare: The term welfare has both a statutory and constitutional basis. Welfare in relation to children is the first and paramount consideration for the court in determining a case. Its statutory basis is to be found in s.3 of the Guardianship of Infants Act 1964 where "welfare" is defined in s.2 of the 1964 Act as compromising "the religious, moral, intellectual, physical and social welfare of the infant". The constitutional basis for the term is said to derive from Art.42.1 (Walsh J. in *B v B* [1975] I.R. 54 at 61; Finlay C.J. in *KC and AC v An Bord Uchtála* [1985] I.L.R.M. 302 at 317). In *State (D and D) v Groarke* [1990] 1 I.R. 305 the withholding of the identity and location of the person who had control of a child may, in exceptional circumstances, be necessary for the welfare of the child.

Subsection (2)

This provides the means by which the statutory function is to be exercised. The Health Service Excutive enjoy a discretion in the subjective exercise of their statutory functions as the phrase "as it considers requisite" implies. In performing the statutory obligation to promote the welfare of children who are not receiving adequate care and attention, the Health Service Executive must adhere to the requirements set out in s.3(2)(*a*)–(*c*). Once these requirements have been adhered to, the Health Service Executive can be said to have fulfilled its statutory function. Whilst the exercise of the statutory function may have attached to it an element of subjectivity in its exercise, this does not mean that the exercise of the function in question is unreviewable. In *Paul Stephens v The Eastern Health Board*, unreported, High Court, July 27, 1994 at 16, Geoghegan J. stated in reviewing the accommodation provided by the Health Board for the applicant that "the court should [not] act as its own expert. It is very much for the experts within the Health Board to form a view as to what is necessary". The judge then, however, stated that the Health Board was not fulfilling its duty under ss.3 and 5 by maintaining the applicant in accommodation that was suitable only as an emergency measure.

The main purpose of subs.(2) is to strike a fair balance between the competing interests of children, parents and the Health Service Executive. The primary objective is to safeguard the welfare of children whose wishes in the matter may be considered where appropriate. This can only be achieved by respecting the rights of parents and the rebuttable presumption that the best interests of the child is served by being brought up within his own family.

Rights and Duties of Parents: The term "'parents" is defined in s.2 as including a surviving parent and where a child has been adopted (a domestic or recognised foreign adoption under the Adoption Acts 1952–1988) the adopter, adopters or surviving adoptive parent. The Health Service Executive has a duty to have regard to the rights of parents whether these derive under the Constitution or otherwise. The marital status of a parent determines the nature of the right owed under the Constitution. Marital parents are afforded the protections conferred by Art.41 and Art.42 of the Constitution (see Casey, *Constitutional Law in Ireland* (3rd ed., Round Hall Ltd, Dublin, 2000), Chap.17 as highlighted by the Supreme Court in *North Western Health Board v HW* [2001] 3 I.R. 622. Non-marital parents are not afforded the same treatment as marital parents (*The State (Nicolaou) v An Bord Uchtála* [1966] I.R. 567). A further distinction arises between non-marital mothers and non-marital fathers. The former has an unenumerated personal constitutional right to the custody of her child (*G v An Bord Uchtála* [1980] I.R. 32) whereas the single father has been declared to have no constitutional right to guardianship of his child (*K v W* [1990] 2 I.R. 437 and endorsed in *W'OR v EH* [1996] 2 I.R. 248). The reference to rights deriving otherwise than under the Constitution in s.3(2)(*b*), for which Health Boards must have regard, relate here to s.6A of the Guardianship of Infants Act 1964 which confers upon the single father no more than a statutory right to apply to be appointed a guardian of his child as opposed to a right to be appointed guardian of the child. Without a s.6A order the single father has no right to custody and thus need not be given notice of any application made by the Health Service Executive under the 1991 Act. A single father may acquire the status of guardian by agreement with the mother of the child (see s.4(4) of the Children Act 1997). The position of the single father is reflected in S.I. No.338 of 1995, District Court (Child Care) Rules 1995 where only the parent with custody or a person acting *in loco parentis* must be served with notice of the various applications the Health Service Executive can make under the 1991 Act. This contrasts with the position in England where specific provision is made for service of proceedings on the single father under the Children Act 1989 (see *Re P (Care Proceedings: Father's Application to be Joined)* [2001] 1

F.L.R. 781; *Re B* (*Care Proceedings: Notification of Father without Parental Responsibility*) [1999] 2 F.L.R. 408).

Where, however, the Health Service Executive proposes to rely upon s.36(1)(c) and place a child with prospective adopters, the Health Service Executive is obliged to adhere to ss.4 and 6 of the Adoption Act 1998. The effect of s.4 of the Adoption Act 1998 is to confer upon the single father the right to give notice to the Adoption Board concerning his wish to be consulted or not in the adoption process and where the identity of the single father is known, the obligation to consult and inform him of the proposed placing of a child for adoption. Section 6 contains similar provisions in relation to post-placement consultation with the single father. Of significance are ss.7F(2) and 19A(3) of the Adoption Act 1952, inserted respectively by ss.4 and 6 of the Adoption Act 1998, which authorise the Adoption Board not to consult with the single father prior to the placement and in the making of an adoption order where the Adoption Board is satisfied that it is not appropriate to do so having regard to the relationship between the mother and the father and the circumstances surrounding the child's conception. Some recent English decisions on a similar issue are: *Re M* (*Adoption: Rights of Natural Father*) [2001] 1 F.L.R. 745; *Re H, Re G* (*Adoption: Consultation of Unmarried Fathers*) [2001] 1 F.L.R. 646.

The different meanings and rights attaching to the term "family" were alluded to under questioning by Minister for State Treacy (see 392 *Dáil Debates* Cols 2105–1207).

Child: This is defined in s.2 as a person under the age of 18 other than a person who is or has been married. This replaces the two categories of minor who were affected by the Children Acts 1908–1989, namely a "child", a person under the age of 15 years and a "young person" who was a person who was 15 years or upwards and under the age of 17 years (s.131 of the Children Act 1908 as amended by s.29 of the Children Act 1941).

Welfare: see subs.(1).

Wishes of the Child: The Health Service Executive in carrying out its general function is required, in a qualified manner, to have regard to the wishes of the child where practicable. In emergency situations it may not be possible to ascertain the views of the child whose general welfare may require summary intervention on the part of a Health Service Executive. The duty may be further qualified by the Health Service Executive's subjective assessment of the child's capacity to understand. If a child is an infant and incapable of communicating, its age renders the ascertaining of views impossible.

Principle of Rearing within the Family: The primary function of the Health Service Executive under the 1991 Act is to promote the welfare of children and if this was the sole consideration of the Health Service Executive it could be seen to be child orientated to the exclusion of the interests of married parents. As there is no definition of "family" set out in this section or the definition section it is presumed that the traditional meaning of family is intended here, that being the family as based upon marriage. In this regard it is important to impose a statutory duty to regard the principle that, generally, the best interests (the term welfare is not used here though little difference in emphasis can be inferred from this omission bearing in mind that the principle in issue here is one of constitutional importance) of the child arise by being brought up within the marital family. The rights of the family and the child as a member of that unit were set out by Finlay C.J. in *Re JH* (*An Infant*) [1985] I.R. 375. This case concerned a custody dispute between a married couple and prospective adopters, a conflict not dissimilar to the intervention of the Health Service Executive under the Act. The rights afforded are subject, however, to circumstances amounting to an "exceptional case" or there being "compelling reasons" for the child not to be raised by the family ([1985] I.R. 275 at 395). Hence the use of the term "generally" here which may be equated with that of the presumption, though rebuttable, which is afforded the family. The constitutional significance of the family unit and in particular the presumption of parental autonomy in making decisions concerning their children has most recently been highlighted in *North Western Health Board v HW* [2001] 3 I.R. 635.

The concept of rearing within the family is also reflected to a certain degree in European Human Rights case law. Article 8 of the Convention provides protection to the right to family life. From Art.8, two specific obligations are imposed upon signatories. First, care proceedings should be of a temporary nature and secondly, where the interests of the child so merit, efforts should be made to re-unite parents with children (see *EP v Italy* (2001) 31 E.H.R.R. 463 and *K and T v Finland* (2001) 31 E.H.R.R. 484).

The most extreme of infringements of the rights of the family will arise in an order under ss.17 and 18 where a child is involuntarily taken into care and for a statutory body to be empowered to initiate such an action, it is imperative that the authorising provisions are seen to constitutionally respect the rights of the family.

Subsection (3)

The primary mandatory obligation imposed on the Health Service Executive by this subsection is to provide child care and family support services, a report of which must be produced annually under s.8 of the 1991 Act. By way of example, the Eastern Health Board provides the following services: child health services; speech and language therapy; dental services; drug misuse; child and adolescence psychiatric services; early childhood support and intervention; child and family support and intervention; child abuse; social work service; fostering; residential care; the "out of hours" service; service for the homeless and out of home young people; family refuges and adoption (for a detailed explanation of these various services see the Eastern Health Board Review of Adequacy Report 1995). The obligation to provide these services is subject to further functions being conferred by statute or directions of the Minister under s.69. The Domestic Violence Act 1996 by virtue of s.6 specifically confers upon the Health Service Executive the authority to seek either a safety or barring order. Under s.7(1) of the 1996 Act a court may order the Health Service Executive to undertake an investigation, during which a supervision order can be made. The Health Service Executive, if directed to investigate, must consider the options of a care or supervision order, the provision of services or assistance or other action. In relation to these options reasons must be given to the court for the exercise or otherwise of the options available (s.7(4)(*a*), (*b*) and (*c*)). In addition to these stated statutory obligations, Barr J. in *MQ v Gleeson* [1998] 4 I.R. 85 details the nature and extent of the Health Board's primary statutory function in promoting the welfare of children. The statutory function includes an obligation to investigate, record, report and conduct a fair hearing where allegations of child abuse arise. Arising from this process the Health Service Executive may also communicate to a third party the results of an investigation. Under s.69 of the 1991 Act the Minister may direct the inspection of premises or services provided by the Health Service Executive (s.69(1)) which is conducted by a person authorised by the Minister (s.69(3)) who can enter and examine the state and management of the premises and the treatment of the children therein as he thinks fit (s.69(4)(*a*)). Further such authorised person may examine records and interview the members of staff (s.69(4)(*b*)).

The Health Service Executive is conferred with a discretionary function in relation to both the provision and maintenance of premises and other functions in this regard as it considers necessary, though this is again subject to Ministerial direction under s.69.

Subsection (4)

This is a consolidating provision in relation to the Health Acts under which functions and powers conferred by earlier Health Acts provisions are to apply under the 1991 Act.

Voluntary care

4.—(1) Where it appears to [the Health Service Executive that a child requires] care or protection that he is unlikely to receive unless he is taken into its care, it shall be the duty of [the Executive] to take him into its care under this section.

(2) Without prejudice to the provisions of *Parts III, IV* and *V*, nothing in this section shall authorise [the Health Service Executive] to take a child into its care against the wishes of a parent having custody of him or of any person acting in loco parentis or to maintain him in its care under this section if that parent or any such person wishes to resume care of him.

(3) Where [the Health Service Executive] has taken a child into its care under this section, it shall be the duty of [the Executive]—

    (a) subject to the provisions of this section, to maintain the child in its care so long as his welfare appears to [the Executive] to require it and while he remains a child, and

    (b) to have regard to the wishes of a parent having custody of him or of any person acting in loco parentis in the provision of such care.

(4) Without prejudice to the provisions of *Parts III, IV* and *VI*, where [the Health Service Executive] takes a child into its care because it appears that he is lost or that a parent having custody of him is missing or that he has been deserted or abandoned, [the Executive] shall endeavour to reunite him with that parent where this appears to [the Executive] to be in his best interests.

[(5) A child who was taken into care under this section by the Health Service Executive before the amendment of this section by the Health Act 2004 and who is in the care of the Health Service Executive immediately before the establishment day of the Health Service Executive shall be deemed for the purposes of this Act to have been taken into care by the Executive and to be in its care on and from that day.]

AMENDMENT

Subsections (1), (2), (3) and (4) amended, and subsection (5) inserted, by s.75 and Schedule 7 of the Health Act 2004, No. 42 of 2004, with effect from January 1 2005 (S.I. 887 of 2004).

DEFINITIONS

    "area": s.2.
    "child": s.2.
    "health board": s.2.
    "parent": s.2.

COMMENCEMENT

Child Care Act, 1991 (Commencement) Order, 1995 (S.I. No. 258 of 1995), which took effect as of October 31, 1995.

NOTE

The purpose of s.4 is to provide a voluntary means of taking children into care with the co-operation of parents or those who are acting *in loco parentis*. No child can be brought into care under s.4 unless the parent agrees. The maintenance of a child in care can be terminated at the request of a parent or person acting *in loco parentis* in which case the child must be immediately returned to that person. It follows that if a parent terminates voluntary care, the child must be returned immediately as the executive has the authority to detain the child against the wishes of the parent.

The operation of the section is contingent upon the child either residing or being found within the Health Service Executive's "area". Further the child must appear in the Health Service Executive's view to be in need of "care or protection" which can only be satisfied by bringing the child into care. Where s.4 operates the Health Service Executive retains a degree of discretion in whether to bring the child into care. It must only do so where the child's "care and protection" cannot otherwise be achieved. This affords the Health Service Executive the opportunity of utilising other services at its disposal to secure the child's "care and protection". Minister for State Treacy gave the examples of home help or social work support (see 403 *Dáil Debates* Col.1918). The principle underlying the section is to have recourse to taking a child into care as a matter of last resort. Other avenues of securing the child's "care and protection" should first be explored. Where, however, the section needs to be utilised, the Health Service Executive should conduct a thorough and conscientious assessment of the child in question to ascertain what action should be taken. This is particularly so where a parent has requested the Health Service Executive to take a child into care (see *R v Tower Hamlets L.B.C. Ex p. B, Lexis Transcript*, January 13, 1997). Failure of the Health Service Executive to properly assess a child's circumstances would properly be redressed by recourse to judicial review proceedings as indicated by Geoghegan J. in *Paul Stephens v The Eastern Health Board*, unreported, High Court, July 27, 1994.

"Care and Protection"

Central to the operation of the Health Service Executive's function of taking a child into care under s.4 is for the child to be in need of "care and protection". There is no definition of this phrase but s.8 sets out examples of circumstances which may constitute want of "care and protection". These include:
– children whose parents are dead or missing;
– children whose parents have deserted or abandoned them;
– children who are homeless;
– children at risk of being neglected or ill treated; and
– children whose parents are unable to care for them due to ill-health or for any other reason.

These circumstances are given by way of example and do not constitute a comprehensive list. Section 4 deliberately omits a definition or list of relevant circumstances to maximise the Health Service Executive's discretion in the matter. The circumstances as set out above contrast sharply with the grounds upon which an emergency care order or a care order may be sough under ss.13 and 18 respectively.

Where the requirements of either s.13 or s.18 were to be found in existence then the Health Service Executive would be obliged to seek an order under either of these sections. In s.4(2) the Health Service Executive is not prejudiced from this course of action where a child is originally taken into care in a voluntary fashion.

"In loco parentis"
    A definition of this phrase is not contained in the Act but O'Hanlon J. in *Hollywood v Cork Harbour Commissioners* [1992] 2 I.R. 457 at 465 described the phrase as "any situation where one person assumes the moral responsibility, not binding in law, to provide for the material needs of another". At 466, O'Hanlon J. stated that this relationship included the provision for both the material needs and the welfare of the child. Further, the relationship in which the concept arises need not be one of blood link. O'Hanlon J. referred to Stirling J.'s passage in *Re Ashton, Ingham v Papillon* [1897] 2 Ch. 574. Whilst any individual is capable of acting *in loco parentis* this function is most likely to carried out by someone who is related to the child in question. (See also *Cubboard v Unitis* (1966) 100 I.L.T.R. 40 uncle/niece relationship and *Waters v Cruikshank* [1967] I.R. 378 uncle/nephew relationship.)

Subsection (3)
    Imposes a duty upon the Health Service Executive, once a child has been taken into care, to maintain the child whilst his welfare so requires it or until the child ceases to be a child (*i.e.* reaches the age of 18). Further the Health Service Executive, whilst maintaining a child, is obliged to regard the wishes of a parent or person who is acting *in loco parentis*.

Subsection (4)
    Imposes upon the Health Service Executive the obligation to endeavour to reunite the child with his parent where the child is lost, the parent with custody is missing, or where the child has been deserted or abandoned. The obligation to reunite in these circumstance is subject to the reunion being in the child's best interest. Whether such a reunion is in the child's best interest is a matter for the Health Service Executive to determine. If the Health Service Executive were to determine that reunion was not in the child's interest, the Health Service Executive would be obliged to obtain a care order under ss.17 or 18 in order to lawfully maintain the child. Where the Health Service Executive considers that reunion with his parents is in the child's best interests, but the Health Service Executive still has some reservation on this issue, an application for a supervision order could be made under s.19.

Deserted or abandoned
    Of the four circumstances in which the Health Service Executive has to consider the reuniting of a child with his parents these two circumstances are the most grave and would require serious consideration before the making of a decision to reunite where the child had been either deserted or abandoned. There need only be the appearance of desertion or abandonment, the Health Service Executive is not obliged to be satisfied as a matter of proven fact that the child has been either deserted or abandoned.
    In relation to desertion there is no case law on the issue of a parent specifically deserting a child and the concept arises most commonly in relation to spousal desertion, though where there are children born to such a relationship one can argue that the child is deserted to the same extent as the spouse. There are four requirements for spousal desertion: factual separation; an absence of a consent to live apart; an intention to desert; and an absence of just cause for leaving. (See Shatter, *Family Law in the Republic of Ireland* (4th ed., Butterworths 1997), [8.35] *et seq.*) It would be unrealistic for the Health Service Executive to satisfy itself of all four of these requirements and the fact that a parent has intentionally separated from a child ought to suffice.
    Abandonment like desertion is not defined though in English law under s.2 of the

Children Act 1948 as amended by s.12 of the Children Act 1975 the term abandonment appears, and has been considered, to mean "to leave to its fate". See *R v Boulden* (1957) C.A.R. 105, where the leaving of children in an unlit house with little food was evidence upon which a jury could find that the children had been abandoned.

Accommodation for homeless children

5.—Where it appears to [the Health Service Executive that a child is homeless, the Executive shall] enquire into the child's circumstances, and [if it] is satisfied that there is no accommodation available to him which he can reasonably occupy, then, unless the child is received into the [care of the Executive] under the provisions of this Act, [the Executive shall take] such steps as are reasonable to make available suitable accommodation for him.

AMENDMENT

Amendments by s.75 and Schedule 7 of the Health Act 2004, No.42 of 2004, with effect from January 1, 2005 (S.I. No.887 of 2004).

DEFINITIONS

"area": s.2.
"child": s.2.
"health board": s.2.

COMMENCEMENT

Child Care Act, 1991 (Commencement) Order 1992 (S.I. No. 264 of 1992) which took effect as of October 1, 1992.

NOTE

Section 5 imposes upon the Health Service Executive the obligation to accommodate homeless children where the child has not been brought into care under the provisions of the Act. Whether or not a child is homeless is dependent upon the Health Service Executive's assessment of the child's circumstances. Where there is no accommodation which the child can reasonably occupy then the child is homeless and the Health Service Executive is obliged to take reasonable steps to provide accommodation where the Health Service Executive does not propose to take a child into care under s.17 or s.18.

The Health Service Executive is obliged not to merely accommodate homeless children but to provide suitable accommodation for the particular child and his circumstances. The word "suitable" was inserted by amendment at Committee stage in the Seanad and proposed by Senator Ryan (see 129 *Seanad Debates* Cols 501–506).

By way of illustration, the Eastern Health Board accommodates child drug abusers in a special short-term residential unit rather than providing bed and breakfast accommodation. Voluntary bodies also co-operate in the provision of accommodation, notably Focuspoint with its "Off The Streets" project.

Provision of adoption service

6.—[(1) The Health Service Executive shall provide or ensure the provision of a service for the adoption of children in accordance with the Adoption Acts 1952 to 1998.]

The Child Care Acts

(2) For the purposes of this section, [the Health Service Executive] may enter into arrangements with any adoption society for the time being registered in the Adoption Societies Register maintained by An Bord Uchtála under *Part IV* of the Adoption Act, 1952.

(3) [The Health Service Executive] may take a child into its care with a view to his adoption and may maintain him in such care in accordance with the provisions of this Act until he is placed for adoption.

(4) Without prejudice to *Parts III, IV* and *VI*, nothing in this section shall authorise [the Health Service Executive] to take a child into its care against the wishes of a parent having custody of him or of any person acting *in loco parentis* or to maintain him in its care under this section if that parent or any such person wishes to resume care of him.

(5) The provisions of *section 10* shall apply with any necessary modifications in relation to any arrangement made under *subsection (2)*.

AMENDMENT

Subsection (1) substituted, and subss.(2), (3) and (4) amended, by s.75 and Schedule 7 of the Health Act 2004, No.42 of 2004, with effect from January 1. 2005 (S.I. No.887 of 2004).

DEFINITIONS

"area": s.2.
"health board": s.2.

COMMENCEMENT

Child Care Act, 1991 (Commencement) (No.2) Order, 1992 (S.I. No.264 of 1992) brought into effect subs.(1), (2) and (5) of s.6 as of October 1, 1992.

Child Care Act, 1991 (Commencement) Order, 1995 (S.I. No.258 of 1995) brought into effect subss.(3) and (4) as of October 31, 1995.

NOTE

Section 6 obliges the the Health Service Executive to either itself provide an adoption service within its functional area or ensure that a service is provided by a voluntary body by arrangement with the Health Service Executive as authorised by s.6(2). The service must be in accordance with the Adoption Acts 1952–1998 which deal with domestic voluntary and involuntary adoptions. Section 8 of the Adoption Act 1991 obliges the Health Service Executive to ensure that an assessment service of prospective adopters of foreign children is available.

Subsection (3)
This enables a child to be taken into care with a view to adoption. Where the taking into care is voluntary, the consent of the parents, mother or guardian of the child is necessary for a valid adoption. Where the taking into care is by virtue of s.13, s.17 or s.18 the subsequent adoption of a child cannot be validly made without an order from the High Court under s.3 of the Adoption Act 1988.

Subsection (4)
This provides the general principle that a parent or person acting *in loco parentis* shall not have a child in their custody taken into care or where voluntarily placed in

care, continue to be maintained against their wishes by the Health Service Executive. This obligation is subject to proceedings under Pt III (emergency protection of children), Pt IV (care proceedings) and Pt VI (maintenance of children in care).

Subsection (5)
This applies, with any necessary modifications, the provisions of s.10 of the Act. Section 10 authorises the Health Service Executive to assist voluntary bodies which engage in child care and family support services. Assistance by way of periodic contribution, grant or contribution in kind may be given (s.10(*a*), (*b*) and (*c*)).

Child care advisory committees

7.—[(1) The Health Service Executive shall establish for each functional area of the Executive a child care advisory committee to advise the Executive on the performance of its functions under this Act and the Executive shall consider and have regard to any advice so tendered to it.]

[(1A) A child care advisory committee that, before the amendment of this section by the Health Act 2004, was established for a functional area of the Health Service Executive and that was in existence immediately before the establishment of the Health Service Executive shall be deemed to have been established by the Executive in compliance with *subsection (1)* of this section for the corresponding functional area of the Executive or for that area as redefined under *section 67(3)* of the Health Act 2004.]

(2) A child care advisory committee shall be composed of persons with a special interest or expertise in matters affecting the welfare of children, including representatives of voluntary bodies providing child care and family support services.

(3) A person shall not receive any remuneration for acting as a member of a child care advisory committee, but [the Health Service Executive] may make payments to any such member in respect of travelling and subsistence expenses incurred by him in relation to the business of the committee.

(4) Payments under this section shall be in accordance with a scale determined by the Minister, with the consent of the Minister for Finance.

(5) The Minister shall give general directions in relation to child care advisory committees which may include directions on any matter relating to the membership, constitution or business of committees (including a provision empowering a committee to co-opt one or more members) and [the Health Service Executive and each child care advisory committee] shall comply with any such directions.

[(5A) Directions given by the Minister in relation to child care advisory committees in existence immediately before the establishment day of the Health Service Executive shall, subject to the amendment or revocation of those directions under *subsection (5B)*, apply to child care advisory committees established or deemed to have been established by the Executive, unless the Minister otherwise directs.]

[(5B) The Minister may amend or revoke directions given in relation to child care advisory committees.]

(6) [The Health Service Executive] may, with the consent of the Minister, and shall, if so directed by the Minister, establish more than one child care

The Child Care Acts

advisory committee for [a function area of the Executive] and where more than one committee is established the provisions of *subsection (1)* shall apply with the necessary modifications.

(7) Each child care advisory committee shall—

(a) have access to non-personal information in relation to child care and family support services in its area,

(b) consult with voluntary bodies providing child care and family support services in its area,

(c) report on child care and family support services in its area, either on its own initiative or when so requested by the [Health Service Executive],

(d) review the needs of children in its area who are not receiving adequate care and protection,

and where more than one child care advisory committee is established in [a functional area of the Health Service Executive], the provisions of this subsection shall apply with the necessary modifications.

AMENDMENT

Subsection (1) substituted, subss.(1A), (5A) and (5B) inserted, and subss.(3), (5), (6) and (7) amended, by s.75 and Schedule 7 of the Health Act 2004, No.42 of 2004, with effect from January 1, 2005 (S.I. No.887 of 2004).

DEFINITIONS

"child[ren]": s.2.
"functions": s.2.
"health board": s.2.
"the Minister": s.2.

COMMENCEMENT

Child Care Act, 1991 (Commencement) (No.3) Order, 1992 (S.I. No. 349 of 1992) took effect as of December 1, 1992.

NOTE

Section 7(1) requires the Health Service Executive to establish child care advisory committees to advise the Health Service Executive upon the performance of its functions under the 1991 Act.

The Health Service Executive is obliged to consider and have regard to such advice, but there is no obligation upon the Health Service Executive to implement any recommendations made.

Subsection (2)

This designates the composition of the advisory committees. The qualifying criteria for members is for the individual to have a special interest or expertise in the welfare of children. Representatives must be appointed from voluntary bodies which provide child care and family support services. The current Child Care Advisory Committee to the Eastern Health Board comprises representatives from the following areas of interest in child care: Adoption and Foster Care; Residential Care; Services for Pre-School children; Education Services; Services for Homeless Children; Child and Adolescent Services;

Support Services for Children and their Families; Probation and Welfare and An Garda Síochána. The representatives from these bodies are appointed by the Health Service Executive and originate from both public bodies and voluntary organisations.

Subsection (3)
This precludes the remuneration of members of the Child Care Advisory Committee.
Travelling expenses and subsistence expenses may be reimbursed to committee members where incurred in relation to the business of the committee.

Subsection (4)
This enables the Minister for Health, with the consent of the Minister for Finance, to determine the scale of travelling and subsistence payments to committee members.

Subsection (5)
This empowers the Minister to give general directions to the Child Care Advisory Committee on matters, including its membership, constitution and business, which includes the power to co-opt one or more members. Both the Health Service Executive and Committees are obliged to comply with any such directions issued. In the Dáil, Minister for State Treacy indicated that Ministerial power to direct under s.7(5) in relation to membership would be exercised by indicating the relevant groups or professional bodies from which the Health Service Executive would appoint members (see 403 *Dáil Debates* Col.1954).

Subsection (6)
Provides that the Health Service Executive may establish, with the consent of the Minister for Health or be directed to establish by the Minister for Health more than one Child Care Advisory Committee within its area to advise the Health Service Executive.

Subsection (7)
This sets out the functions and rights of the Child Care Advisory Committee. Its functions are fourfold which are to: have access to non-personal information in relation to child care and family support services within the area; consult with voluntary bodies providing child care and family support services within the area; report upon child care and family support services which the committee can do of its own initiative or if requested by the Health Service Executive; and to review the needs of children in its area who are not receiving adequate care and protection. If the Health Service Executive area has more than one Child Care Advisory Committee s.7(7) shall apply to each committee.
This subsection was an amendment proposed by Deputy Yates and accepted by Minister for State Treacy. In the absence of regulations governing the operation of such committees, the Dáil generally felt that Child Care Advisory Committees should have a statutory basis from which to function (see 403 *Dáil Debates* Cols 2007– 2008). Section 7(7)(*c*) was further amended by Senator Ryan's proposal to enable the Committee to report on child care and family support services of its own initiative (see 129 *Seanad Debates* Col.507).
Included in the Eastern Health Board's 1995 Annual Report On Child Care And Family Support Services are two Child Care Advisory Sub Committee reports on Teenage Pregnancy and Adoption and Children in Care.

Review of services

8.—[(1) The Health Service Executive shall—

(*a*) not later than 6 months after the establishment day of the Executive, prepare for each health board the report that, but for the amendment of this section by the Health Act 2004, the health board would have been required to have prepared under this section, and

(*b*) annually thereafter prepare a report on the adequacy of the child care and family support services available in each functional area of the Executive.]

(2) Without prejudice to the generality of *subsection (1)*, [the Health Service Executive] in preparing a report under this section shall have regard to the needs of children who are not receiving adequate care and protection and, in particular—

(*a*) children whose parents are dead or missing,

(*b*) children whose parents have deserted or abandoned them,

(*c*) children who are in the care of [the Executive],

(*d*) children who are homeless,

(*e*) children who are at risk of being neglected or ill-treated, and

(*f*) children whose parents are unable to care for them due to ill-health or for any other reason.

[(3) The Health Service Executive shall give notice of the preparation of a report under *subsection (1)* to—

(*a*) each child care advisory committee, and

(*b*) such bodies as the Executive sees fit whose purposes include the provision of child care and family support services,

and shall have regard to any views or information furnished by such committees or bodies in the preparation of the report.]

(4) [The Health Service Executive] shall submit a copy of any report prepared under this section to the Minister and may make copies of any such report available to such bodies as are mentioned in *subsection (3)(b)*.

AMENDMENT

Subsections (1) and (3) substituted, and subss.(2) and (4) amended, by s.75 and Schedule 7 of the Health Act 2004, No.42 of 2004, with effect from January 1, 2005 (S.I. No.887 of 2004).

DEFINITIONS

"area": s.2.
"child[ren]": s.2.
"health board": s.2.
"parents": s.2.
"the Minister": s.2.

COMMENCEMENT

Child Care Act, 1991 (Commencement) (No. 3) Order 1992 (S.I. No. 349 of 1992) took effect as of December 1, 1992.

Note

This section imposes upon the Health Service Executive the obligation to produce a report on the child care and family support services available within its area. Specific guidelines as to the content of the report are set out, as is the requirement to give notice of preparation of such a report to relevant bodies. The Health Service Executive is obliged to submit a copy of the report to the Minister for Health. The obligation to report falls under the general duty of the Health Service Executive to promote the welfare of children within its area under s.3.

Subsection (1)

This imposes an obligation to produce a report annually on the adequacy of child care and family support services. This provision was amended by Deputy Yates' proposal at Committee Stage in the Dáil where the original version of the section contained no specific time limits within which the first and subsequent reports had to be produced (see 403 *Dáil Debates* Cols 2010–2011).

Subsection (2)

Sets out specific categories of children whom the Health Service Executive in preparing a report is obliged to regard in addition to reviewing the adequacy of child care and family support services. These categories include: children whose parents are dead or missing; children whose parents have deserted or abandoned them; children who are in the care of the Health Service Executive; children who are homeless; children who are at risk of being neglected or ill-treated; and children whose parents are unable to care for them due to ill-health or for any other reason.

Minister for State Treacy added to these categories those children mentioned in s.8(2)(*c*) who are in the care of the Health Service Executive and been either fostered or placed in residential care (see 403 *Dáil Debates* Col.2012).

Further amendments to s.8 were suggested in the Seanad and adopted by the Minister for State in the Dáil whereby the category of child mentioned in s.8(2)(*d*) was included in the section (see 129 *Seanad Debates* Cols 516–517 and 410 *Dáil Debates* Col.431).

Subsection (3)

This obliges the Health Service Executive to give notice to any child care advisory committee in its area when preparing a report under subs.1. The Health Service Executive retains a discretion in giving notice of the preparation of a report to bodies providing child care and family support services. Where, however, notice has been given to the committee or bodies in question, the Health Service Executive is obliged to regard the views or information supplied by them in the preparation of the report.

Subsection (4)

Once a report is prepared under this section the Health Service Executive is obliged to submit such report to the Minister for Health and may make copies available to those bodies mentioned in s.8(3)(*b*) (voluntary bodies providing child care and family support services). It is curious that the child care advisory committee is excluded from mention in this subsection concerning the furnishing of reports and on a strict interpretation the Health Service Executive would not be obliged to make available a report to the committees. This, however, is entirely unreasonable in light of the Health Service Executive's positive obligation to regard information and views submitted to them by such committees. On the basis of this interaction with the preparation of the report, child care advisory committees ought to be entitled to copies of such reports. In any event the Health Service Executive could be directed by the Minister for Health under s.69 to comply with a direction issued under that section to make available a report to a child care advisory committee.

Provision of services by voluntary bodies and other persons

9.—(1) […].

(2) [Nothing in the Health Act 2004 shall empower the Health Service Executive] to delegate to a voluntary body or any other person the duty conferred on it under *section 4* to receive certain children into care or the power to apply for an order under *Part III*, *IV* or *VI*.

AMENDMENT

Subsection (1) deleted and subs.(2) amended by s.75 and Schedule 7 of the Health Act 2004, No.42 of 2004, with effect from January 1, 2005 (S.I. No.887 of 2004).

DEFINITIONS

"health board": s.2.
"the Minister": s.2.

COMMENCEMENT

Child Care Act, 1991 (Commencement) Order, 1992 (S.I. No. 123 of 1992) took effect as of June 1, 1992.

NOTE

This section enables the Health Service Executive to delegate to voluntary and other bodies functions in relation to child care and family support services. The right of the Health Service Executive to enter into arrangements is subject to Ministerial directions but the Health Service Executive may determine the terms and conditions of any arrangement entered into by it with the voluntary bodies or other individuals. The nature and extent of the services to be provided by voluntary bodies or other individuals must be those which the Health Service Executive is empowered to provide under the Act. In this regard s.9(2) specifically excludes from delegation to such voluntary bodies or other individuals any function in relation to the receiving into care of children under s.4 or by virtue of applying for an order under Pts III, IV or VI of the Act.

Assistance for voluntary bodies and other persons

10.—[(1)] [The Health Service Executive] may, subject to any general directions given by the Minister and on such terms or conditions as it thinks fit, assist a voluntary body or any other person who provides or proposes to provide a child care or family support service similar or ancillary to a service which [the Executive] may provide under this Act—

   (*a*) by a periodic contribution to funds of the body or person;
   (*b*) by a grant;
   (*c*) by a contribution in kind (whether by way of materials or labour or any other service).

[(2) Assistance given under this section to a voluntary body or other person that is a service provider as defined in section 2 of the Health Act 2004 shall be deemed for the purpose of Part 9 of that Act to have been given to the voluntary body or other person under section 39 of that Act.]

AMENDMENT

Existing section renumbered as subs.(1) and amended, and subsection (2) inserted, by s.75 and Schedule 7 of the Health Act 2004, No.42 of 2004, with effect from January 1, 2005 (S.I. No.887 of 2004).

DEFINITIONS

"health board": s.2.
"the Minister": s.2.

COMMENCEMENT

Child Care Act, 1991 (Commencement) Order, 1992 (S.I. No. 123 of 1992) took effect as of June 1, 1992.

NOTE

This enables the Health Service Executive to provide assistance to voluntary bodies or other person providing child care and family support services. The authority to assist is subject to Ministerial direction. The assistance may be given on such terms and conditions as the Health Service Executive considers fit. The voluntary body or other person must be providing or propose to provide a child care or family support service in order for assistance to be given. The service given can be similar to one provided by the Health Service Executive or one which is ancillary to a service provided by the Health Service Executive. The assistance can take any of the following forms: periodic payment to funds; grant; or by contribution in kind (by the provision of materials or labour).

Research

11.—(1) The Minister may conduct or assist other persons in conducting research into any matter connected with the care and protection of children or the provision of child care and family support services.

(2) [The Health Service Executive] may conduct or assist other persons in conducting research into any matter connected with the functions assigned to the board under this Act.

AMENDMENT

Subsection (2) amended by s.75 and Schedule 7 of the Health Act 2004, No. 42 of 2004, with effect from January 1, 2005 (S.I. No.887 of 2004).

DEFINITIONS

"functions": s.2.
"health board": s.2.
"the Minister": s.2.

COMMENCEMENT

Child Care Act, 1991 (Commencement) (No. 2) Order, 1992 (S.I. No. 264 of 1992) took effect as of October 1, 1992.

NOTE

This section concerns the conducting of research. The Minister for Health is conferred with discretionary authority to conduct or to assist other persons in conducting research into any matter relating to the care and protection of children or the provision of child care and family support services.

The Health Service Executive is likewise conferred with a discretionary power to conduct or assist others in conducting research into any matter relating to the Executive's functions under the Act.

PART III

PROTECTION OF CHILDREN IN EMERGENCIES

NOTE

Part III of the Child Care Act 1991 provides two means of securing the protection of children in emergency situations. This is achieved by bringing a child into the care of the Health Service Executive either by removal of a child without warrant by a member of the gardaí or by application to the District Court for an emergency care order. There are further provisions in relation to informing parents or person acting *in loco parentis* of the taking into care of the child and the imposition of an obligation upon the Health Service Executive of a duty to provide residential centres for children brought into care under Pt III of the Act.

Power of Garda Síochána to take a child to safety

12.—(1) Where a member of the Garda Síochána has reasonable grounds for believing that—

   (a) there is an immediate and serious risk to the health or welfare of a child, and

   (b) it would not be sufficient for the protection of the child from such immediate and serious risk to await the making of an application for an emergency care order by [the Health Service Executive] under *section 13,*

the member, accompanied by such other persons as may be necessary, may, without warrant, enter (if need be by force) any house or other place (including any building or part of a building, tent, caravan or other temporary or moveable structure, vehicle, vessel, aircraft or hovercraft) and remove the child to safety.

(2) The provisions of *subsection (1)* are without prejudice to any other powers exercisable by a member of the Garda Síochána.

(3) Where a child is removed by a member of the Garda Síochána in accordance with *subsection (1)*, the child shall as soon as possible be delivered up to the custody of the [Health Service Executive].

(4) Where a child is delivered up to the custody of [the Health Service Executive] in accordance with *subsection (3)*, [the Executive] shall, unless it

returns the child to the parent having custody of him or a person acting *in loco parentis*, make application for an emergency care order at the next sitting of the District Court held in the same district court district or, in the event that the next such sitting is not due to be held within three days of the date on which the child is delivered up to the custody of [the Executive], at a sitting of the District Court, which has been specially arranged under *section 13(4)*, held within the said three days, and it shall be lawful for [the Executive] to retain custody of the child pending the hearing of that application.

[(5) Where a child was removed to safety in accordance with *subsection (1)* of this section or *section 254(4)* of the Children Act 2001 before the amendment of those provisions by the Health Act 2004 and the child is not delivered up to the custody of the health board concerned before the establishment day of the Health Service Executive—

    (*a*) the child shall as soon as possible be delivered up to the custody of the Executive, and

    (*b*) *subsection (4)* of this section applies in relation to the child as though the child had been delivered up to the Executive in accordance with *subsection (3)* of this section.]

AMENDMENT

Subsection (5) inserted, and subss.(1)(*b*), (3) and (4) amended by s.75 and Schedule 7 of the Health Act 2004, No. 42 of 2004, with effect from January 1, 2005 (S.I. No.887 of 2004).

DEFINITIONS

    "area": s.2.
    "child": s.2.
    "health board": s.2.

COMMENCEMENT

Child Care Act, 1991 (Commencement) Order, 1995 (S.I. No. 258 of 1995) took effect as of October 31, 1995.

NOTE

Section 12 provides for the protection of children in emergency situations whereby a child can be brought into care without a court order. The wide-ranging power vested in the gardaí is one which should only be resorted to in extreme cases. The circumstances must be so extreme as not to justify the application for an emergency care order under s.13.

Subsection (1)

Authorises a member of An Garda Síochána to remove a child to the care of the Health Service Executive where he\she has reasonable grounds to believe that there is both an immediate and serious risk to the health or welfare of the a child and that the awaiting of an application for an emergency care order under s.13 would not protect the child from the immediacy and seriousness of the risk to his health or welfare. Neither the term "health" nor "welfare" is defined but health can relate to either physical or psychological health. The term "welfare" has both statutory and constitutional implications (see Note to s.3 "welfare", and also *O'B v O'B* [1984] I.R. 182 on the meaning of welfare in the context of the Family Law (Protection of Spouses and Children) Act 1981). Of assistance in identifying a risk to health or welfare are the grounds for a care order under s.18 which include: assault; ill-treatment; neglect; sexual abuse; present or future avoidable impairment or neglect to the health, welfare or development of the child. The Department of Health and Children "National Guidelines for the Protection and Welfare of Children", 1999, identify four forms of abuse that fall within what the Department considers "child abuse". These are physical abuse, sexual abuse, emotional abuse, and neglect. Whilst these are not legal definitions they may be instructive in identifying in a practical way the criteria for a risk to health or welfare. The risk to the child must be current, actual or existing owing to the need to remove the child prior to obtaining an emergency care order, which ordinarily requires two days notice prior to the hearing of an emergency care order (see S.I. No.93 of 1997, District Court Rules 1997, r.5(1)).

Fundamental to the exercise of this emergency and pre-emptive power by the gardaí is the belief that there are reasonable grounds that the health or welfare of the child is at risk. A member of the Garda Síochána will not always personally hold information as to a risk and such revelations are likely to be made by an individual or family member informing either the gardaí or a social worker. Section 3 of the Protections [for Persons Reporting Child Abuse Act 1998 confers immunity from an award of damages where a person reports incidents of child abuse. The immunity conferred operates provided the person reporting has acted reasonably and in good faith. In light of the Department of Health and Children guidelines as updated by "Putting Children First", a discussion document on mandatory reporting, the exercise of the power vested in the gardaí under s.12 would need to transcend the procedures set out in the above documents for dealing with child abuse. In this regard the risk to the child would have to be so immediate and so serious as to justify bypassing the notification process between gardaí and social workers where abuse is suspected or known (see Appendix A of "Putting Children First"), and also to by bypass the investigation and assessment process, including the obtaining of parental consent to a medical examination as a starting point and the convening of a case conference (see "Child Abuse Guidelines" Department of Health, 1987). A member of the gardaí may be accompanied by "such other persons as may be necessary" (invariably a social worker) in the removal to safety of a child at risk. Children can be removed from any place, premises, structure or a number of means of transport. The reference in s.12(1)(*b*) to vehicles, vessels, aircraft and hovercraft may envisage the prevention of an attempted abduction and removal from the jurisdiction by such means. The gardaí may enter the variety of premises stated in subs.(1)(*b*) and may use force if necessary to effect entry. Whilst force may be used to enter, where the need arises, the section does not explicitly authorise the removal of the child by force and where a parent, guardian or person acting *in loco parentis* is unwilling to allow a child be removed, the gardaí would have to apply under s.13 for an emergency care order authorising the removal of the child. If, however, the life of the child was at risk, it would be difficult to imagine a court holding that the removal was unlawful in such circumstances.

Subsection (2)
Provides that the gardaí, in exercising their power under subs.(1), are not prejudiced in exercising other statutory or common law powers that they possess. Where a breach of the criminal law has occurred, the gardaí could exercise powers of arrest or in the related area of domestic violence (arrest without warrant for breach of an order under s.18 of the Domestic Violence Act 1996).

Subsection (3)

Once a child has been removed in accordance with subs.(1), the gardaí must deliver up custody of the child so removed to the Health Service Executive in the area of the Health Service Executive in which the child is for the time being. The gardaí, and not the person or persons accompanying the gardaí, must deliver up the child as soon as is possible. In the interests of the child's welfare, particularly in light of the manner in which the child is to be put into care, it would be undesirable for the child to be maintained at a garda station, and the child should be brought immediately from the place of residence to the custody of the Health Service Executive.

In these circumstances the Health Service Executive has mere physical control of the child. The Health Service Executive is not vested with any parental or guardianship rights which only arise where a care order is made under s.18. The Health Service Executive, where a child has been delivered up by a member of the gardaí under this section, is obliged to inform or cause to inform a parent exercising custody or person acting *in loco parentis* of the delivery up to the Health Service Executive. Section 37 imposes a general duty upon the Health Service Executive to facilitate reasonable access to parents, a person acting *in loco parentis* and any person, in the Health Service Executive's view, who has a bona fide interest in the child.

Subsection (4)

This renders lawful the retention of custody of the child by the Health Service Executive between the time of delivering up the child until the time than an application for an order of the District Court is made under s.13, which is the emergency care order procedure.

The Health Service Executive must apply for an order under s.13 if the child has not been returned to a parent or person acting *in loco parentis*. The maximum duration for which a child may be held in the custody of the Health Service Executive under s.12 is three days.

Where no sitting of the District Court in the district will take place within three days of the date on which the child is delivered up, then an application may be made to any Judge of the District Court under s.13(4)(*b*), which application at a specially arranged sitting must be made within the same three-day period.

Emergency care order

13.—(1) If a justice of the District Court is of opinion on the application of [the Health Service Executive] that there is reasonable cause to believe that—

(*a*) there is an immediate and serious risk to the health or welfare of a child which necessitates his being placed in the care of [the Health Service Executive], or

(*b*) there is likely to be such a risk if the child is removed from the place where he is for the time being,

the justice may make an order to be known and in this Act referred to as an "emergency care order".

(2) An emergency care order shall place the child under the care of [the Health Service Executive] for a period of eight days or such shorter period as may be specified in the order.

(3) Where a justice makes an emergency care order, he may for the purpose of executing that order issue a warrant authorising a member of the Garda Síochána, accompanied by such other members of the Garda Síochána or such

other persons as may be necessary, to enter (if need be by force) any house or other place specified in the warrant (including any building or part of a building, tent, caravan or other temporary or moveable structure, vehicle, vessel, aircraft or hovercraft) where the child is or where there are reasonable grounds for believing that he is and to deliver the child into the custody of the [Health Service Executive].

(4) The following provisions shall have effect in relation to the making of emergency care orders—

    (*a*) any such order shall, subject to *paragraph* (*b*), be made by the justice for the district in which the child resides or is for the time being;

    (*b*) where a justice for the district in which the child resides or is for the time being is not immediately available, an order may be made by any justice of the District Court;

    (*c*) an application for any such order may, if the justice is satisfied that the urgency of the matter so requires, be made *ex parte*;

    (*d*) an application for any such order may, if the justice is satisfied that the urgency of the matter so requires, be heard and an order made thereon elsewhere than at a public sitting of the District Court.

(5) An appeal from an emergency care order shall not stay the operation of the order.

(6) It shall not be necessary in any application or order under this section to name the child if such name is unknown.

(7)(*a*) Where a justice makes an emergency care order, he may, of his own motion or on the application of any person, give such directions (if any) as he thinks proper with respect to—

    (i) whether the address or location of the place at which the child is being kept is to be withheld from the parents of the child, or either of them, a person acting *in loco parentis* or any other person;

    (ii) the access, if any, which is to be permitted between the child and any named person and the conditions under which the access is to take place;

    (iii) the medical or psychiatric examination, treatment or assessment of the child.

    (*b*) A direction under this subsection may be given at any time during the currency of the order and may be varied or discharged on the application of any person.

AMENDMENT

Subsections (1), (2) and (3) amended by s.75 and Schedule 7 of the Health Act 2004, No. 42 of 2004, with effect from January 1, 2005 (S.I. No.887 of 2004).

DEFINITIONS

    "area": s.2.
    "child": s.2.
    "health board": s.2.
    "parent[s]": s.2.

COMMENCEMENT

Child Care Act, 1991 (Commencement) Order, 1995 (S.I. No. 258 of 1995) took effect as of October 31, 1995.

NOTE

The application for an order under s.13 arises in an emergency situation. Only the Health Service Executive may make the application. The application by virtue of s.29(1) requires it to be held *in camera* and S.I. No.93 of 1997, District Court Rules 1997, r.4(1) authorises the presence of court officers, legal representatives and witnesses and such other persons as the judge, in his discretion, permits to be present. Section 29(2) makes applicable s.33(1) and (2) of the Judicial Separation and Family Law Reform Act 1989 which provisions relate respectively to court personnel (judges, solicitors and barristers) not wearing wigs and gowns and to the conducting of proceedings in as informal a manner as is practicable and consistent with the administration of justice (see S.I. No.93 of 1997, District Court Rules 1997, Ord.84, r.2(3)).

The application must be made immediately to a Judge of the District Court in the district court area in which the child resides or where the child is for the time being (s.13(4)(a)). The reason for the alternative basis for the District Court's jurisdiction is because a child may be placed in the care of the Health Service Executive by the gardaí under s.12(1) in an area which is different to that where the child resides.

Where a Judge of the District Court is not immediately available, any Judge of the District Court may grant an order.

Ordinarily an application under s.13(1) requires the service of notice of the application upon the respondent (parent having custody or person acting *in loco parentis*) two days prior to the date fixed for the hearing of the application (See S.I. No.93 of 1997, District Court Rules 1997, Ord.84, r.5(i)). In cases of urgency an *ex parte* application may be made (see s.13(4)(c) and S.I. No.93 of 1997, District Court Rules 1997, Ord.84, rr.5(2)(a) and (b)) which can be heard and granted at a place elsewhere than at a public sitting of the District Court (for example, at the Judge's home). Such urgent ex parte applications in places other than a public sitting of the District Court can be made to either a District Judge of the district in which the child resides or is for the time being or any Judge of the District Court, where a Judge of the district in which the child resides or is for the time being is not immediately available. The Canadian Supreme Court has considered the constitutional validity of emergency care type orders in circumstances where the parent has no notice of the application for the order. In *KLW v Winnipeg* [2000] S.C.C. 48 a majority upheld the constitutional validity of s.21(1)(2) of the Child and Family Services Act 1985–1986 on the basis that a balance between the parents' rights and the State's interest in protecting the child was adequately set where removal of a child was restricted to cases where the agency, on reasonable grounds, believed that the child was at serious risk of harm and there was a prompt post-removal hearing.

The European Court of Human Rights (ECHR) has considered emergency care orders in a number of recent decisions where children have been immediately removed from their mothers at birth. Emergency care orders clearly violate the protection afforded to family life guaranteed by Art.8 of the European Convention for the Protection of Human Rights and Fundamental Freedoms ("the Convention"). Invariably the application for an emergency care order will both be in accordance with law and for a legitimate aim as emergency care orders are necessary to protect a child and thus satisfy the legitimate aim of protection of health, morals or more particularly the rights of the child. The crucial issue is whether circumstances surrounding the application for the emergency care order can be said to be necessary in a democratic society.

The ECHR extensively examined emergency care orders in *K and T v Finland* (2001) 31 E.H.R.R. 18, [2001] 1 F.L.R. 707 (affirmed in (2003) 36 E.H.R.R. 18). Here a schizophrenic mother of two children, P and M, by different fathers gave birth to a third child, J, in June of 1993. J was the subject of an emergency care order within six hours of birth of which the applicant had no notice and was only informed after the care orders had been made. M was in care at the time of J's birth and was also made the subject of an emergency care order. The applicant's access to P was restricted by court order following a custody dispute with P's father. The applicant's initial access was one supervised visit per month in a foster home. In 1995 the applicant gave birth to another child, R, whom the applicant proved capable of caring for. A single three-hour monthly visit to the two children until the age of 12 was recommended. The Court noted that the application for emergency care orders necessitated not consulting with the parents and as such the effect of their abrupt removal from the family without notice was justified. In addition the application for emergency care orders fell within the margin of appreciation afforded contracting states but ultimately the latitude to be afforded depended upon the seriousness of the threat to the child and the possibility of reuniting the child with the family. The Court also noted that an emergency care order was an extremely harsh measure which required extraordinary compelling reasons for the removal of a child against the will of the mother immediately after the birth and was as a consequence of a procedure in which neither the applicant nor her partner had been involved. On the facts of the case, there was no reason to justify the emergency care order for J. Similarly in *Haase v Germany* [2004] 2 F.L.R. 39 the prohibition on contact and access to seven children, one of whom was seven days old was found to be in breach of Art.8. Further, both the use of emergency procedures to remove the children and the failure to sufficiently involve the parents in the decision-making process fell foul of the Convention. *Johansen v Norway* (1997) 23 E.H.R.R. 33 provides a good example of an Art.8 violation. The applicant's second child was placed in temporary care shortly after birth owing to the social services concern for the applicant mother's poor physical and medical condition. Within five months a decision was made to place the child in permanent foster care with a view to adoption. The decision also directed the termination of both the mother's parental rights and access to the child as well as rendering secret the address of the foster home. The decision was held to violate Art.8 of the Convention and in particular the measures were considered too far-reaching and inconsistent with the overall obligation to reunite parent and child. The Court did note that in exceptional circumstances pertaining to the child's best interests that it would be justifiable to impose restrictions of this nature. Two important factors existed at the time of the decision to terminate parental rights and contact which made the decision unjustifiable. First, the mother had enjoyed access to her child for a six-month period. Secondly, the mother had improved her lifestyle to the extent that she was capable of providing an upbringing for her child. Here the social services gave greater consideration to the adoption of the child rather than properly considering and effecting a reunion of the applicant with her child.

Where a violation of the Convention is asserted, the Court will closely scrutinise the circumstances leading to the taking of a child into care and the subsequent decisions relating to the care of the child. In this regard not all emergency care orders and restrictions on access will breach the convention. In *L v Finland* (2001) 31 E.H.R.R. concerns over child sexual abuse allegations justified the use of an emergency care order even though the concerns were later unproven. Subsequently the children in this case were placed in care on the basis of a risk to their future development whereby restrictions on the father's access were justified in light of the allegations of sexual abuse. More particularly the Court noted that children's express desire not to meet their justified total restriction of his, the grandfather's, access.

Not alone can the application for an emergency care order violate Art.8 but also the decision-making process leading to the application and the implementation of the order once obtained can fall foul of Art.8. In *W v UK* (1988) 10 E.H.R.R. 29 the failure to give notice and information to the mother concerning the intended adoption and of the intention to terminate access to her child constituted a violation of the right to family life. These restrictions amounted to insufficient involvement by the mother with the child in the decision-making process amounting to an interference with the right to family life. Likewise in *Olsson v Sweden* (1989) 11 E.H.R.R. 259 a decision to separate children and place them considerable distances from their parents with limited and restricted access and without sufficient reasons for so doing constituted a violation of Art.8. The Court reasoned that the very obligation to reunite the family was weakened by the impediment of not having regular and easy access to their children. See also *EP v Italy* (2001) 31 E.H.R.R. 17 where the court stressed that the Italian authorities had failed to take reasonable steps to re-establish the parent-child relationship in denying the mother access to her daughter in care.

Subsection (1)

This sets out two grounds upon which an emergency care order may be made. It should be noted that the District Judge must be of the opinion that there is reasonable cause to believe either of the grounds set out in s.13(1)(*a*) or (*b*). This contrasts with the requirements of an interim care order (s.17), care order (s.18) and supervision order (s.19) where the District Judge must be satisfied of the requirements set out in the relevant section. Owing to the urgency of the circumstances and the need for immediate protection of the child, the temporary duration of the order (a maximum of eight days, s.13(2)) and thus the limited but nonetheless serious impact of the order on both the parent or person acting *in loco parentis* and the child himself, justify that the lesser requirement of being of the opinion as opposed to that of being satisfied. The standard of proof is likely to be that of the balance of probabilities (see *Re H* [1996] 1 All E.R. 1 which relates to the standard of proof in relation to allegations of sexual abuse).

Under s.13(1)(*a*) the District Judge's opinion that there is reasonable cause to believe is twofold. First, that there is both an immediate and serious risk to the health or welfare of a child. The use of the word "is" indicates that there must be a present or current risk to the child's health or welfare. Secondly, that the immediate and serious risk necessitates the child being placed in the care of the Health Service Executive. Notwithstanding the presence of an immediate and serious risk to the child, there may be circumstances which do not necessitate the taking of the child into care. In an abusive and hostile domestic environment, the risk to a child could be alleviated by removing the abusive and hostile party either by the other applying for a barring or safety order under s.2 or s.3 of the Domestic Violence Act 1996 or by the Health Service Executive applying on behalf of that other party under s.6 of the 1996 Act. It is only where the health or welfare of the child can only be secured by the taking into care of the child that an order under s.13 can be made. Regard here should be had to the Supreme Court decision in *The State DD v Groarke* [1990] 1 I.R. 305 concerning the abuse by one parent. The Supreme Court held that the Court must positively inquire into whether the welfare of the child requires the removal from the innocent parent and the Court would only be justified in so removing the child where the innocent parent was unable to protect the child from the abusing parent.

For an example of the risk to a child in the operation of the similar "place of safety order" under the Children Act 1908 see the facts of *Re FO'D; Southern Health Board v An Bord Uchtála* [1995] 2 I.L.R.M. 369, which concerned the making of an involuntary adoption order under the Adoption Act 1988. Once an order is made it can be enforced by the issuing of a warrant to a member of the gardaí to enforce the order by entering any premises under s.13(3).

Section 13(1)(*b*) provides an alternative ground upon which a District Judge may make an emergency care order. Where the removal of a child from the place where he is for the time being is likely to put the child at an immediate and serious risk then an order may be made. Examples of the circumstances in which an application would be made under this provision are where the child has been taken into care under s.12(1) by a member of the gardaí and placed in the care of the Health Service Executive or where a child has been voluntarily placed into the care of the Health Service Executive under s.4. A further circumstance might be where the child has been admitted to hospital for non-accidental injuries and an order could be granted to prevent the child leaving hospital care.

Subsection (2)

The effect of an emergency care order is to place the child in the care of the Health Service Executive. The duration of the order is stated to be for a period not exceeding eight days or for a shorter period as ordered by the District Judge. The necessity of a minimum duration of separation between the removal of the child from his parents and the subsequent determination of the child's future custody was a matter of great constitutional importance as pointed out by Keane J. in *DC v Midland Health Board*, unreported, High Court, July 31, 1986, albeit in relation to s.24 of the Children Act 1908.

Once in the care of the Health Service Executive, the Executive is limited in what it can do in relation to the child. Unlike a care order under s.18(3), where the Health Service Executive is in essence conferred with parental authority over the child in relation to all aspects of the child's welfare, s.13, like s.17 (interim care order), merely places the child under the care of the Health Service Executive. The Health Service Executive, apart from physically maintaining the child for the duration of the order, can intervene in aspects of the child's welfare only by direction of the court as set out in s.13(7). Further directions in relation to the child's welfare whilst under the care of the Health Service Executive under an emergency care order may be applied for by the Health Service Executive under s.13(7)(*a*).

Subsection (3)

This authorises the District Judge to issue a warrant to a member of the gardaí to execute the emergency care order. The garda may be accompanied by other members of the gardaí and other persons as are considered necessary (for example, social workers and medical personnel). Force may used to enter a variety of premises set out in s.13(3) (see Note to s.12(1)(*b*)). The warrant to enter to remove may relate to a specific place or such place where there are reasonable grounds to believe the child is. Such a provision is necessary, particularly so where the parent or guardians has been given notice of the application for an emergency care order, and thus have the opportunity to remove the child from his normal place of residence and relocate to another address. Before removal of a child the order directing the delivery up of the child must be shown to or given to the person having actual custody of the child (s.14(1)), and this is deemed to have occurred where the person is present in court on the making of the order (s.14(2)). Failure to deliver up a child on foot of an order under s.13 carries a maximum fine of €634.87 or six months imprisonment on summary conviction (s.34(1)).

On the specific requirements of the contents of warrants under s.24 (place of safety order) of the Children Act 1908 see the judgment of Keane J. in *The State (DC) v The Midland Health Board*, unreported, High Court, July 31, 1986.

Subsection (4)

Section 13(4)(*a*) allows the District Judge of the district in which the child resides or is for the time being to make the order. Where such a District Judge is not immediately available any Judge of the District Court may make an order (s.13(4)(*b*) and see S.I. No.93 of 1997, District Court Rules 1997, Ord.84, r.6(1)). An ex parte application for an emergency care order may be made where the District Judge is satisfied that the matter is an urgent one (s.13(4)(*c*) and if the need arises the *ex parte* application may be made and heard, again if the District Judge is satisfied that the matter is an urgent one, elsewhere than at a public sitting of the District Court (s.13(4)(*b*) and S.I. No.93 of 1997, District Court Rules 1997, Ord.84, rr.5(2)(*a*) and (*b*)).

Subsection (5)

This provides that an appeal shall not operate as a stay on the order.

Subsection (6)

This provides that the name of the child who is the subject of an emergency care application and subsequent order need not be given where the name is unknown. This provision is in keeping with the emergency nature of the application.

Subsection (7)

Once a District Judge has made an emergency care order this subsection confers a discretion, on the Judge, to issue directions (see s.47), of his own motion or upon application of any person (for example Health Service Executive, parent, guardian or person acting *in loco parentis*). The directions which can be made relate to first, withholding the location or address where the child is being kept from either or both parents, any person acting *in loco parentis* or any other person. Note, however, should be had of *MF v Superintendent of Ballymun Garda Station* [1991] 1 I.R. 189 where the Supreme Court stated in the context of a "place of safety order" under the Children Act 1908 that it would only be in exceptional circumstances that the location of a child placed in care be withheld from a parent.

The second direction which may be made relates to the granting or refusing of access to the child by any named person. Where access is granted, conditions relating to that access may be made. The ECHR has considered the issue of access in care proceedings in *Johansen v Norway* (1997) 23 E.H.R.R. 33, *K and T v Finland* (2001) 31 E.H.R.R. 18, [2001] F.L.R. 707 affirmed in (2003) 36 E.H.R.R. 18 which hold that a breach of the right to respect for family life can arise by restricting a parent's access to children in care. In *L v Finland* (2001) 31 E.H.R.R. 30, however, the ECHR found no violation of Art.8 where subsequent to an emergency care order the applicant father was refused access to his daughters for a period of 14 weeks.

The third direction which may be given under s.13(7)(a) concerns a direction that the child undergo medical or psychiatric examination, treatment or assessment but not for the purposes of s.25(15) of the Mental Health Act 2001, which expressly excludes a psychiatric examination, treatment or assessment. In *A and B v Eastern Health Board* [1998] 1 I.R. 464 the High Court held that a termination of a pregnancy constituted both medical and psychiatric treatment for the child who was in the care of the Health Board. In *North Western Health Board v HW and CW* [2001] 3 I.R. 622 Hardiman J. indicated that the use of directions for having a P.K.U. test conducted on a child against the wishes of the parents would call into question the constitutionality of the 1991 Act. Where a child has been placed in the care of the Health Service Executive under this section the District Court retains the decision-making power in relation to the child. The authority of the District Court to make directions clearly defines the respective roles of the Court and the Health Service Executive at this stage of care proceedings.

Any direction, if not made at the time of the making of the emergency care order may be made during the currency of the order. Further, any direction made may be varied or discharged, by application of any person. Applications for both a direction after the making of an emergency care order and applications to discharge or vary must be on notice and served two days prior to the hearing of the application, depending upon who makes the application, to the Health Service Executive, either or both of the parents, any person acting *in loco parentis* or any other person as appropriate (see S.I. No.93 of 1997, District Court Rules 1997, Ord.84, r.7(1) and (2)).

For the rules concerning the service of documents required under S.I. No.93 of 1997 District Court Rules 1997, see Ord.84, r.3(1)(*a*)–(*d*).

Notification to be given by [Health Service Executive]

14.—(1) Where a child is delivered up to, or placed in the custody of, [the Health Service Executive under this Part, the Executive] shall as soon as possible inform or cause to be informed a parent having custody of him or a person acting *in loco parentis* of that delivery or placement unless that parent or person is missing and cannot be found.

(2) For the purposes of this section, a person shall be deemed to have been informed of the placing of a child in the custody of [the Health Service Executive] under *section 13* if he is given or shown a copy of the emergency care order made under that section or if that person was present at the sitting of the court at which such order was made.

AMENDMENT

Subsections (1) and (2) amended by s.75 and Schedule 7 of the Health Act 2004, No. 42 of 2004, with effect from January 1, 2005 (S.I. No.887 of 2004).

DEFINITIONS

"child": s.2.
"health board": s.2.
"parents": s.2.

COMMENCEMENT

Child Care Act, 1991 (Commencement) Order, 1995 (S.I. No. 258 of 1995) took effect as of October 31, 1995.

NOTE

Section 14 imposes upon the Health Service Executive the statutory obligation to inform a parent having custody or a person acting *in loco parentis* of a child who has been delivered up to the Health Service Executive by the power conferred upon the gardaí under s.12 or by means of the granting of an emergency care order by the District Court under s.13 which places the child in the care of the Health Service Executive. Reference here should be made to the Note to s.13 and s.13(7) on the ECHR case law therein discussed. The obligation is merely to inform of the delivery up or placing into the care of the Health Service Executive. There is no obligation to inform the relevant person of the whereabouts of the child. The Health Service Executive may have applied, in appropriate circumstances, for a direction under s.13(7)(1)(*a*) withholding the whereabouts of the child from the parent with custody or the person acting *in loco parentis.* The section enables either the Health Service Executive itself to inform or delegate the function to a third party to inform the parent or person acting *in loco parentis* of the delivery or placement of a child. Notice of the delivering up or making of the emergency care order placing the child has to be given as soon as is possible thereafter. There is no obligation on the Health Service Executive to inform where the parent having custody or person acting *in loco parentis* is missing or cannot be found.

Subsection (2)
Provides that a parent having custody or person acting *in loco parentis* shall be deemed to be informed of the placing of a child in the care of the Health Service Executive under s.13 where that person is shown or given a copy of the emergency care order made under s.13 or if the person was present in the court at the making of the order.

Provision of accommodation for purposes of *Part III*

15.—[The Health Service Executive] shall provide or make arrangements with the registered proprietors of children's residential centres or with other suitable persons for the provision of suitable accommodation for the purposes of this Part.

AMENDMENT

Amended by s.75 and Schedule 7 of the Health Act 2004, No. 42 of 2004, with effect from January 1, 2005 (S.I. No.No.887 of 2004).

DEFINITIONS

"health board": s.2.
"residential centres": s.59.
"registered proprietor": s.59.

COMMENCEMENT

Child Care Act, 1991 (Commencement) Order, 1995 (S.I. No. 258 of 1995) took effect as of October 31, 1995.

NOTE

Section 15 obliges the health service executive to provide or make arrangements for accommodation for children placed in care under this part of the Act. This section obliges the Health Service Executive to either themselves provide suitable accommodation for children in residential centres or enter into arrangements with proprietors of residential centres or other suitable persons.

Arrangements can only be made with registered proprietors of residential centres (see Pt VIII, ss.59–67 on the statutory requirement to register residential centres and the regulations governing them, S.I. No.259 of 1995, Child Care (Placement of Children in Residential Care) Regulations 1995 and S.I. No.397 of 1996, Child Care (Standards in Children's Residential Centres) Regulations 1996). There is a statutory prohibition on unregistered children's residential centres. The Health Service Executive may also enter into arrangements with other suitable persons for the accommodation of children under this Part. Such persons are likely to be foster parents with whom the placement of children is governed by s.39 and regulated by S.I. No.260 of 1995, Child Care

(Placement of Children in Foster Care) Regulations 1995 or with relatives as set out in s.41 and governed by S.I. No.261 of 1995, Child Care (Placement of Children with Relatives) Regulations 1995.

PART IV

CARE PROCEEDINGS

Duty of [Health Service Executive] to institute proceedings

16.—Where it appears to [the Health Service Executive that a child] requires care or protection which he is unlikely to receive unless a court makes a care order or a supervision order in respect of him, it shall be the duty of the [Executive] to make application for a care order or a supervision order, as it thinks fit.

AMENDMENT

Amendments by s.75 and Schedule 7 of the Health Act 2004, No. 42 of 2004, with effect from January 1, 2005 (S.I. No.887 of 2004).

COMMENCEMENT

Child Care Act, 1991 (Commencement) Order, 1995 (S.I. No. 258 of 1995) took effect as of October 31, 1995.

DEFINITIONS

"area": s.2.
"child": s.2.
"health board": s.2.

NOTE

Section 16 imposes upon the Health Service Executive a statutory duty to institute care proceedings. The nature of the duty imposed is general and confers a wide degree of discretion upon the Health Service Executive. The Health Service Executive is only obliged to institute care proceedings where it appears to them that it is unlikely that the child will receive care or protection unless a care or supervision order is made. To this extent the section implies that the conditions exist, albeit in the Health Service Executive's view, for a successful application for a care or supervision order. Even where it does appear to the Health Service Executive that proceedings are required to safeguard the care or protection of a child, the Health Service Executive retains a discretion as to what order to seek.

It should be noted that s.23 overcomes any difficulty that might arise in relation to the residence requirement not being satisfied and thus invalidating the making of a care order. Section 23 enables a court to render valid a care order in circumstances where the original order is invalid.

Where the Health Service Executive fails to act or chooses one order in favour of another, such a failure to act or choice of order may be subject to judicial review proceedings. Owing, however, to the wide discretion conferred upon the Health Service Executive in determining what course of action to take, the likelihood of success of such judicial review proceedings are uncertain save in the clearest of cases and extremity of circumstances. The duty to act under this section is to be viewed in light of the general duty imposed in s.3 to promote the welfare of children (see Note to s.3) and the overriding requirement to vindicate the constitutional rights of the child.

In relation to the institution of care proceedings it is appropriate to again reiterate that, from the ECHR perspective, care proceedings should be viewed as a last resort.

Care proceedings constitute an intrusion into the right to respect for family life and whilst signatories enjoy a margin of appreciation surrounding the institution of care proceedings, such proceedings should be seen in light of two general principles. First, such should be of a temporary nature and secondly, where the interests of the child so merit, efforts should be made to re-unite parents with children (see *Scozzari and Giunta v Italy* (2002) 35 E.H.R.R. 12, *EP v Italy* (2001) 31 E.H.R.R. 463, *K and T v Finland* (2001) 31 E.H.R.R. 484, *Olsson v Sweden (No.1)* (1989) 11 E.H.R.R. 259).

Interim care order

17.—(1) Where a justice of the District Court is satisfied on the application of [the Health Service Executive] that—

    (*a*) an application for a care order in respect of the child has been or is about to be made (whether or not an emergency care order is in force), and

    (*b*) there is reasonable cause to believe that any of the circumstances mentioned at *paragraph* (*a*), (*b*) or (*c*) of *section 18(1)* exists or has existed with respect to the child and that it is necessary for the protection of the child's health or welfare that he be placed or maintained in the care of [the Executive] pending the determination of the application for the care order,

the justice may make an order to be known and in this Act referred to as an "interim care order".

(2) An interim care order shall require that the child named in the order be placed or maintained in the care of the [Health Service Executive]—

    (*a*) for a period not exceeding [twenty-eight days], or

    (*b*) where the [Health Service Executive] and the parent having custody of the child or person acting *in loco parentis* consent, for a period exceeding [twenty-eight days],

and an extension or extensions of any such period may be granted (with the consent, where an extension is to exceed eight days, of the persons specified in *paragraph* (*b*)) on the application of any of the parties if the justice is satisfied that grounds for the making of an interim care order continue to exist with respect to the child.

(3) An application for an interim care order or for an extension of such an order shall be made on notice to a parent having custody of the child or to a person acting *in loco parentis* except where, having regard to the interests of justice or the welfare of the child, the justice otherwise directs.

(4) Where an interim care order is made, the justice may order that any directions given under *subsection (7)* of *section 13* may remain in force subject to such variations, if any, as he may see fit to make or the justice may give directions in relation to any of the matters mentioned in the said subsection and the provisions of that section shall apply with any necessary modifications.

AMENDMENT

The amendment to para.(*a*) of subs. (2), and the amendment in the second set of brackets in para.(*b*) of subs.(2), by s.267 of the Children Act 2001, No.24 of 2001, which came into effect on May 1 2002 (S.I. No.151 of 2002).

Amendments to subss.(1), (1)(*b*), (2) and (2)(*b*){in first set of brackets} by s.75 and Schedule 7 of the Health Act 2004, No. 42 of 2004, with effect from January 1, 2005 (S.I. No.887 of 2004).

DEFINITIONS

"child": s.2.
"health board": s.2.
"parents": s.2.

COMMENCEMENT

Child Care Act, 1991 (Commencement) Order, 1995 (S.I. No. 258 of 1995) took effect as of October 31, 1995.

NOTE

Section 17 provides for the making of an interim care order on the application of the Health Service Executive to the District Court. The order is temporary in nature though extensions of the order may be sought. In addition, directions may be given in relation to any of the matters provided for in s.13(7), or where directions already exist pursuant to s.13(7), such directions may remain in force or be varied. In any proceedings under this section the court is obliged by s.24 to consider the welfare of the child as the first and paramount consideration and where practicable, give due consideration to the wishes of the child, having regard to his age and understanding. These considerations must be assessed in the context of the constitutional and other rights and duties of parents.

Subsection (1)

This sets out the conditions which must be established for the granting of an order. Firstly, the application must be brought by the Health Service Executive and made to the District Court. In light of s.16, the application must be made to a District Judge of the district in which the child resides or is found. There is no express provision for seeking an order from a District Judge in a district different to that in which the child resides or is found in either this section or S.I. No.93 of 1997, District Court Rules 1997. Where an application is made, notice of the application must be served upon the respondent (a parent having custody or person acting *in loco parentis*) two days prior to the hearing (see s.17(3) and S.I. No.93 of 1997, District (Child Care) Rules 1997, Ord.84, r.9(1)).

Secondly, the District Judge must be satisfied of the requirements set out in s.17(1)(*a*) and (*b*), as opposed to being "of the opinion" of the requirements in s.13 for an emergency care order (see 403 *Dáil Debates* Col.2239, Minister for State Treacy). The requirement of being satisfied is identical to that for a care order under s.18. For an authoritative view of the standard and burden of proof in such applications see the House of Lords' decision in *Re H (Minors)* [1996] 1 All E.R. 1 and the General Note to s.18.

Thirdly, the District Judge must be satisfied that an application for care order has been or is about to be made. The former can be easily established by production of documents and the latter, perhaps, by an undertaking given to the court to institute proceedings immediately. The fact that no application was made for an emergency care order will not prejudice the application for an interim care order nor will the existence of an emergency care order affect an application under s.17.

Fourthly, the District Judge must be satisfied that there is reasonable cause to believe that any of the circumstances set out in s.18(1)(*a*), (*b*) or (*c*), which relate respectively to: the child being assaulted, ill-treated, neglected or sexually abused; the child's health, development or welfare has been or is being avoidably impaired or neglected; or the child's health development or welfare is likely to be avoidably impaired or neglected. The reasonable cause to believe will be held by the Health Service Executive and the District Judge must be satisfied of this belief. It should be noted that the circumstances giving rise to the reasonable cause to believe can either exist in that it is current or ongoing or that there has existed but that there no longer exists such reasonable cause to believe. This latter basis for the belief where the risk did exist, but no longer exists, would cater for a situation where a child has been brought into the care of the Health Service Executive under either s.12 or s.13 in an emergency situation. Once the child is in the care of the Health Service Executive and an application is made for an interim care order, the circumstances set out in s.18(1)(*a*), (*b*) or (*c*), grounding the application, cannot be said to currently exist. This approach reflects the House of Lords decision in *Re M (A Minor)* [1994] 3 All E.R. 298 which held that the relevant date for satisfying the court as to the threshold conditions required under the relevant UK legislation was the date on which the local authority initiated the procedure for protection under the Act. In the Dáil, Minister for State Treacy indicated that if an interim care order was to be available, it was to be so on clear and precise grounds so as to avoid the constitutionality of the section being called in question (see 403 *Dáil Debates* Cols 2240–2241).

Fifthly, it must be proven that the protection of the health or welfare of the child requires him to be either placed or maintained in the care of the Health Service Executive pending the determination of the application for a care order. Where these requirements are satisfied the District Judge is entitled to make an interim care order. The order can be enforced by a warrant issued under s.35 (see Ord.84, r.9(2) of S.I. No.93 of 1997, District Court Rules 1997) authorising the entry of premises by a garda, with force if necessary, to remove and deliver up the child to the Health Service Executive (see General Note to s.13(3) which is in similar terms to s.35). The District Judge has a discretion in issuing a warrant to enforce an interim care order. The failure to deliver up a child on presentation of an order is subject on summary conviction to a fine not exceeding €634.87 or a term of imprisonment not exceeding six months or both (s.34).

Subsection (2)

This provides that the effect of the interim care order is that the child must be either placed or maintained in the care of the Health Service Executive. This imposes upon the Health Service Executive a statutory duty to care for the child and Pt VI of the Act (ss.36–48) deals with children in the care of the Health Service Executive and the options available to the Health Service Executive in caring and maintaining children. While an interim order is in force the Health Service Executive is dependent upon the obtaining of directions under s.13(7) (as applied, with any necessary modifications, by this section) in caring for the child. The Health Service Executive is vested with limited authority over the child when an interim care order is made, in contrast with a care order, which vests in the Health Service Executive authority akin to that of a parent (see s.18(3)).

The duration of an interim care order is stated to be for a period no longer than 28 days (s.17(2)(*a*)) as amended by s.267 of the Children Act 2001 or where the Health Service Executive and a parent or person acting *in loco parentis* consents, to a period exceeding 28 days (s.17(2)(*b*)) as amended by s.267 of the Children Act 2001.

A single or multiple extensions may be granted but the District Judge must be satisfied that the grounds for an interim care order continue to exist. Any of the parties to the interim care order may apply for an extension on notice to the other party and in accordance with Ord.84, r.9(3) of S.I. No.93 of 1997, District Court Rules 1997. An extension to an order exceeding 28 days may be granted with the consent of the relevant person, provided it would appear, that the grounds for an interim care order continue to exist at the making of the application for the extension.

A parent or person acting *in loco parentis* can only consent to the period exceeding 28 days provided the extension to the order can first be granted.

Subsection (3)

This provides that applications for interim care orders and extensions thereto shall be on notice to the parent having custody or person acting *in loco parentis*. The notice requirements are set out in Ord.84, r.9(1) of S.I. No.93 of 1997, District Court Rules 1997. In exceptional circumstances an application for an interim care order or extension thereto may be made otherwise than on notice (ex parte) as directed by a District Judge. In addition to the requirements of s.17(1)(*a*) and (*b*), the ex parte application must be on the basis of the interests of Justice or that the welfare of the child so requires it.

Subsection (4)

This provision concerns the ordering of directions. Where directions are in force under s.13(7) (on foot of an emergency care order), such may remain in force, subject to any variation made by the District Judge on the granting of the interim care order. Where no directions are in force, the District Judge may order directions in accordance with s.13(7) (see Note to s.13(7)).

Care order

18.—(1) Where, on the application of [the Health Service Executive with respect to a child], the court is satisfied that—

    (*a*) the child has been or is being assaulted, ill-treated, neglected or sexually abused, or

    (*b*) the child's health, development or welfare has been or is being avoidably impaired or neglected, or

    (*c*) the child's health, development or welfare is likely to be avoidably impaired or neglected,

and that the child requires care or protection which he is unlikely to receive unless the court makes an order under this section, the court may make an order (in this Act referred to as a "care order") in respect of the child.

(2) A care order shall commit the child to the care of the [Health Service Executive] for so long as he remains a child or for such shorter period as the court may determine and, in such case, the court may, of its own motion or on the application of any person, extend the operation of the order if the court is satisfied that grounds for the making of a care order continue to exist with respect to the child.

(3) Where a care order is in force, the [Health Service Executive] shall—

    (*a*) have the like control over the child as if it were his parent; and

    (*b*) do what is reasonable (subject to the provisions of this Act) in all the circumstances of the case for the purpose of safeguarding or

promoting the child's health, development or welfare;
and shall have, in particular, the authority to—
  (i) decide the type of care to be provided for the child under section 36;
  (ii) give consent to any necessary medical or psychiatric examination, treatment or assessment with respect to the child; and
  (iii) give consent to the issue of a passport to the child, or to the provision of passport facilities for him, to enable him to travel abroad for a limited period.

(4) Any consent given by [the Health Service Executive] in accordance with this section shall be sufficient authority for the carrying out of a medical or psychiatric examination or assessment, the provision of medical or psychiatric treatment, the issue of a passport or the provision of passport facilities, as the case may be.

(5) Where, on an application for a care order, the court is satisfied that—
  (*a*) it is not necessary or appropriate that a care order be made, and
  (*b*) it is desirable that the child be visited periodically in his home by or on behalf of [the Health Service Executive],
the court may make a supervision order under *section 19*.

(6) Between the making of an application for a care order and its determination, the court, of its own motion or on the application of any person, may give such directions as it sees fit as to the care and custody of, or may make a supervision order in respect of, the child who is the subject of the application pending such determination, and any such direction or supervision order shall cease to have effect on the determination of the application.

(7) Where a court makes a care order, it may in addition make an order requiring the parents of the child or either of them to contribute to the [Health Service Executive] such weekly or other periodic sum towards the cost of maintaining the child as the court, having regard to the means of the parents or either of them, thinks fit.

(8) An order under *subsection (7)* may be varied or discharged on application to the court by the parent required to contribute or by the [Health Service Executive].

AMENDMENT

Subsections (1), (2), (3), (4), (5)(*b*), (7) and (8) amended by s.75 and Schedule 7 of the Health Act 2004, No.42 of 2004, with effect from January 1, 2005 (S.I. No.887 of 2004).

DEFINITIONS

"area": s.2.
"child": s.2.
"health board": s.2.
"parents": s.2.

COMMENCEMENT

Child Care Act, 1991 (Commencement) Order, 1995 (S.I. No. 258 of 1995) took effect as of October 31, 1995.

NOTE

This section relates to the most important order that a Court may make in terms of the effect it has on the child, his parent or person acing *in loco parentis*, and indeed the Health Service Executive which will in effect take control and care of the child. The section sets out the specific grounds for and duration of an order. Further the section is specific in relation to the effect of the order and the authority conferred upon the Health Service Executive on the making of an order. There is provision for the making of a supervision order where a care order is thought inappropriate and the ordering of directions during the interim between the application for an order and the determination of that application.

Even on the making of a care order, the court not alone can make directions but is under an obligation to do so as held by McCracken J. in *Eastern Health Board v McDonnell* [1999] 1 I.R. 174, [1999] 2 I.L.R.M. 382. The authority to make such directions stemmed from both s.24 and s.47 of the Act. Here the High Court upheld a number of specific directions, which imposed a number of obligations on the Health Board pending the hearing of the adjournment of the matter (see General Note to s.47). In addition a court can order that a parent or parents contribute to the cost of maintaining the child whilst in the care of the Health Service Executive. The court is obliged to conduct the hearing of the proceedings in accordance with the statement of principle set out in s.24 which concerns the rights and duties of parents, both constitutional and otherwise, and the welfare of the child as the first and paramount consideration as well as regarding the wishes of the child where practicable.

Subsection (1)

This identifies the circumstances in which an application may be made for a care order. Only the Health Service Executive may apply for an order. Order 84, r.10(1) of S.I. No.93 of 1997 District Court Rules 1997, requires the service of notice of the application for a care order at least seven days prior to the hearing. The notice must be served upon either the parent or person acing *in loco parentis*.

Having satisfied the procedural requirements the Health Service Executive must then satisfy the District Judge that one of the three available grounds for a care order exists, and that the child requires care or protection which he is unlikely to receive unless the care order is made. In relation to the first of these grounds actual proof of, as opposed to suspicions of, assault, ill-treatment, neglect or sexual abuse should be presented to satisfy the District Judge of their existence. Regard here should be had to two instructive House of Lords decisions concerning children in care, *Re M (A Minor)* [1994] 3 All E.R. 298 and *Re H (Minors)* [1996] A.C. 563, [1996] 2 W.L.R. 8, [1996] 1 All E.R. 1. The former decision concerns the relevant date for determining whether there is a risk to the child, the latter decision concerns the standard of proof for establishing the threshold conditions and particularly allegations of sexual abuse.

Evidential issues

Proof of the requisite ground has been assisted by the introduction of Pt III of the Children Act 1997. Part III took effect as of January 1, 1999. Section 28 of the Children Act 1997 abolished the requirement that a child between the age of seven and 14 give evidence on oath or affirmation. All that is required is that the court be satisfied that the child is capable of giving an intelligible account which is relevant to the proceedings. This, in turn, will dependent upon the child's level of maturity and understanding. In *Southern Health Board v CH* [1996] 2 I.L.R.M. 142 at 151 O'Flaherty J. noted that in the context of admitting hearsay evidence, that: "a courtroom is, in general, an unsuitable environment for a child of such tender years ...". Section 28(4) of the Children Act

1997 also provides that the unsworn evidence of a child may corroborate the sworn or unsworn evidence of another person. In the case of a child over the age of 14 but who suffers from a mental disability, s.28(3) treats such a child as a child under the age of 14. Section 19 of the Children Act 1997 enables the court to deem or presume the age of a child for the purpose of giving evidence under Pt III of the Act.

Apart from giving direct evidence, a child may also give evidence indirectly via live television link by virtue of s.21 of the Children Act 1997. A number of conditions attach to this means of giving evidence. First, leave of the court must first be obtained and second, the evidence must be video recorded. The evidence can be given whilst the child is either in the State or not, and either in person or through an intermediary. The giving of evidence, both direct and in cross-examination, is subject to the normal rules of evidence except for the necessity to identify any person during the proceedings where the child has stated that the person in question was known to the child prior to the commencement of the proceedings. This exception, however, is subject to the court directing otherwise.

Section 22 of the Children Act 1997 provides that a child may also give evidence via an intermediary either where the child is present in court or through a live television link. An application to use an intermediary must be made and is subject to the court's discretion. In addition the court must be satisfied having regard to the age or mental condition of the child that all or any questions put to the child, should be put through an intermediary. The court may also determine that the questions be put to the child in a manner that conveys the meaning of the question asked rather than in actual words.

Hearsay

The most significant aspect of the Children Act 1997 relates to the admission of hearsay evidence. Section 23 of the Children Act 1997 expressly provides for the admission of hearsay evidence subject to a number of requirements. First, the child must be unable to give evidence by reason of age or that the giving of direct evidence or by live television link would not be in the interests of the child's welfare. Keane J. in *Re M, S & W (Infants)* [1999] 2 I.L.R.M. 321 approved a number of factors set out in McLaughlin J.'s judgment in *R v Khan* [1990] 2 R.S.C. 531 to determine the competence of a child to give evidence. In the context of admitting hearsay evidence as to child sexual abuse the factors relevant to competence included: timing, demeanour, the personality of the child, the intelligence and understanding of the child, and the absence of any reason to expect fabrication in the statement. Secondly, s.23(2)(a) provides that where it is not in the interests of justice to admit hearsay evidence, the court can decline to admit the evidence. Section 23(2)(b) specifically identifies as a relevant consideration in admitting hearsay evidence the potential unfairness to any party of the admission. Costello P.'s judgment in *Re M., S & W (Infants)* [1996] 1 I.L.R.M. 370 identified a number of factors relevant to the decision to admit hearsay evidence of child sexual abuse. These included the fact that a contemporaneous note of the child's evidence was taken, the evidence of the hearsay witness was clear and unhesitating, the witness has no background information on the child or the parents in question and were thus objective and independent and the witness did not prompt the child. Further helpful factors are contained in Ward L.J.'s judgment in *Re N* [1996] 4 All E.R. 225; [1997] 1 W.L.R. 153; [1996] 2 F.L.R. 214, also in the context of sexual abuse and admitting hearsay evidence of such. The Court noted that the following factors should be considered: whether the diagnosis of sexual abuse emanated from a person with a high level of expertise such as a child psychologist or psychiatrist; was the child's evidence contaminated by a pressured interview; was there a time lapse between the allegations and the interview; was there an absence of repeated complaint by the child; and was a parent present during the interview. Thirdly, the party wishing to adduce hearsay evidence must give notice of such intention to the other parties and furnish particulars of the hearsay evidence. In the case of a report or video recording, a copy of such should be forwarded within sufficient time to allow the other party to assess the evidence and produce evidence in rebuttal. Where the hearsay evidence is contained in a videotaped interview, the judgments of Keane J. in *Re M, S & W (Infants)* [1999] 2 I.L.R.M. 321 and Ward L.J.'s judgment in *Re N* [1996] 4 All E.R. 225; [1997] 1 W.L.R. 153; [1996] 2 F.L.R. 214 are quite instructive. Keane J. in the former decision noted that a videotape constituted a different form of hearsay evidence to oral testimony as the judge could see and hear the exact statement and assess what weight and credibility should attach to it. It did, however, require the judge to consider that the child is not cross-examined, that the testimony is unsworn, that there is no objection made to the questions posed and that the questioning is conducted by someone who is not a lawyer. Those considerations aside, Keane J. recommended the application of Ward L.J.'s three principles in the latter case. They were that the statement was a hearsay statement and admitted as an exception to the rule against hearsay and subject to whatever weight and credibility the judge afforded the statement with particular vigilance of pressure on the child and the use of leading questions; that expert evidence is necessary to explain and interpret the relevance of body movement, use of language, vocal intonation and signs of fascination; and that the expertise of the interviewer would have to be to a very high standard. Keane J. indicated that it was desirable that the experience of the interviewer approximated that of a clinically experienced child psychologist or child psychiatrist. It should be noted that s.23 merely entitles the court to admit hearsay evidence. Section 23 is subject to the checks and balances contained in s.24 and s.25. Section 24 outlines a number of factors the court should consider in deciding what weight to attach to the evidence. The factors are: the timing of the child's statement in relation to the occurrence of the matter stated; whether the evidence constituted multiple hearsay; whether any person involved has a motive to conceal or misrepresent matters; whether the original statement was an edited account or was made in collaboration with another for a particular purpose; and the circumstances in which the evidence is adduced as hearsay are such as to suggest an attempt to prevent proper evaluation of its weight. In *Re M, S & W (Infants)* [1996] 1 I.L.R.M. 370 Costello P. indicated that where a bitter matrimonial dispute existed it would be unsafe to rely upon hearsay evidence of parental misconduct towards a child. In *Re N* [1996] 4 All E.R. 225; [1997] 1 W.L.R. 153; [1996] 2 F.L.R. 214 the Court of Appeal held the expert testimony to be wholly unreliable as the mother was present during the interview and elicited answers from the child. Section 25 provides a further check on the admissibility of hearsay evidence by enabling a court to hear evidence as to its credibility or lack thereof. A case decided prior to the introduction of the Children Act 1997 may shed some light on how to assess whether the hearsay statement made is credible. In *Re N* [1996] 4 All E.R. 225; [1997] 1 W.L.R. 153; [1996] 2 F.L.R. 214, Ward L.J. defined the role of the expert witness in the admission of hearsay evidence, albeit in relation to sexual abuse allegations. Ward L.J. noted that the role of the expert witness was to cover such matters as nuances of emotion and behaviour, gestures and body movements, the use or non-use of language and its imagery, the vocal inflections and intonations, the pace and pressure of the interview, the child's verbal and intellectual abilities, or lack of them, or any signs of or the absence of signs of fantasising. Ward L.J. categorically stated that the expert witness could not give an opinion as to whether an individual perpetrated abuse. The role of the expert was summarised as constituting: first, evidence of the expert's belief in the truth of what a child has said is ordinarily inadmissible as such trespasses upon the judicial domain and usurps judicial function, and secondly, an expert's evidence will be couched in terms that a certain fact is consistent with or inconsistent with an allegation of abuse which renders the child's evidence capable or incapable of being accepted by the judge as true. Section 25(*a*) and (*b*) enables a cross-examining party to adduce evidence that could have been elicited from the child had the child given evidence. In addition, s.25(*c*) enables the admission of evidence of inconsistency of statements made by a child as evidence that the child has contradicted himself. Evidence sought to be introduced under s.25(*b*) or (*c*) requires leave of the court. In conjunction with the admission of hearsay evidence and evidence as to credibility of such, s.26 broadly defines the type of document that may be admitted in evidence and the manner in which it may be admitted to include photocopied versions of original documents or reports, faxed, emailed or otherwise electronically transmitted versions of documents as well as video tapes or digital recordings of pictures and sounds.

In *Eastern Health Board v Mooney*, unreported, High Court, March 20, 1998, Carney J. held that hearsay evidence was admissible in proceedings under the Child Care Act 1991 where the witnesses are competent, compellable and available. In addition foster parents were compellable witnesses who could be called by motion of the District Court Judge where it was appropriate to do so.

Expert's evidence

The role of the expert witness has identified a number of evidential principles applicable in care proceedings in the English courts. Fundamentally the role of the expert witness is to advise and the role of the court to assess and make a determination on the evidence presented. The court is not obliged to unreservedly accept the evidence of the experts in a case as demonstrated by *Re B (A Minor) (Care: Expert Evidence)* [1996] 1 F.L.R. 667. This case involved the non-accidental injury of a child where the father was identified as the perpetrator but the mother exonerated of the serious injuries suffered. The trial judge disagreed with the consultant paediatrician, the guardian and social worker all of whom advised adoption as opposed to the interim care order directed by the trial judge. The Court of Appeal noted that it was the judge's function to weigh and assess the evidence but where the judge fundamentally disagreed with the expert opinion, it was not sufficient for the judge to merely substitute his opinion without disclosing reasons and the evidence relied upon. *Re J (Expert Evidence: Hearsay)* [1999] 2 F.L.R. 661 is a good example of the court assessing and weighing all the evidence in deciding not to take a child into care. Further difficulties have arisen where there is no consensus amongst the experts involved in the care proceedings or where the experts have different areas of expertise. In *Re A (Non-Accidental Injury: Medical Evidence)* [2001] 2 F.L.R. 657 the experts agreed that the child's death could not be explained as a cot death or arising from natural causes. While there was retinal haemorrhaging, there was no cerebral haemorrhaging, the absence of the latter caused division amongst the experts as to what conclusions could be drawn from the existence of the former alone. A majority of the experts agreed that on the balance of probabilities, the child's death was non-accidental and arose from a shaking incident. The remaining experts were unable to identify the cause of death in the absence of cerebral haemorrhaging. The High Court rejected the application of the Bolam test (*Bolam v Friern Hospital Management Committee* [1957] 1 W.L.R. 582, [1957] 2 All E.R. 118) to care proceedings whereby a court was obliged to accept a respectable thesis when it is supported by a responsible body of opinion despite there being contradictory evidence or opinion. Here the court favoured the majority view as to the child's cause of death as all other possible explanations had been excluded.

In some recent cases from the English Courts, attempts have been made to impose a higher burden of proof on local authorities seeking to take children into care arising from serious injures. The Court of Appeal recently rejected that the *R v Cannings* [2004] EWCA 1 decision made any inroads into care proceedings. In *Re U (Serious*

Injury: Standard of Proof) [2004] 3 W.L.R. 753 and *Re B* [2004] 2 F.L.R. 263 the House of Lord's position in *Re H (Minors) (Sexual Abuse: Standard of Proof)* [1996] A.C. 563, [1996] 2 W.L.R. 8, [1996] 1 F.L.R. 80, [1996] 1 All E.R. 1 was applied (see also *North Yorkshire C.C. v SA* [2003] 2 F.L.R. 849).

Issue estoppel

Issue estoppel has arisen as a matter for consideration in the English courts. The most recent decision on the issue is *Re B (Minors) (Care Proceedings: Issue Estoppel)* [1997] 2 All E.R. 29, [1997] 3 W.L.R. 1, [1997] Fam. 117, Hale J. (as she then was) considered a number of earlier decisions (*B v Derbyshire C.C.* [1992] 2 F.L.R. 538 and *Re S (Discharge of Care Order)* [1995] 2 F.L.R. 639) on this issue and concluded that a flexible approach should be adopted to the finding of facts in other proceedings. The most pertinent circumstances where this issue is likely to arise in care proceedings would be where a parent, for example, in a custody dispute under s.11 of the Guardianship of Infants Act 1964 is found as a fact to have assaulted, ill-treated or sexually abused a child. The Health Service Executive may wish to rely on those findings of fact in subsequent care proceedings. Another potential scenario could be where the Health Service Executive may wish to rely on findings of fact in earlier care proceedings or criminal proceedings where it was established that a parent harmed a child. The Health Service Executive may attempt to adduce such findings in care proceedings concerning other children. In *Re B (Minors) (Care Proceedings: Issue Estoppel)* [1997] 2 All E.R. 29, [1997] 3 W.L.R. 1, [1997] Fam. 117, Hale J. stated that there was no strict rule of issue estoppel binding on the parties to care proceedings. The court retains a discretion on whether to decline a full hearing on matters determined in earlier proceedings. Where a party wishes to challenge the findings made in earlier proceedings, the court should be made aware of the findings and evidence upon which they are based prior to exercising the discretion. The exercise of the discretion would be guided by the following considerations: the public interest of finality in litigation; that delay in concluding proceedings is prejudicial to the child; that the child's welfare was not served by relying upon erroneous earlier findings; that the discretion should be exercised to achieve justice; the importance of previous findings in the context of current proceedings and whether a rehearing would result in a substantially different finding in light of whether the previous finding arose from a full hearing and if so whether the accuracy of such finding could have been appealed as well as whether there was any new evidence or information casting doubt upon the earlier findings. In *S, S and A (Care Proceedings: Issue Estoppel)* [1995] 2 F.L.R. 244 the court declined to accept findings of fact from two earlier care proceeding cases as in the first set of proceedings there had been no specific finding of fact giving rise to issue estoppel and in the second set of proceedings the finding was reached on the basis of written evidence and in the absence of the alleged abuser.

Regard should be had to the ECHR decision in *Buchberger v Austria* (2003) 37 E.H.R.R. 13 where a violation of both Arts 6 and 8 of the Convention was found. Here in the course of an appeal new evidence was submitted to the court of which the mother was not informed prior to the hearing and which evidence resulted in the care orders being made. The failure to disclose the new evidence amounted to the mother having an insufficient involvement in the proceedings. Such constituted a violation of the right to respect for family life and the right to a fair trial.

The section provides three categories of harm, any of which, if proven, enables the court to grant a care order. The wording of s.18(1)(a)–(c) indicates that there is no requirement to prove who perpetrates the harm in question. But in light of the dictum in *The State (DD) v Groarke* [1990] 1 I.R. 305 which mandates an inquiry into an innocent parent's ability to care for a child abused by the other parent prior to placing a child in care, a difficulty can arise where the identity of the abusing parent cannot be established. The House of Lords has addressed this issue of "uncertain perpetrator" in *Lancashire C.C. v B* [2000] 2 A.C. 147, [2000] 2 All E.R. 97, [2000] 2 W.L.R. 590, [2000] 1 F.L.R. 583. This case concerned a child who suffered serious head injuries from violent shaking. While both parents were at work the child was cared for by a childminder and otherwise by the parents. It could not be established who had caused the injuries but this deficiency did not preclude the making of a care order. Thus only proof that the harm has been suffered is required rather than additionally establishing who was the perpetrator of the harm.

Parental concession

Proof of harm may be easily established by parental concession or agreement as to any of the requirements of s.18(1)(*a*)–(*c*) existing. The concession must factually establish the threshold requirement and not merely amount to a consent to the care order. Thus in *Stockport Metropolitan BC v D* [1995] 1 F.L.R. 873 the court held that an investigation into the threshold criteria was unnecessary where the father admitted sexually abusing the child. Likewise in *Re B (Agreed Findings of Fact)* [1998] 2 F.L.R. 968 the Court of Appeal noted the benefit of obviating the need for a 10-day trial. In this case the mother accepted that she was an inadequate parent to the extent of satisfying the threshold criteria but denied a charge of administering an overdose of salt to the child. The Court of Appeal refused to allow the care proceedings to proceed with an investigation of the overdose allegation and the Court was satisfied the threshold criteria were met on the basis of the mother's concession. In *M (Threshold Criteria: Parental Concession)* [1999] 2 F.L.R. 728, however, the parental concession as to the threshold criteria was rejected and a full investigation into the children's circumstances was warranted to determine whether the threshold criteria were met. This case involved an adoptive father who was tried and acquitted of sexually abusing each of the three adopted children. Following the acquittal the adopted parents did not want the children returned to them and conceded the threshold criteria for a care order had been met. The Court of Appeal rejected the threshold criteria had been met on the parents' concession. A number of important reasons for this position were advanced. First, the Court doubted whether the physical chastisement of the children constituted the threshold requirement. Secondly, there was the potential for future contact between the adoptive mother and one of the children, which required a court adjudication on the issue of sexual abuse. Thirdly a similar determination was necessary for any assistance a therapist could offer the children. Finally and most interestingly, the children had to be given the opportunity of putting their evidence before the court for adjudication. Such was in the interest of justice in light of the ordeal of a criminal trial in which their credibility had been impugned.

In *Re B (Threshold Criteria: Fabricated Illness)* [2004] 2 F.L.R. 200 the court held that the threshold criteria could be met by adducing cogent circumstantial evidence identifying the mother, on the balance of probabilities, as having deliberately introduced an infection to the child whilst in hospital. The evidence in question constituted medical evidence on which there was disagreement amongst the experts as to whether deliberate introduction of infection was the cause of the child's illness. In addition there was considerable non-medical evidence establishing the mother as the probable perpetrator of the child's illness. On appeal to the Court of Appeal (*Re U (Serious Injury: Standard of Proof); Re B* [2004] 2 F.L.R. 263) the trial judge was found to have erred in relying upon the minority medical evidence suggesting deliberate introduction of infection. The non-medical evidence, however, was sufficient to establish the threshold criteria as in that the mother was responsible for the child's illness.

Witness anonymity may be afforded to professional social workers in care proceedings but only in highly exceptional cases. The Court of Appeal in *Re W (Care Proceedings: Witness Immunity)* [2003] 1 F.L.R. 329 held that immunity similar to that available in criminal proceedings could be afforded to social workers but threats from adults who face separation from their children was a professional hazard and not an exceptional one.

Threshold criteria
The four components to the first ground set out in s.18(1)(a) are not defined and the following is set out as a guide rather than as legal definition.

An assault on a child will invariably amount to physical abuse manifested by bruising, fractures, tender and swollen joints, burns and scalds and intentional poisoning (see Department of Health "Child Abuse Guidelines" 1987 for practical suggestions on identifying physical abuse). In the spirit of the legislation and for the purpose of securing the welfare of children, the consideration of the issue should centre on the child's welfare rather than any mental state of mind of the wrongdoer. This approach is reflected in the Supreme Court decisions of *Re M, S and W (Infants)* [1996] I.L.R.M. 370 and *Southern Health Board v CH* [1996] 2 I.L.R.M. 142. While the former decision concerned wardship proceedings and the latter an application under s.58 of the Children Act of 1908, in both cases the Court stressed that the function of the application was to assess the child's welfare rather than determine whether the parent had actually sexually abused the child. Both cases concerned the admissibility of hearsay evidence of sexual abuse. This inquisitorial approach to care proceedings is also evident in a number of English decisions. *Re N (A Minor)* [1996] 4 All E.R. 225, [1997] 1 W.L.R. 153, [1996] 2 F.L.R. 214 also concerned the issued of hearsay evidence and allegations of sexual abuse. This investigative approach is evident in recent House of Lords decisions concerning proof of the threshold criteria for the making of a care order where the focus is upon the risk to the child's welfare, past, present or future, rather than proving, as a matter of fact, that a parent or guardian caused the injury in question (see *Lancashire C.C. v B* [2000] 2 A.C. 147, [2000] 2 All E.R. 97, [2000] 2 W.L.R. 590, [2000] 1 F.L.R. 583 and *Re O (Children) (Non-Accidental Injury)* [2004] 1 A.C. 523, [2003] 2 All E.R. 305, [2003] 2 W.L.R. 1075, [2003] 1 F.L.R. 1169).

Ill-treatment may arise for example by clothing or nutritional deprivation, in addition to general forms of non-physical abuse such as emotional abuse which can arise by persistent or severe emotional ill-treatment or rejection. Long term exposure to domestic violence may emotionally affect a child (see s.31 of the Children Act 1989 which is the English equivalent of a care order under s.18 of the 1991 Act and the definitions as set out in s.31(9) of the 1989 Act).

Neglect connotes a failure on the part of a parent or person acting *in loco parentis* to care properly or adequately for a child. There may be cases where, owing to impecuniosity, a child is neglected which is not attributable to any deliberate fault on the part of the parent (see by way of example the case of *The State (Kavanagh) v O'Sullivan* [1933] I.R. 618, concerning ss.3 of the Custody of Children Act 1891 on abandoned or deserted children and see also Department of Health, "Putting Children First" a discussion document on mandatory reporting, where at p.48 neglect is described as "persistent or severe neglect, whether wilful or unintentional, which results in serious impairment of the child's health, development or welfare"). This approach concentrates upon the welfare of the child rather than an investigation into the conduct and mental state of the wrongdoer.

Sexual abuse of children should not be confined to actual physical violation of the child by rape. The Department of Health "Putting Children First", a discussion document on mandatory reporting describes sexual abuse as "the use of children for sexual gratification". This includes sexual assault, allowing children to view sexual acts or be exposed to, or involved in, pornography, exhibitionism and other perverse activities. See *Re H (Minors)* [1996] A.C. 563, [1996] 2 W.L.R. 8, [1996] 1 ALL E.R. 1 on the standard and burden of proof in cases of alleged sexual abuse that is likely to occur where the alleged abuser had been acquitted of a previous charge.

See also the Supreme Court decision in *Southern Health Board v CH and CH* [1996] 2 I.L.R.M. 142 and contrast the approach of the Court of Appeal in *Re N (A Minor)* [1997] 1 W.L.R. 153 on the admissibility of hearsay evidence in relation to child sexual abuse allegations and care proceedings, noted in [1997] Fam. Law 464.

The second ground for a care order is set out in s.18(1)(*b*). Where a District Judge is satisfied that a child's health, development or welfare has been or is being avoidably impaired or neglected, a care order may be granted. The phrase "has been or is being" overcomes the difficulty of a situation where a child has been brought into care in an emergency situation, and thereby removed from the risk, and thus at the time of the application for a care order, the child could not be said to be currently at risk. In *Re M (A Minor)* [1994] 2 A.C. 424 at 440 Lord Templeman explained the phrase "is being" as meaning that a local authority "cannot apply for a care order unless at the date of the application the child is suffering or is likely to suffer significant harm. Once a local authority has grounds for making the application the court has jurisdiction to grant that application. If between the date of the application and the date of the judgment of the court, circumstances arise which make a care order unnecessary or undesirable, the local authority can withdraw its application for a care order or the court can refuse to make a care order".

The Court of Appeal has further considered how and when the threshold criteria can be established. In *Re G (Care Proceedings)* [2001] 1 W.L.R. 2100, [2001] 2 F.L.R. 1111, the Court endorsed the principle set out by Lord Templeman but added that a local authority could rely upon evidence and information that arises after the date of intervention as well as later events provided the evidential material in question goes to establish the circumstances warranting the intervention in the first place.

The neglect or impairment can be to the child's health, development or welfare. Health will obviously include physical and mental (both psychiatric and psychological). Development as a term could be broadly interpreted; it could include physical, social, emotional, behavioural and educational (see *F v Suffolk C.C.* (1981) 125 S.J. 307 which determined that development includes physical, mental and emotional). Welfare is a very broad concept including many aspects of the requirements of a child's upbringing. It has both a statutory and constitutional basis and incorporates the intellectual, physical, social and moral aspects to a child's upbringing. Whether neglect to a child's religious welfare could be the subject of a care order is questionable (see Note to s.3(2)(*b*)(i)).

The use of the term "avoidably" in s.18(1)(a) and (b), it is submitted applies to both the concepts of "impaired" and "neglected" in the subsections. The section is silent on the source of the impairment or neglect. If the source of the impairment or the neglect of an individual, then the use of the term "avoidably" suggests that the conduct amounting to impairment or neglect is deliberate or conscious. Alternatively, the impairment of neglect may arise from force of circumstances where no individual can be identified for the impairment or neglect but nonetheless the impairment or neglect to the child's health, development or welfare can be avoided. Thus the existence of an individual responsible for the impairment or neglect may not be necessary to satisfy the requirements of the subsections.

The third ground upon which a care order may be granted is that the child's health, development or welfare is likely to be avoidably impaired or neglected. Whilst the previous ground requires that there is or has been neglect or impairment to the child's health, development or welfare, and that there is evidence to this extent, this ground operates on the premise that there has not yet been or there is insufficient proof that there has been neglect or impairment but that it is likely in the future. Of the three grounds this is the most difficult to satisfy in terms of proof.

Central to this ground is the term "likely to be". The House of Lords (see *Re H (Minors)* [1996] A.C. 563, [1996] 2 W.L.R. 8, [1996] 1 All E.R. 1) have held this to mean that there is a real possibility that the child would suffer. The higher standard of showing that the harm was probable, in that it was more likely than not, did not apply. The burden lay upon the applicant and the standard of proof was that of the ordinary civil one. Further any conclusion that a child was suffering and was likely to suffer (future harm) had to be based upon facts and not just suspicion. More recently the Court of Appeal has considered this issue in *Re C and B (Care Order: Future Harm)* [2001] 1 F.L.R. 611. Here a 10-month-old child and newborn baby were removed from the mother in the maternity hospital. The basis for the removal was the fact that two elder siblings had been placed in care following the eldest child's revelations of sexual abuse by the grandfather. The Court of Appeal held that although there was no immediate harm to the younger children, there was evidence supporting a real possibility of future harm. The Court noted, however, that any action proposed must be proportionate to the nature and gravity of the risk of harm. In the instant case the local authority acted expeditiously without first exploring options other than placing the children in care. There were no long-term difficulties which rendered the parents incapable of parenting the children. The local authority was obliged to support and effect a reunification of the family unless the risks were so high as to warrant care proceedings. There was no evidence to justify the removal of either child by interim care order or emergency care order procedures respectively. In so concluding Hale L.J. noted the ever-present importance of the ECHR and stated that while circumstances may warrant peremptory action of this nature, the present case was a clear example where a full hearing should be held prior to intervention.

In addition to satisfying the District Judge as to one of the above grounds there is the further obligation to establish that the child requires care or protection which he is unlikely to receive unless the court makes a care order in respect of the child. This involves speculation as to the future welfare of the child. The House of Lords has considered how this requirement can be established in "uncertain perpetrator" cases.

In *Re O (Children) (Non-Accidental Injury)* and *Re B (Children) (Non-Accidental Injury)* [2003] 2 All E.R. 305, [2004] 1 A.C. 523, [2003] 2 W.L.R. 1075, [2003] 1 F.L.R. 1169 the Court held that where it could be established that one parent was a perpetrator of abuse but that the other parent could not be exonerated of participation in the abuse, in considering the future welfare of the child and whether to make a care order, the court could not exclude from consideration the possibility that the other parent or carer contributed to the abuse of the child. The House of Lords did stress that an inability to identify the perpetrator did not amount to a finding of failing to protect a child. The Court also stressed that in these circumstances the burden of proof did not shift to the parent or carer to exculpate themselves of suspicion of abuse. This position was in line with the earlier decision of *Lancashire C.C. v B.* [2000] 2 A.C. 147, [2000] 2 All E.R. 97, [2000] 2 W.L.R. 590, [2000] 1 F.L.R. 583. The House of Lords also went on to consider the proposition of a court entertaining an unproven allegation for the purposes of determining the future welfare of a child. The Court noted that the "threshold criteria" are intended to protect the family from intrusion by state bodies but this has to be balanced against the duty of the court to assess the child's welfare. If a court did take into consideration unproven allegations of abuse or harm in determining the future welfare of the child such would remove the protection afforded by the threshold criteria. This position reflects the earlier decision in *Re M and R (Minors) (Expert Opinion: Evidence)* [1996] 4 All E.R. 239, [1996] 2 F.L.R. 195 where the Court of Appeal indicated that the same principle applied where allegations of abuse were withdrawn as opposed to being unproven (see *Re R (Care: Disclosure: Nature of Proceedings)* [2002] 1 F.L.R. 755.

Where one of the requisite grounds has been established but care or protection can be provided to the child without the making of a care order, then a care order cannot be made. The making of a care order is discretionary and may not be made where the District Judge considers it not to be necessary or inappropriate. Where this is the case, the District Judge has the alternative option of making a supervision order under s.18(5)(*a*) and (*b*) and in accordance with s.19.

A care order can be enforced by the issue of a warrant under s.35 (see Ord.84, r.10(3) of S.I. No.93 of 1997, District Court Rules 1997). The penalty for failing to deliver up a child on foot of a care order may be, on summary conviction, a fine not exceeding €634.87 or six months imprisonment or both (see s.34).

Subsection (2)
This sets out the effect and duration for which a care order may be made and the circumstances in which it can be extended. A care order commits a child to the care of the Health Service Executive. The duration of the commission to care can be for so long as the child remains a child (i.e. to the age of 18, or until married if before 18, see s.2). A care order can be for a shorter period which is for the court to determine. In this event, where an extension of an expiring care order is sought, that extension may only be granted provided the grounds for the making of a care order continue to exist and the District Judge is so satisfied. The requirement to re-establish the grounds for a care order in an application to extend was inserted by amendment at Committee Stage in the Seanad. The rationale for such was stated to be to provide criteria for the original provision that was thought to be vague.

The net effect is to safeguard against excessive and unnecessary extensions (see 129 *Seanad Debates* Cols 527–528, Minister for State Treacy). The application for an extension may be made on the court's own motion or on the application of any other person. An application to extend a care order must be on notice to the respondent at least seven days prior to the hearing (see Ord.84, r.11 of S.I. No.93 of 1997, District Court Rules 1997).

Any care order made may be appealed under s.21 with or without a stay attaching to its execution and may be varied under s.22(1)(*a*).

Subsection (3)
This confers upon the Health Service Executive, once a care order is made, the authority to control and make decisions in relation to the child as if the Health Service Executive were the child's parents. The Health Service Executive, subject to the provisions of the Act (see in particular s.3) may do what is reasonable for safeguarding or promoting the child's health, development or welfare. The authority conferred is a broad one and enables, in effect, the Health Service Executive to act in relation to a child as if it was the parent of the child. All matters of maintaining and rearing the child fall to the Health Service Executive to determine according to the circumstances. Apart from the general authority conferred, the Health Service Executive is specifically conferred with the authority to determine firstly, the type of care to be provided for the child under s.36. Secondly, the Health Service Executive can consent to medical or psychiatric examination, treatment or assessment except for the purposes of s.25(2) of the Mental Health Act 2001. Any medical or psychiatric intervention must be necessary and would include the giving of an informed consent to medical procedures involving invasive surgery, if and where the need arose. Thirdly, the Health Service Executive may consent to the issue of a passport or consent to the provision of passport facilities to enable the child travel abroad. Such travel is stated to be only for a limited period

and probably relates to foreign holidays or educational trips abroad. The wording would prohibit the consenting to the issue of a passport for the purpose of a child in care being the subject of a foreign adoption.

Subsection (4)
This provision was inserted for the sake of absolute certainty on the giving of consent to medical and psychiatric assessment or treatment. In light of the constitutional right to bodily integrity and indeed the need to safeguard the health of a child in particular circumstances, this provision ensures that there is no doubt surrounding the giving of such consent to medical or psychiatric treatment or examination. The same certainty as to the validity of the consent to the issue of a passport or provision of passport facilities likewise applies.

Subsection (5)
This enables a District Judge to make a supervision order (see s.19) on an application for a care order by the Health Service Executive, provided, that it is not necessary or appropriate that a care order be made and that it is desirable that the child be visited periodically in his home by or on behalf of the Health Service Executive (see Note to s.19). Both of these requirements must be established, though the latter requirement is not that stringent owing to the term "desirable" and the fact that the visits to the child's home are periodic. Ord.84, rr.12 and 14 of S.I. No.93 of 1997, District Court Rules 1997 require that the order be derived upon the respondent.
The "not necessary or appropriate" formula may arise where one of the grounds in s.18(1) has been established to the satisfaction of the District Judge, but that the need to make a care order for the child's care or protection has not been so established. In these circumstances where there is a risk to the child, it would be in the interest of the child that a supervision order be made to monitor the child's situation in his home.

Subsection (6)
This provides that pending the hearing of a care order, the District Judge of his own motion or an application of any person, may give either a direction as to the care and custody of the child or make a supervision order in respect of the child who is the subject of the care order application. The direction or supervision order as made are interim in nature and cease to have effect on the determination of the care order. Any application made under this subsection must be on notice to the respondent at least two days prior to the hearing, unless the application is made viva voce at the hearing of the care order. Where an order is made, it must be duly served upon the respondent (see Ord.84, r.13 of S.I. No.93 of 1997, District Court Rules 1997).

Subsection (7)
This provides that on the making of a care order, the court may make an order directing the parents of the child to contribute to the cost of the child's maintenance by the Health Service Executive. Such sums are payable to the Health Service Executive. The sum are payable weekly or by other periodic sums. In calculating the sum, the court must have regard to the means of the parents or either of them. An order directing a parent or parents to contribute must be served upon the parent or parents in accordance with Ord.84, r.15(1) of S.I. No.93 of 1997, District Court Rules 1997. A parent or parents, jointly or individually, may apply to vary or discharge a contribution order (s.18(8)) and this must be on notice to the Health Service Executive or Health Service Executive of the parent or parents as the case may be, of seven days prior to the hearing of the application (see Ord.84, r.15(2) of S.I. No.93 of 1997, District Court Rules 1997).

Supervision order

19.—(1) Where, on the application of [the Health Service Executive with respect to a child], the court is satisfied that there are reasonable grounds for believing that—

(*a*) the child has been or is being assaulted, ill-treated, neglected or sexually abused, or

(*b*) the child's health, development or welfare has been or is being avoidably impaired or neglected, or

(*c*) the child's health, development or welfare is likely to be avoidably impaired or neglected,

and it is desirable that the child be visited periodically by or on behalf of the [Health Service Executive], the court may make an order (in this Act referred to as a "supervision order") in respect of the child.

(2) A supervision order shall authorise [the Health Service Executive] to have the child visited on such periodic occasions as [the Health Service Executive] may consider necessary in order to satisfy itself as to the welfare of the child and to give to his parents or to a person acting *in loco parentis* any necessary advice as to the care of the child.

(3) Any parent or person acting *in loco parentis* who is dissatisfied with the manner in which [the Health Service Executive] is exercising its authority to have a child visited in accordance with this section may apply to the court and the court may give such directions as it sees fit as to the manner in which the child is to be visited and [the Health Service Executive] shall comply with any such direction.

(4) Where a court makes a supervision order in respect of a child, it may, on the application of [the Health Service Executive], either at the time of the making of the order or at any time during the currency of the order, give such directions as it sees fit as to the care of the child, which may require the parents of the child or a person acting *in loco parentis* to cause him to attend for medical or psychiatric examination, treatment or assessment at a hospital, clinic or other place specified by the court.

(5) Any person who fails to comply with the terms of a supervision order or any directions given by a court under *subsection (4)* or who prevents a person from visiting a child on behalf of [the Health Service Executive] or who obstructs or impedes any such person visiting a child in pursuance of such an order shall be guilty of an offence and shall be liable on summary conviction to a fine not exceeding €634.87 or, at the discretion of the court, to imprisonment for a term not exceeding 6 months or both such fine and such imprisonment.

(6) A supervision order shall remain in force for a period of 12 months or such shorter period as may be specified in the order and, in any event, shall cease to have effect when the person in respect of whom the order is made ceases to be a child.

(7) On or before the expiration of a supervision order, a further supervision order may be made on the application of [the Health Service Executive] with effect from the expiration of the first mentioned order.

AMENDMENT

Subsections (1), (2), (3), (4), (5) and (7) amended sby s.75 and Schedule 7 of the Health Act 2004, No.42 of 2004, with effect from January 1, 2005 (S.I. No.887 of 2004).

COMMENCEMENT

Child Care Act, 1991 (Commencement) Order, 1995 (S.I. No. 258 of 1995) took effect as of October 31, 1995.

DEFINITIONS

"area": s.2.
"child": s.2.
"health board": s.2.
"parents": s.2.

NOTE

This section provides for the making of a supervision order. A supervision order enables a child to be monitored in his home by the Health Service Executive without the child having to be taken into care. In this way the welfare of the child can be assessed and safeguarded, with the making of directions if necessary, without the need to remove the child from his domestic surroundings. The application can arise either under this section or under s.18(5) where a District Judge does not consider a care order necessary or appropriate. The grounds for the making of a supervision order are identical to those for a care order (see Note to s.18(1)) under s.18 but the level of proof required is lesser than that for a care order in that the District Judge need only "be satisfied" that the Health Service Executive has reasonable grounds to believe one of the three circumstances exist in s.19(1). The main issue for a court is to decide whether a care or supervision order should be made, if at all. The key question in these circumstances is whether a supervision order is proportionate to the present risk to the child.

The essence of a supervision order was described in *Re T (A Minor) (Care or Supervision Order)* [1994] 1 F.L.R. 103 as involving the advising, assisting and befriending of the supervised child where the parents have full responsibility for care and upbringing. *Re D (Care or Supervision Order)* [2000] Fam. Law 600 provides some helpful points on whether to make a supervision order rather than a care order. First, if the balance in favour of making either a care order or a supervision order is equal, the court should adopt the least intrusive approach and question whether: (i) the stronger order is needed to protect the child; (ii) the risks could be met by a supervision order; (iii) the parent could protect the child without sharing parental responsibility with the authority; (iv) parental co-operation could only be obtained through the more draconian order; (v) the child's needs could be met by advising, assisting and befriending him rather than by sharing parental responsibility of him; and (vi) there have been any improvements seen by objective observers during the current proceedings which would indicate the future, and the range of powers allotted to a supervision order, including its duration. In *Re O (Supervision Order)* [2001] 1 F.L.R. 923, Hale L.J. identified some important points in deciding whether to make a care or supervision order. First, to regain parental authority over a child, an application to discharge a care order must be made and is time consuming. Secondly, it gives the local authority parental responsibility for the child coupled with the power to control the parents' exercise of that responsibility. Thirdly and perhaps most pertinently in light of the impact of human rights jurisprudence in care proceedings, the order sought must be a proportionate response to the risk presented in light of the well-established right to respect for family life protected by Art.8 of the European Convention on the Protection of Human Rights and Fundamental Freedoms.

Two English cases illustrate when it may be appropriate to seek a supervision order rather than a care order. In *Re O (Supervision Order)* [2001] 1 F.L.R. 923 the Court of Appeal upheld a decision to make a supervision order even though there was a risk of significant harm arising from the mother's mental problems and the father's conviction for indecent assault. The parents' self esteem in not having a care order made and the fact that the domestic situation would not deteriorate so fast as to warrant the making of a care order were factors considered by the court in awarding a supervision order. In *Re C (Care Order or Supervision Order)* [2001] 2 F.L.R. 466 the father caused serious brain damage from a violent assault to his two-year-old child. On discharge from hospital the mother and child spent time in a residential unit during which time the mother proved herself capable of caring adequately for the child. The future risks to the child constituted the mother failing to maintain her current standards, failing to assess the child's needs or proving incapable of meeting the needs or allowing a violent person into her home. The risks as identified were low in light of the mother's co-operation and thus a supervision order was proportionate in the circumstances.

The section deals with the effect of an order (s.19(2)); the making of directions in relation to the order (s.19(3)); the power of the court to order medical or psychiatric treatment or assessment (s.19(4)); offences in relation to failing to comply with an order (s.19(5)); duration (s.19(6)) and renewal of orders (s.19(7)).

Subsection (1)

This sets out the requirements that must be established for a supervision order. Only the Health Service Executive may apply for a supervision order for a child that resides in the area of the Health Service Executive.. The Health Service Executive has a discretion in making the decision whether or not to apply for a supervision order and may decide to apply for a supervision order instead of a care order where the Executive considers such appropriate. The Health Service Executive must satisfy the court of any one of the three grounds set out in s.19(1)(*a*), (*b*) or (*c*) to the extent that there are reasonable grounds for their belief. Further it must be established that it is desirable that the child be visited periodically by or on behalf of the Health Service Executive. The application for a supervision order must be on notice to the respondent and served at least seven days prior to the hearing of the order (see Ord.84, r.16(1) of S.I. No.93 of 1997, District Court Rules 1997). Once an order is made it must be served on each respondent (see Ord.84, r.16(2) of S.I. No.93 of 1997, District Court Rules 1997).

The grounds for a supervision order are that there is a reasonable belief firstly, that the child is or has been assaulted, ill-treated, neglected or sexually abused. Secondly that the child's health, development or welfare has been or is being avoidably impaired or neglected. Thirdly, the child's health, development or welfare is likely to be avoidably impaired or neglected.

Subsection (2)

This sets out the effect of a supervision order which authorises the Health Service Executive to itself, or through a third party, visit the child. The Health Service Executive has a discretion as to when and how often such visits shall occur. The number of visits which the Health Service Executive is entitled to conduct must be sufficient to satisfy the Health Service Executive that the child's welfare is being secured. The Health Service Executive can tender advice to the parents or person acting *in loco parentis* to the child on such visits.

Subsection (3)

This enables a parent or person acting *in loco parentis* who is aggrieved with the manner in which the Health Service Executive is exercising its authority of having the child visited to apply to the District Court for directions in relation to the supervision of the child. This is a complaints procedure and it should be the first means to be utilised in seeking to redress any complaint. The District Judge on application is empowered to make directions in relation to the supervision with which the Health Service Executive is obliged to comply. Such applications must be on notice to the Health Service Executive at least seven days prior to the hearing and any directions made must be served upon all the parties (see Ord.84, r.17 of S.I. No.93 of 1997, District Court Rules 1997).

Subsection (4)

This enables a District Judge to make directions in relation to the supervision of the child either at the time of the making of the supervision order or at any time during its currency. The application is brought by the Health Service Executive and must be on notice to the parents or person acting *in loco parentis* at least seven days prior to the hearing date (see Ord.84, r.17 of S.I. No.93 of 1997, District Court Rules 1997). Whilst the District Judge can make any direction that he considers fit for the care of the child, there is specific authority to compel attendance for medical or psychiatric treatment or assessment except for the purposes of s.25(2) of the Mental Health Act 2001. The Court can specify the location (hospital, clinic or other place) at which the child is to attend.

Subsection (5)

This provides for the maximum penalties which may be imposed on summary conviction for either a failure to comply with a supervision order or a direction made under subs.4. The same penalties apply to the offence of a person who prevents, obstructs or impedes the visiting of a child. The penalties for an offence under this section are either or both a fine not exceeding €634.87 or a term of imprisonment not exceeding six months or both.

Subsection (6)

This provides the maximum duration of a supervision order, which is 12 months. An order for a shorter period may be made and any order made ceases to have effect on expiry or upon the child reaching the age of 18.

Subsection (7)

This provides that a further supervision order may be made on or before the expiration of a supervision order. The Health Service Executive must apply for a further supervision order and should apply for such before or on the expiration of the supervision order. The further supervision order takes effect upon the expiration of the supervision order.

Proceedings under Guardianship of Infants Act, 1964, Judicial Separation and Family Law Reform Act, 1989, etc.

20.—[(1) Where in any proceedings under *section 7, 8, 11, 11B* or *Part III* of the Guardianship of Infants Act, 1964, or in any case to which—

      (*a*) *section 3(3)* of the Judicial Separation and Family Law Reform Act, 1989,

      (*b*) *section 6(b)* of the Family Law Act, 1995, or

(c) *section 5(2)* of the Family Law (Divorce) Act, 1996,
relates, or in any other proceedings for the delivery or return of a child, it appears to the court that it may be appropriate for a care order or a supervision order to be made with respect to the child concerned in the proceedings, the court may, of its own motion or on the application of any person, adjourn the proceedings and direct [the Health Service Executive] to undertake an investigation of the child's circumstances.]

(2) Where proceedings are adjourned and the court gives a direction under *subsection (1)*, the court may give such directions as it sees fit as to the care and custody of, or may make a supervision order in respect of, the child concerned pending the outcome of the investigation by the [Health Service Executive].

(3) Where the court gives a direction under *subsection (1)*, the [Health Service Executive] shall undertake an investigation of the child's circumstances and shall consider whether it should—

(a) apply for a care order or for a supervision order with respect to the child,

(b) provide services or assistance for the child or his family, or

(c) take any other action with respect to the child.

(4) Where [the Health Service Executive] undertakes an investigation under this section and decides not to apply for a care order or a supervision order with respect to the child concerned, it shall inform the court of—

(a) its reasons for so deciding,

(b) any service or assistance it has provided, or it intends to provide, for the child and his family, and

(c) any other action which it has taken, or proposes to take, with respect to the child.

[(5) Where, before the amendment of this section by the Health Act 2004, the Health Service Executive was directed to undertake an investigation into a child's circumstances and the investigation has not been undertaken or all matters relating to or arising from the investigation have not been concluded before the establishment day of the Health Service Executive—

(a) any direction given under this section by the court to the Health Service Executive in respect of the child concerned shall be deemed to have been given to the Executive,

(b) the investigation may be completed by the Executive, and

(c) *subsections (3)* and *(4)* apply as though all of the investigation had been undertaken and completed by the Executive.]

AMENDMENT

Subsection (1) substituted by s.17 of the Children Act 1997, No.40 of 1997, which came into effect on January 8, 1998 (s.1(2) of the 1997 Act).

Subsection (1) subsequently amended, subss.(2), (3) and (4) amended, and subs.(5) inserted by s.75 and Schedule 7 of the Health Act 2004, No.42 of 2004, with effect from January 1, 2005 (S.I. No.887 of 2004).

COMMENCEMENT

Child Care Act, 1991 (Commencement) Order, 1995 (S.I. No. 258 of 1995) took effect as of October 31, 1995.

DEFINITIONS

"area": s.2.
"child": s.2.
"health board": s.2.
"parents": s.2.

NOTE

This section enables the interaction of certain provisions of the Act with other proceedings concerning the welfare of children or for the delivery or return of a child. Two statutes are specifically referred to, the Guardianship of Infants Act 1964 and the Judicial Separation and Family Law Reform Act 1989.

The relevant provisions of the 1964 Act concern s.7, which provides for the appointment of testamentary guardians on the death of parents or guardians which the court may refuse to order where a dispute arises concerning the appointment. Section 8 of the 1964 Act concerns the power of the court to appoint guardians over a child where the child has no guardian or the parent or parents failed to appoint a testamentary guardian on their death. Section 11 of the 1964 Act concerns applications for directions concerning the welfare of children and particularly for orders granting sole custody and access for the father or mother. Section 11B enables a relative or person acting *in loco parentis* to apply for access to a child. Part III of the 1964 Act concerns the enforcement of the right to custody. Of particular relevance is s.14 where a court can refuse an order requested by a parent or guardian for a child to be produced to that parent or guardian where the child has been abandoned or deserted. Section 16 deals with the authority of the court to refuse an order requiring the delivery up of a child to a parent or guardian, unless the parent or guardian is a fit person to have custody of the child, where that parent or guardian has abandoned or deserted a child or allowed the child to be maintained at another person's expense.

The relevant sections of the Judicial Separation and Family Law Reform Act 1989 are s.3(3), which concerns orders as to the welfare of, custody of and access to children on the grant of judicial separation; s.11(*b*), which concerns the making of a custody or access order whilst an application for a judicial separation is pending; and s.16(*g*), which concerns orders as to welfare of, custody of or access to children which may be applied for after the grant of a judicial separation.

This section was amended by s.17 of the Children Act 1997 which makes this section applicable to applications under s.11 of the 1964 Act in judicial separation and divorce proceedings. Reference in this section is also made to proceedings concerning the delivery or return of children. Reference here should be made to the Child Abduction and Enforcement of Custody Orders Act 1991 which implements the Hague and Luxembourg Conventions on the return of wrongfully removed children (see *Saunders v Mid Western Health Board* [1989] I.L.R.M. 229, on the interaction of the Children Act 1908 with a wardship order from an English court and the role of the Health Service Executive in taking a child into care in an emergency situation). Note should also be taken of the provisions of the Domestic Violence Act 1996, s.6 of which authorises the Health Service Executive to apply for safety, barring and interim barring orders on behalf of aggrieved persons and particularly s.7 which authorises a court to direct an investigation into the circumstances of a dependent person to whom proceedings under the Domestic Violence Act 1996 relate.

Where in the course of any of the above proceedings it appears to the court that a care or supervision order would be appropriate, the court may of its own motion or upon the application of any person adjourn those proceedings. Where the proceedings are adjourned the court will direct the Health Service Executive of the area in which the child resides, or is for the time being, to undertake an investigation of the child's circumstances. Where the Health Service Executive is not a party to these proceedings, the Clerk is obliged to notify the relevant Health Service Executive of the order directing an investigation (see r.21(1) of S.I. No.338 of 1995, District Court (Child Care) Rules 1995).

Subsection (2)

This provides for the making of interim supervision or custody orders in relation to the child and for the giving of directions pending the outcome of the Health Service Executive's investigation as directed under s.20(1). The discretion to make these orders lies with the court. Any application made must be in accordance with Ord.84, r.19 of S.I. No.93 of 1997, District Court Rules 1997 and must be served upon each person directly affected thereby.

Subsection (3)

This specifies the obligation imposed upon the Health Service Executive where an order directing the investigation of the child's circumstances has been made. The Health Service Executive must investigate the child's circumstances and specific consideration must be given to the following: whether or not to apply for a care or supervision order; whether to provide services or assistance for the child or his family; and whether to take any other action with respect to the child.

Subsection (4)

This sets out the obligation the Health Service Executive must fulfil having undertaken an investigation in accordance with a direction under s.20(1) and having made a decision not to apply for a care or supervision order, the Health Service Executive is obliged to inform the court of the following: the reasons for not seeking a care or supervision order; any service or assistance it has provided or intends to provide for the child and his family; and any other action it has taken or intends to take with respect to the child.

Effect of appeal from orders

21.—An appeal from an order under this Part shall, if the court that made the order or the court to which the appeal is brought so determines (but not otherwise), stay the operation of the order on such terms (if any) as may be imposed by the court making the determination.

COMMENCEMENT

Child Care Act, 1991 (Commencement) Order, 1995 (S.I. No. 258 of 1995) took effect as of October 31, 1995.

NOTE

This provides for a stay on the operation of any order under this part where the order is appealed. A stay can only be granted by the court making the order or the court hearing an appeal from the making of an order. A stay cannot be granted in any other circumstances and the court making that determination may attach terms to the stay. The orders affected by this section are an interim care order (s.17), a care order (s.18), a supervision order (s.19) or an interim order as to the care, custody or supervision of the child under s.20(2). Section 23G makes applicable this section to a special care order and interim special care order. An order as to directions made is likewise subject to a stay (see Ord.84, r.21 of S.I. No.93 of 1997, District Court Rules 1997).

Variation or discharge of orders etc.

22.—The court, of its own motion or on the application of any person, may—

    (*a*) vary or discharge a care order or a supervision order,

    (*b*) vary or discharge any condition or direction attaching to the order, or

    (*c*) in the case of a care order, discharge the care order and make a supervision order in respect of the child.

DEFINITIONS

    "child": s.2.

COMMENCEMENT

    Child Care Act, 1991 (Commencement) Order, 1995 (S.I. No. 258 of 1995) took effect as of October 31, 1995.

NOTE

    This section provides for applications to vary and discharge care and supervision orders and any directions or condition attaching thereto. Where there is an application to discharge a care order, the care order may be discharged and a supervision order made. An application may be brought by any person or by the court of its own motion. Notice of any application under this section must be served upon the respondent at least seven days prior to the hearing and any order made varying, discharging or making a supervision order must be served upon each person directly affected thereby (see Ord.84, r.20 of S.I. No.93 of 1997, District Court Rules 1997).

Powers of court in case of invalidity of orders

23.—Where a court finds or declares in any proceedings that a care order for whatever reason is invalid, that court may of its own motion or on the application of any person refuse to exercise any power to order the delivery or return of the child to a parent or any other person if the court is of opinion that such delivery or return would not be in the best interests of the child and in any such case the court, of its own motion or on the application of any person, may—

    (*a*) make a care order as if it were a court to which an application had been made by [the Health Service Executive] under *section 18*,

    (*b*) make an order remitting the matter to a justice of the District Court for the time being assigned to the district court district where the child resides or is for the time being or was residing or was at the time that the invalid order was made or the application therefor was made; and where the matter has been so remitted [the Health Service Executive]shall be deemed to have made an application under section 18,

(c) direct that any order under *paragraph* (*a*) shall, if necessary, be deemed for the purposes of this Act to have been made by a justice of the District Court for the time being assigned to a district court district, specified by the court, or

(d) where it makes an order under *paragraph* (*b*), make a temporary order under *paragraph* (*a*) pending the making of an order by the court to which the matter or question has been remitted.

AMENDMENT

Paragraphs (*a*) and (*b*) amended by s.75 and Schedule 7 of the Health Act 2004, No.42 of 2004, with effect from January 1, 2005 (S.I. No.887 of 2004).

DEFINITIONS

"child": s.2.
"health board": s.2.
"parent": s.2.

COMMENCEMENT

Child Care Act, 1991 (Commencement) Order, 1995 (S.I. No. 258 of 1995) took effect as of October 31, 1995.

NOTE

This is a safety net provision that relates only to care orders that when originally made are invalid. Where a child is in care and the order authorising that care is invalid this provision enables the status quo concerning the child's care to be maintained whilst a new order authorising the care is obtained. Whatever reason for the invalidity, the court of its own motion or on the application of any other person may refuse to order the delivery or return of the child to a parent or any other person. The refusal to return or deliver up is contingent upon the court being of the opinion that it is not in the best interests of the child to return or deliver up the child. In this way the child may be lawfully maintained by the Health Service Executive while a new application is made for a care order. The terms of the provision are very broad and enable the welfare of the child, who is considered to require care, to be safeguarded against technical or fundamental matters invalidating care orders and thereby facilitating the automatic return of a child to his parents or person acting *in loco parentis*. The provision was not originally included in the draft legislation and was inserted at Report Stage in the Dáil, the amendment having been agreed to in the Seanad. Minister for State Treacy indicated the reason for the insertion being that he "did not want to leave anything to chance or permit technicalities to take precedence over the well-being of the child" (see 129 *Seanad Debates* Cols 536–540 and 403 *Dáil Debates* Cols 2334–2335).

Having refused to return or deliver up the child, the Court of its own motion or on the application of any person may make any of the following orders. Firstly the Court (District or Circuit on appeal) may make a care order as if it were the court to which the application for a care order had been made. A District Court might make an order under this section where the child has been transferred to the care of the Health Service

Executive in an area different to that to which the original care order relates and for which the Health Service Executive has no order enabling it to validly maintain the child.

Secondly, the matter may be remitted to a Judge of the District Court in a district where the child resides or is for the time being (for example, under an emergency care order) or where the child resided or was at the time when the invalid order was made or applied for. Where a matter is so remitted the Health Service Executive is deemed to have applied for that order under s.18. No order is made here which enables the Health Service Executive to retain care of the child and a temporary order under s.23(*d*) would have to be sought to keep the child in care whilst the application for a care order is pending. The application procedure for a care order is deemed to have been validly conducted. A hearing of the merits of the application must still be conducted.

Thirdly, a court may deem an order under para.(*a*) (a care order) to have been made by a District Court Judge in a district as specified by the court. The care order, when made by the court, can then be dealt with by the District Court in the district in which the child is residing. This enables a District Judge to make a care order for a child who resides in a different district court district and the order when made is deemed to be an order made under the jurisdiction of that other district court district. This order is an alternative to the next order available under this section.

Fourthly, where a District Judge makes an order remitting the application to a district of the District Court as specified, the District Court making the order to remit may make a temporary care order pending the determination of the District Court to which the application has been remitted. This order is an alternative to the above order.

This section should be read in light of s.48(2) which provides for void care orders where a prosecution under ss.21 or 24 of the Children Act is dismissed for want of prosecution or the defendant is acquitted. It is suggested this section applies to orders under s.48(2).

[PART IVA

CHILDREN IN NEED OF SPECIAL CARE OR PROTECTION

AMENDMENT

Part IVA, ss. 23A to 23N, inserted by s.16 of the Children Act 2001, No.24 of 2001. The insertion, with the exception of s.23D, came into effect on September 23, 2004 (S.I. No.548 of 2004).

[Duty of [Health Service Executive] where child requires special care or protection

[23A.—(1) Where it appears to [the Health Service Executive that a child] requires special care or protection which he or she is unlikely to receive unless a court makes an order under this Part in respect of the child, being either—

(*a*) an order under *section 23B* (in this Part referred to as a 'special care order'), or

(*b*) an order under *section 23C* (in this Part referred to as an 'interim special care order'),

it shall, subject to *subsection (2)*, be the duty of [the Health Service Executive] to apply for whichever of such orders is appropriate in the particular circumstances.

(2) Before applying for an order under this Part [the Health Service Executive] shall—
- (*a*) arrange for the convening of a family welfare conference (within the meaning of the *Children Act, 2001*) in respect of the child, and
- (*b*) where, on the conclusion of the conference proceedings, it proposes to apply for a special care order in respect of the child, seek the views of the Special Residential Services Board established under *section 226* of that Act on the proposal.

(3) Where a parent or guardian of a child requests [the Health Service Executive] to apply for an order under this Part in respect of the child and [the Executive] decides not to do so, it shall inform the parent in writing of the reasons for its decision.]

[(4) Where, before the amendment of this section by the *Health Act 2004*, the Health Service Executive arranged for the convening of a family welfare conference in respect of a child but the health board did not apply for an order under this Part in respect of the child before the establishment day of the Health Service Executive, the Executive shall be deemed for the purpose of an application by it for such order in respect of the child to have complied with the requirement of *subsection (1)(a)*.]

[(5) Where, before the amendment of this section by the Health Act 2004, the Health Service Executive sought the views of the Special Residential Services Board on the health board's proposal to apply for an order under this Part in respect of a child but the health board did not apply for the order before the establishment day of the Health Service Executive, the Executive shall be deemed for the purpose of an application by it for such order in respect of the child to have complied with the requirement of *subsection (2)(b)*.]

<small>AMENDMENT</small>

Section 23A inserted by s.16 of the Children Act 2001, No.24 of 2001, with effect from September 23 2004 (S.I. No.548 of 2004).

Subsections (1), (2) and (3) amended, and subss.(4) and (5) inserted by s.75 and Schedule 7 of the Health Act 2004, No.42 of 2004, with effect from January 1, 2005 (S.I. No.887 of 2004).

[Special care order

[**23B.**—(1) A court may, on the application of [the Health Service Executive with respect to a child] and having taken into account the views of the Special Residential Services Board referred to in *section 23A(2)(b)*, make a special care order in respect of the child if it is satisfied that—
- (*a*) the behaviour of the child is such that it poses a real and substantial risk to his or her health, safety, development or welfare, and
- (*b*) the child requires special care or protection which he or she is unlikely to receive unless the court makes such an order.

(2) A special care order shall commit the child to the care of the [Health Service Executive] for so long as the order remains in force and shall authorise it to provide appropriate care, education and treatment for the child and, for that purpose, to place and detain the child in a special care unit provided by or

on behalf of the [Health Service Executive] pursuant to *section 23K.*

(3) Where a child is detained in a special care unit pursuant to a special care order, the [Health Service Executive] may take such steps as are reasonably necessary to prevent the child from—

    (*a*) causing injury to himself or herself or to other persons in the unit, or

    (*b*) absconding from the unit.

(4)(*a*) Subject to *subsections* (*5*) and (*6*), a special care order shall remain in force for a period to be specified in the order, being a period which is not less than 3 months or more than 6 months.

    (*b*) The court may, on the application of the [Health Service Executive], extend the period of validity of a special care order if and so often as the court is satisfied that the grounds for making the order continue to exist with respect to the child concerned.

(5) If, while a special care order is in force in respect of a child, it appears to the [Health Service Executive] that the circumstances which led to the making of the order no longer exist with respect to the child, [it shall], as soon as practicable, apply to the court which made the order to have the order discharged.

(6) A special care order shall cease to have effect when the person in respect of whom it was made ceases to be a child.

(7) Where a special care order is in force, the [Health Service Executive] may—

    (*a*) as part of its programme for the care, education and treatment of the child, place the child on a temporary basis in such other accommodation [as it] is empowered to provide for children in its care under *section 36,* or

    (*b*) arrange for the temporary release of the child from the unit on health, education or compassionate grounds, and any such placement or arrangement shall be subject to its control and supervision.

(8) Subject to this section, *subsections* (*3*), (*4*), (*6*), (*7*) and (*8*) of *section 18* shall apply in relation to a special care order as they apply in relation to a care order, with any necessary modifications.]

AMENDMENT

Section 23B inserted by s.16 of the Children Act 2001, No.24 of 2001, with effect from September 23, 2004 (S.I. No.548 of 2004).

Subsections (1), (2), (3), (4)(*b*), (5) and (7) amended by s.75 and Schedule 7 of the Health Act 2004, No.42 of 2004, with effect from January 1, 2005 (S.I. No.887 of 2004).

[Interim special care order

[**23C.**—(1) Where a judge of the Children Court is satisfied on the application of [the Health Service Executive]—

    [(*a*) That the Executive is complying with the requirements of *section 23A(2)* in relation to the making of an application for a special care order in respect of a child or is deemed under section *23A(4)* and (5) to have complied with those requirements], and

    (*b*) that there is reasonable cause to believe that—

(i) the behaviour of the child is such that it poses a real and substantial risk to his or her health, safety, development or welfare, and

(ii) it is necessary in the interests of the child, pending determination of the application for a special care order, that he or she be placed and detained in a special care unit provided under *section 23K*,

the judge may make an interim special care order in respect of the child.

(2) An interim special care order shall require that the child named in the order be placed and detained in a special care unit—

(*a*) for a period not exceeding twenty-eight days, or

(*b*) where the [Health Service Executive]and the parent having custody of the child or a person acting *in loco parentis* consent, for a period exceeding twenty-eight days,

and the judge concerned may be order extend any such period, on the application of any of the persons specified in paragraph (*b*) and, where the period of the extension exceeds twenty-eight days, with the consent of those persons, if he or she is satisfied that the grounds for making the interim special care order continue to exist with respect to the child.

(3) An application for an interim special care order or for an extension of a period mentioned in *subsection (2)* shall be made on notice to a parent having custody of the child or a person acting *in loco parentis* or, where appropriate, to the [Health Service Executive], except where, having regard to the welfare of the child, the judge otherwise directs.

(4) *Subsections (3)* to *(7) of section 13* shall apply in relation to an interim special care order as they apply in relation to an emergency care order, with any necessary modifications.]

AMENDMENT

Section 23C inserted by s.16 of the Children Act 2001, No. 24 of 2001, with effect from September 23 2004 (S.I. No.548 of 2004).

Paragraph (1)(*a*) substituted, and subsections (1), (2)(*b*) and (3) amended by s.75 and Schedule 7 of the Health Act 2004, No.42 of 2004, with effect from January 1, 2005 (S.I. No.887 of 2004).

[Duty of Garda Síochána where child needs special care or protection

[**23D.**—(1) Where a member of the Garda Síochána has reasonable grounds for believing that—

(*a*) the behaviour of a child is such that it poses a real and substantial risk to the child's health, safety, development or welfare,

(*b*) the child is not receiving adequate care or protection, and

(*c*) it would not be sufficient for the protection of the child from such risk to await the making of an application for an interim special care order by [the Health Service Executive] under section 23C,

the member shall endeavour to deliver or arrange for the child to be delivered to the [custody of the Executive and shall inform it] of the circumstances in which the child came to the notice of the Garda Síochána.

(2) Where—

    (*a*) a child is delivered to the custody of [the Health Service Executive] or comes to its notice in the circumstances described in subsection (1), and

    (*b*) it appears to [the Health Service Executive] that the child requires care or protection which he or she is unlikely to receive unless a court makes an order under this Part in respect of the child,

[the Health Service Executive] shall proceed in accordance with *section 23A*.]

AMENDMENT

Provision is made for the insertion of the above s.23D by s.16 of the Children Act 2001, No.24 of 2001. However, at the date of publication of this volume, s.16 of the 2001 Act has not yet been brought into effect for the purposes of making the insertion of this section.

Subsections (1), (1)(*c*) and (2) amended by s.75 and Schedule 7 of the Health Act 2004, No.42 of 2004, with effect from January 1, 2005 (S.I. No.887 of 2004).

[Notification by Health Service Executive

[**23E.**—(1) Where a child is placed in a special care unit pursuant to an interim special care order, the [Health Service Executive] shall as soon as possible inform or cause to be informed a parent having custody of the child or a person acting *in loco parentis* of the placement unless the parent or person is missing and cannot be found.

(2) For the purposes of this section, a person shall be deemed to have been informed of the placing of a child in a special care unit if the person is given or shown a copy of the interim special care order or if the person was present at the sitting of the court at which the order was made.]

AMENDMENT

Section 23E inserted by s.16 of the Children Act 2001, No.24 of 2001, with effect from September 23 2004 (S.I. No.548 of 2004).

Subsection (1) by s.75 and Schedule 7 of the Health Act 2004, No.42 of 2004, with effect from January 1, 2005 (S.I. No.887 of 2004).

[Variation or discharge of special care orders

[**23F.**—(1) Without prejudice to *section 23B(5)*, the court may, of its own motion or on the application of any person, vary or discharge a special care order.

(2) In discharging a special care order, the court may, of its own motion or on the application of [the Health Service Executive] either—

    (*a*) make a supervision order in respect of the child, or

    (*b*) if the court is of opinion that—

        (i) the child requires care and protection which he or she is unlikely to receive unless he or she remains in the care of [the Health Service Executive], or

        (ii) the delivery or return of the child to a parent or any other

person would not be in the best interests of the child,
make a care order in respect of the child.]

AMENDMENT

Section 23F inserted by s.16 of the Children Act 2001, No.24 of 2001, with effect
from September 23 2004 (S.I. No.548 of 2004)
Subsection (2) amended by s.75 and Schedule 7 of the Health Act 2004, No.42 of
2004, with effect from January 1, 2005 (S.I. No.887 of 2004).

[Appeals

[**23G.**—*Section 21* shall apply to an appeal from an interim special care
order or a special care order as it applies to an appeal from an order under *Part
IV*.]

AMENDMENT

Section 23G inserted by s.16 of the Children Act 2001, No.24 of 2001, with effect
from September 23 2004 (S.I. No.548 of 2004).

[Powers of court in case of invalidity of order

[**23H.**—*Section 23* shall apply to a special care order as it applies to a care
order, with the modification that the court may, as an alternative to making a
special care order, make a care order in respect of the child.]

AMENDMENT

Section 23H inserted by s.16 of the Children Act 2001, No.24 of 2001, with effect
from September 23 2004 (S.I. No.548 of 2004).

[Application of *Part V*

[**23I.**—Part V shall apply to proceedings relating to an application for an
interim special care order or a special care order, with any necessary
modifications.]

AMENDMENT

Section 23I inserted by s.16 of the Children Act 2001, No.24 of 2001, with effect
from September 23 2004 (S.I. No.548 of 2004).

[Application of *Part VI*

[**23J.**—*Section 37, 42, 45* and *47* shall apply to a child who is committed to
the care of [the Health Service Executive] pursuant to an interim special care
order or a special care order.]

AMENDMENT

Section 23J inserted by s.16 of the Children Act 2001, No.24 of 2001, with effect from September 23, 2004 (S.I. No.548 of 2004).

Amended by s.75 and Schedule 7 of the Health Act 2004, No.42 of 2004, with effect from January 1, 2005 (S.I. No.887 of 2004).

[Provision of special care units by [the Health Service Executive]

[23K.—[(1) For the purposes of *sections 23B* and *23C*, the Health Service Executive may, with the Minister's approval, provide special care units and maintain special care units whether provided by the Executive or provided by the Health Service Executive before the establishment day of the Executive.]

[(1A) The Health Service Executive may, subject to its available resources and any general directions issued by the Minister, make arrangements with a voluntary body or other person for the provision and operation of a special care unit by that body or person on behalf of the Executive.]

[(1B) *Section 38(2)* to *(9)* of the Health Act 2004 shall apply with the necessary modifications in respect of an arrangement under this section with a voluntary body or other person for the provision and operation of a special care unit and the body or person making such arrangement with the Health Service Executive is for the purpose of Part 9 of that Act a service provider as defined in *section 2* of that Act.]

(2) The Minister shall not approve of the provision of a special care unit unless—

(*a*) having caused the unit to be inspected by a person authorised in that behalf by the Minister, and

(*b*) having considered a report in writing of the inspection, he or she is satisfied that the requirements of regulations under this section will be complied with by [the Health Service Executive], voluntary body or other person, as the case may be, in relation to the unit.

(3) The duration of an approval of a special care unit by the Minister shall be 3 years from the date of approval, and thereafter the Minister may renew the approval for a further period, or further periods, of the like duration.

(4) The Minister, on approving of a special care unit, shall cause a certificate to that effect to be issued to the [Health Service Executive] and the certificate shall without further proof, unless the contrary is shown, be admissible in any proceedings as evidence that the unit has been approved of by the Minister for the purposes of *sections 23B* and *23C*.

[(4A) A certificate issued by the Minister to the Health Service Executive before the amendment of this section by the Health Act 2004 shall be deemed to have been issued to the Health Service Executive.]

(5) The Minister may cancel such a certificate if he or she is of opinion that the special care unit concerned is no longer suitable for use as such a unit or is no longer required for that purpose.

(6) The Minister shall make regulations with respect to the operation of special care units provided by or on behalf of [the Health Service Executive] under this section and for securing the welfare of children detained therein.

(7) Without prejudice to the generality of *subsection (6)*, regulations under

this section may prescribe requirements as to—

(*a*) the maintenance, care and welfare of children while being detained in special care units,

(*b*) the staffing of those units,

(*c*) the physical standards in those units, including the provision of adequate and suitable accommodation and facilities,

(*d*) the periodical review of the cases of children in those units and the matters to be considered in such reviews,

(*e*) the records to be kept in those units and the examination and copying of any such records or of extracts therefrom by persons authorised in that behalf by the Minister, and

(*f*) the periodical inspection of those units by persons authorised in that behalf by—

[(i) in case the units were provided in accordance with an arrangement referred to in *subsection (1A)*, the Health Service Executive, and]

(ii) in any other case, the Minister n accordance with *section 69.*

[(8) *Section 10(1)* and (2) shall apply with any necessary modifications in relation to a voluntary body or other person with whom the Health Service Executive enters into an arrangement referred to in *subsection (1A)*.]

(9) Nothing in this section shall empower [the Health Service Executive] to delegate to a voluntary body or any other person the power to apply for an order under *section 23B* or *23C*.

(10) Where a child is detained in a special care unit provided under [*subsection (1A)*], the provisions of *section 23B(3)* shall apply in relation to the voluntary body or other person providing or operating the unit.

(11) Nothing in this section shall authorise the placing of a child in a special care unit otherwise than in accordance with an interim special care order or a special care order.]

AMENDMENT

Section 23K inserted by s.16 of the Children Act 2001, No.24 of 2001, with effect from September 23, 2004 (S.I. No.548 of 2004)

Subsections (1), (7)(*f*)(i) and (8) substituted, subs.(1A), (1B) and (4A) inserted and subss.(2), (4), (6), (9) and (10) amended by s.75 and Schedule 7 of the Health Act 2004, No.42 of 2004, with effect from January 1, 2005 (S.I. No.887 of 2004).

See the Child Care (Special Care) Regulations 2004, S.I. No.550 of 2004, made pursuant to the powers conferred by this section. The Regulations set out various requirements to be complied with by the Health Service Executive in relation to the placing of children in special care units, the conduct of special care units provided by the Health Service Executive or a voluntary body or any other person, the care, supervision, visiting and review of children placed in special care units and the discharge of children from such units, in accordance with the relevant provisions of this Act of 1991 as amended by the Children Act 2001.

[Recovery of absconding child

[23L.—Section 46 shall apply to the recovery of a child who absconds from a special care unit.]

AMENDMENT

Section 23L inserted by s.16 of the Children Act 2001, No.24 of 2001, with effect from September 23, 2004 (S.I. No.548 of 2004).

[Amendment of section 4

[**23M.**—References in *section 4* to *Parts III, IV* and *VI* shall be construed as including references to this Part.]

AMENDMENT

Section 23M inserted by s.16 of the Children Act 2001, No.24 of 2001, with effect from September 23, 2004 (S.I. No.548 of 2004).

[Restriction

[**23N.**—A child on being found guilty of an offence may not be ordered to be placed or detained in a special care unit.]

AMENDMENT

Section 23N inserted by s.16 of the Children Act 2001, No.24 of 2001, with effect from September 23, 2004 (S.I. No.548 of 2004).

DEFINITIONS

"area": s.3 of the Children Act 2001
"child": s.3 of the Children Act 2001
"family welfare conference": s.3 of the Children Act 2001
"guardian": s.3 of the Children Act 2001
"legal guardian": s.3 of the Children Act 2001
"minister": s.3 of the Children Act 2001
"parent": s.3 of the Children Act 2001
"prescribed": s.3 of the Children Act 2001
"relative": s.3 of the Children Act 2001

NOTE

The 1991 Act is amended by the insertion of Part IVA. The essential effect of the amendment is to authorise the detention of children in special care units where the child's welfare warrants special care under this Part rather than care with relatives, foster parents or in residential care under Pt IV. The section provides for new types of order know as an interim special care order (hereinafter ISCO) and a special care order (hereinafter SCO). Parents or a guardian possess an important right to request the Health Service Executive to apply for an order under Pt IVA (s.23A(3)). The legislation does provide for applying for an order where the child is in the care of the Health Service Executive (s.23B(1)). In addition the gardaí have powers similar to those in s.12 of this Act of 1991 save for the fact that the language of s.23D imposes a duty on the gardaí to deliver a child who is in need of special care, to the Health Service Executive, whereas s.12 of this Act confers a power on the Gardai to take a child to safety where there is an immediate and serious risk to the heath or welfare of the child. This new Part IVA provides for the obligation to seek the orders set out in this Part and also provides for the effect, duration and obligations arising from an ISCO and an SCO. This Part also provides for the provision and maintenance of special care units (SCUs).

The need to amend this Act can be traced back to the decision of Geoghegan J. in *FN v The Minister for Education* [1995] 1 I.R. 409, [1995] 1 I.L.R.M. 297 which, in relation to the first constitutional issue, dealt with one of two fundamental constitutional issues. This decision apparently held that the State was constitutionally obliged to place and maintain in a secure residential unit a child in order to ensure the appropriate religious, moral, intellectual, physical and social education for the child. *FN v The Minister for Education* [1995] 1 I.R. 409, [1995] 1 I.L.R.M. 297 was followed in a number of similar cases including: *DT v Eastern Health Board*, unreported, HC, March 14, 1995; *GL v Minister for Justice*, unreported, High Court, March 24, 1995; *DD v The Eastern Health Board*, unreported, High Court, May 3, 1995; *PS v Eastern Health Board*, unreported, High Court, July 27, 1995; *Comerford v Minister for Education* [1997] 2 I.L.R.M. 234; *DG v The Eastern Health Board* [1997] 3 I.R. 511, [1998] 1 I.L.R.M. 241; *DB v Minister for Justice* [1999] 1 I.R. 29, [1999] 1 I.L.R.M. 93; *DH v Minister for Justice*, unreported, High Court, May 23, 2000. In *FN v The Minister for Education* [1995] 1 I.R. 409, [1995] 1 I.L.R.M. 297, however, Geoghegan J. declined to make the declaration and order sought, thus technically making his comments on the rights of the child and the State's obligation arising thereunder obiter remarks. Further, in *DG v The Eastern Health Board* [1997] 3 I.R. 511, [1998] 1 I.L.R.M 241, the Supreme Court attempted to address the second fundamental issue namely whether the High Court possessed the inherent jurisdiction to civilly detain a child to vindicate the child's constitutional right to have his welfare protected. This in turn presupposed that there existed a constitutional right that the court could vindicate. More recently Keane C.J. and Murphy J. have expressed opinions on the existence of such a constitutional right. In *TD v Minister for Education* [2001] 4 I.R. 259 Keane C.J. had grave reservations whether the courts had the authority to declare socio-economic rights to be unenumerated constitutional rights guaranteed under Art.40. Murphy J. rejected the existence of such a right and dismantled the constitutional framework upon which it was based, namely Geoghegan J.'s reliance in *FN v The Minister for Education* [1995] 1 I.R. 409, [1995] 1 I.L.R.M. 297 upon an obiter *dictum* in *G v An Bord Uchtála* [1980] I.R. 32.

Part IVA as inserted by s.16 of the Children Act 2001 has clarified the latter of these two fundamental constitutional issues. The courts now unequivocally possess the authority to direct that a child who falls within the requirements of the Part can be civilly detained. The courts possessed no such authority under this Act of 1991 and thus recourse to the inherent jurisdiction of the High Court was necessary to attempt to deal with such disturbed children. The requirements for obtaining SCOs and the restrictions that accompany an order now comply with the European Convention on the Protection of Human Rights and Fundamental Freedoms. This is evident from *DG v Ireland* (2002) 35 E.H.R.R. 33 in which the State was held to be in breach of Art.5 in depriving the applicant of his right to liberty. *DG v Ireland* (2002) 35 E.H.R.R. 33 is the follow on from *DG v The Eastern Health Board* [1997] 3 I.R. 511, [1998] 1 I.L.R.M 241 in which the Supreme Court held that it was constitutionally permissible to detain DG in a juvenile prison albeit for a limited period and only in exceptional circumstances. The ECHR held that the detention of children in itself did not amount to a violation of the right to liberty provided the detention falls within the *Bouamar v Belgium* (1989) 11 E.H.R.R. 1 exception, namely, that the detention, even in a juvenile prison, is an interim custody measure preliminary to a future regime of supervised education. DG's detention in St Patrick's was in breach of Art 5(1)(*d*) in that neither educational supervision was provided in the institution nor was it an interim measure to be followed speedily by the provision of an educational regime. The ECHR also noted that St Patrick's Institution was neither appropriate nor secure. These failings contributed to the breach of Art.5. The combination of ECHR and Supreme Court decisions suggest that it remains permissible both under the Constitution and the Convention to utilise a juvenile prison to detain a child but only as an interim measure which must be immediately followed by the provision of educational supervision in accordance with Art 5(1)(d).

The Art.5(1)(d) exception of educational supervision has been held not to amount to strict notions of classroom teaching. In *Koniarska v UK*, unreported, ECHR decision, October 12, 2000 (cited in *Re K (Secure Accommodation Order: Right to Liberty)* [2001] 1 F.L.R. 526) the ECHR held in relation to secure detention orders under the Children Act 1989 that educational supervision embraces many aspects of the exercise of parental rights by a local authority for the benefit and protection of the person concerned. The minor in this case was a psychopath who was a danger to herself and others, but as she was 17 years old she was not obliged to attend school. She argued that the s.25 of the Children Act 1989 order existed not for the purpose of educational supervision but simply detention. Here there was no breach of Art.5 as the child had attended some life and social skill programmes but thereafter refused to attend. The fact that the child was not obliged to attend the programmes did not affect the fact that an extensive educational programme was provided from which the child benefited to a limited extent.

Article 13 of S.I. No.550 of 2004, Child Care (Special Care) Regulations 2004 specifically obliges the Health Service Executive to ensure that appropriate educational facilities and services are available for children placed in SCUs. Article 14 of S.I. No.550 of 2004, Child Care (Special Care) Regulations 2004 expressly provides that regard shall be had to the child's religious, ethnic, cultural identity and spoken language of the child. No child detained in a SCU can be subject to corporal punishment or other form of physical violence, deprived of food or drink, subjected to physical, emotional or psychological detrimental treatment or treatment that is cruel, inhuman or degrading (art.15 of S.I. No.550 of 2004, Child Care (Special Care) Regulations 2004).

There are two sets of criteria that must be met before a court can make an SCO. The Health Service Executive must first engage in a consultation process and then satisfy the court that the circumstances warrant an SCO.

S.I. No.548 of 2004, Children Act 2001 (Commencement) (No.2) Order 2004 brought into effect Pt 2 of the 2001 Act save ss.7(1)(a), 10(2) and 13(2) which respectively relate to the convening of a family welfare conference by direction of the Children Court under s.77 of the 2001 Act, the adjournment of the conference and the communication by the family welfare conference with the Children Court. S.I. No.548 of 2004 also brought into effect Pt 3 of the 2001 Act save for s.23D which relates to garda powers of detention and delivery of a child in need of special care and attention. S.I. No.548 of 2004 took effect as of September 23, 2004.

Section 23A(1) imposes a positive statutory obligation to apply for either an ISCO or an SCO in specified circumstances. The obligation is contingent on the child requiring special care or protection which is unlikely to be achieved unless either an ISCO or an SCO is made. Before an application for either order is made, however, the Health Service Executive must first convene a "family welfare conference" (s.7 of the 2001 Act) and if the Health Service Executive proposes to apply for an order, there is a further consultation obligation with the Special Residential Services Board (s.226 of the 2001 Act).

The convening of a family welfare conference is governed by ss.7–15 the Children Act 2001. Section 7 of the Children Act 2001 (the 2001 Act) obliges the Health Service Executive to appoint a coordinator to act as chairperson of the family welfare conference (s.7(1)(b) and s.7(2) of the 2001 Act). The Health Service Executive is authorised to direct the family welfare conference to consider such matters as the Health Service Executive considers appropriate (s.7(3) of the 2001 Act).

The family welfare conference is obliged to determine whether a child is in need of special protection for the purposes of Pt IVA (s.8(1)(*a*) of the 2001 Act). If the determination is positive, the family welfare conference must recommend that the Health Service Executive apply for an SCO (s.8(1)(*b*) of the 2001 Act). If the determination is negative, then the family welfare conference must make a recommendation as to the care and protection of the child and in particular whether the Health Service Executive should apply for a care or supervision order (s.8(1)(*c*) of the 2001 Act). Note should be had here of the important power conferred upon a court under s.77 of the Children Act 2001. Section 77 authorises a court before which a child is charged with an offence to adjourn and, if appropriate, dismiss the charge where the court directs the Health Service Executive to convene a family welfare conference. It must appear appropriate to the court that the child in question receives care to the extent that an application is made for a care or supervision order, though the Health Service Executive may, on the conclusion of the family welfare conference, recommend an application for an SCO. Note here also should be had of s.23N which precludes the placing or detaining of a child in a special care unit where the child has been found guilty of an offence. Any recommendation made by the family welfare conference must be a unanimous recommendation subject to the coordinator's right to regard a person's disagreement as unreasonable and dispense with the dissenting person's opinion (s.8(2) of the 2001 Act) thereby making the recommendation unanimous. Where there is other disagreement, the Health Service Executive must determine the outcome of the unresolved issues.

Section 9(1)(*a*)–(*f*) of the 2001 Act specifies a number of individuals who are entitled to attend the family welfare conference. The individuals are: the child the subject matter of the conference; the parents or guardian of the child; any guardian *ad lite*m; any other relative of the child as determined by the coordinator after consultation with the parents or guardian of the child; an officer or officers of the Health Service Executive concerned and any other person who, in the opinion of the coordinator, after consultation with the parents or guardian, would make a positive contribution to the conference because of that person's knowledge of the child or the child's family or because of some particular expertise. The above individuals are entitled to be informed in writing by the coordinator of any recommendations made by the conference. Section 12(*a*)–(*g*) lists the individuals entitled to the recommendations which include a body other than the Health Service Executive who has referred the child to conference and such person at the discretion of the coordinator should be informed (s.12(*f*) and s.12(*g*)).

The right of any of the above individuals to attend is subject to the coordinator's right to exclude a person either before or during the conference where the participation of the individual is not in the interest of the conference or the child (s.9(2) of the 2001 Act). The coordinator is obliged to take all reasonable steps to give notice of the time, date and venue of the conference to the individuals entitled to attend (s.9(3) of the 2001 Act), but failure to notify a person to attend or non attendance of a person entitled to attend will not invalidate the proceedings (s.9(4)).

The right of the child and parents or guardians to be notified, attend and participate in the family welfare conference are important from both a constitutional and ECHR basis. Such involvement ensures the rights of the family collectively and individually are protected in accordance with Art.41 of the Constitution which the Health Service Executive is statutorily obliged to do under s.3 of the 1991 Act. Decisions such as *B v UK* (1988) 10 E.H.R.R. 87 stress the importance of the ECHR jurisprudence on the need for parents to be involved in the decision-making process of placing the child in the care of the State, in this case the parents were neither informed of nor participated in a case conference which resolved to place the child in long-term foster care (see also *W v UK* (1988) 10 E.H.R.R. 29). But the right of the coordinator to exclude an individual, particularly a parent or guardian, either before or during a family welfare conference and the possibility of failing to notify such individuals could affect the rights of parents.

Such parental rights are identified in the above cases and decisions to exclude parents or fail to inform may very well lead to judicial review applications in the event of adverse decisions by the coordinator. Perhaps the most significant aspect to the family welfare conference is the potential length of time involved in holding the conference and making recommendations to the Health Service Executive. Time is of the essence in care proceedings in light of two fundamental human rights principles, the right to an expeditious trial of the matter and the impact delay can have on the obligation of State authorities to attempt to re-unite the family once care proceedings are initiated (see *EP v Italy* (2001) 31 E.H.R.R. 17 and *H v UK* (1988) 10 E.H.R.R. 95). The potential for delay can be compounded by the requirement under s.23C(2)(*b*) to seek the views of the Special Residential Services Board where an SCO is sought.

Any information, statement or admission made in the course of a family welfare conference is privileged and is inadmissible in evidence in any court proceedings (Children Act 2001, s.14(1)), which reflects the position in England where confidentiality and maintaining frankness outweigh the public interest in investigating crime and inter-agency co-operation (see *Re C (A Minor) (Care Proceedings: Disclosure)* [1997] 2 W.L.R. 322 and *Re M (Care Proceedings: Disclosure: Human Rights)* [2001] 2 F.L.R. 1316).

S.I. No.549 of 2004 Children (Family Welfare Conference) Regulations 2004 provides for the convening, attendance, procedures and records relating to a family welfare conference. S.I. No.549 of 2004 took effect as of September 24, 2004.

Section 23A

This imposes a mandatory obligation on the Health Service Executive to apply for either an SCO or an ISCO depending on the Health Service Executive's assessment of the child's needs. It must appear to the Health Service Executive that the child requires special care or protection which is unlikely to be achieved unless the court makes an order under the section. Further the child must require "special care or protection". This phrase is not defined in the Act but reference to cases such as *DT v Eastern Health Board*, unreported, High Court, March 14, 1995; *GL v Minister for Justice*, unreported, High Court, March 24, 1995; *DD v The Eastern Health Board*, unreported, High Court, May 3, 1995; *PS v Eastern Health Board*, unreported, High Court, July 27, 1995; *Comerford v Minister for Education* [1997] 2 I.L.R.M. 234; *DG v The Eastern Health Board* [1997] 3 I.R. 511, [1998] 1 I.L.R.M. 241; *DB v Minister for Justice* [1999] 1 I.R. 29, [1999] 1 I.L.R.M. 93; *DH v Minister for Justice*, unreported, High Court, May 23, 2000; *DG v The Eastern Health Board* [1997] 3 I.R. 511, [1998] 1 I.L.R.M 241 and *TD v Minister for Education* [2001] 4 I.R. 259 identify the factual circumstances warranting the special care or protection. These include children constituting a danger to themselves and others, suffering severe personality disorders, engaging in child prostitution and in the English case of *A Metropolitan B.C. v DB* [1997] 1 F.L.R. 767 the secure detention of a post-partem crack-cocaine mother.

The Health Service Executive's obligation to apply for an order is subject to the convening of a family welfare conference, and if that conference decides that an ISCO or SCO should be applied for, to then seek the views of the Special Residential Services Board. There would appear to be no compulsion to act on the views of the Special Residential Services Board, i.e. the Health Service Executive only consults the SRSB after the conference has made a decision to apply for an order, but the section is silent as to what effect the view of the SRSB should or could have on the decision already taken.

The Health Service Executive has one further obligation under s.23 and that is to inform the parent of the reasons not to apply for an order where either a parent or guardian has requested the Health Service Executive to apply for an order. This implies that parents have a right to request that the Health Service Executive seek an SCO.

Section 23A appears to burden the Health Service Executive with a series of consultations which may delay an application for an order. These consultations are, however, a necessary hurdle in safeguarding the rights of all concerned. Primarily, the child's right to liberty will be infringed, and thus before any action is taken, all necessary safeguards must be adopted beforehand. In addition, the constitutional rights of parents are severely affected by an order.

Section 23B

This provides for the making of an SCO and for the effect, duration of the order once made. An SCO amounts to depriving the child of liberty and thus it is not surprising that the requirements for the making of an order are stringent. Section 23B(1)(*a*) and (*b*) require the court to be satisfied that the behaviour of the child is such that it poses a real and substantial risk to his or her health, safety, development or welfare and the child requires special care or protection which is unlikely to be received unless an order is made. The phrase "real and substantial" is not defined in the legislation but the factual circumstances warranting the declaration made in the cases listed in the General Note to s.23A would constitute a real and substantial risk to the health, safety, development or welfare. A number of English decisions identify the circumstances warranting secure detention of children such as sexual aggression to others in *Re K (A Child) (Secure Accommodation Order: Right to Liberty)* [2001] Fam. 377 and self harm and assaulting others in *LM v Essex C.C.* [1999] 1 F.L.R. 988.

It can be clearly stated that a secure detention order constitutes a restriction of the right to liberty for the purposes of Art.5 of the European Convention on Human Rights and Fundamental Freedoms but such a restriction is not incompatible with Art.5 as it is justified within the provision of Art.5(1)(*d*) as identified by the Court of Appeal in *Re K (A Child) (Secure Accommodation Order: Right to Liberty)* [2001] Fam. Law 377.

More problematic, however, may be the constitutional validity of such an order, particularly in light of the statements by Keane C.J. and Murphy J. in *TD v Minister for Education* [2001] 4 I.R. 259. Both judges questioned whether a child possessed an unenumerated constitutional right to have their welfare protected. If no such right exists, it is difficult to see how the courts have the authority to justify depriving a child of the right to liberty. That said, however, these new provisions providing for SCOs and ISCOs benefit from the presumption of constitutionality and it is suggested that whatever the judicial views on the constitutional rights of children, the provisions of the Children Act 2001 are constitutionally valid measures owing to their restrictive nature. The purpose of an SCO or ISCO once made is limited to providing care, education and treatment which complies, it is suggested with Art.5(1)(*d*) of the European Convention and is a proportionate, balanced and constitutionally valid means of providing for children who require special care and attention. Further, the duration of an SCO is stated to be for a minimum of three months and a maximum of six months (s.23B(4)(*a*)) subject to an extension or extensions (s.23B(4)(*b*)), discharge (s.23B(5)) and termination (s.23B(6)). In *DK v Crowley* [2002] 2 I.R. 744 the Supreme Court, in the context of interim barring orders, stressed the importance of strict and precise time limits on the operation of the order in question. The conditions attaching to the making of an SCO are strict and precise which should be the case considering the effect that an order has.

The language of s.23B(1)(*a*) and (*b*) contrasts sharply with s.18 which sets out the requirements for a care order. Primarily but not exclusively, the risk to the child's health, safety, development or welfare must emanate from the child's behaviour, though the manner in which a child conducts himself may make the child vulnerable to a risk emanating from a third party such as child prostitution. In addition, the risk must be a current and existing one in that the inherent risk is imminent. The language of s.23B(1)(*a*) suggests that events have occurred in relation to the child that currently constitute a risk, rather than anticipated events occurring which may constitute a risk to the child in the future. The section appears to envisage dealing with children with a history of deteriorating personal difficulties that now warrant more drastic action in requiring secure accommodation. While *Re M (A Minor)* [1994] 3 All E.R. 298 and *Re H (Minors)* [1996] A.C. 563, [1996] 2 W.L.R. 8, [1996] 1 ALL E.R. 1 have not yet been considered by an Irish court, both decisions are persuasive authorities on the relevant date for determining the risk to the child and the standard of proof for establishing the threshold criteria.

A court is also obliged by virtue of s.23B(1) to consider the views of the Special Residential Services Board in an application by the Health Service Executive for an SCO but not necessarily to act or not act on those views.

When an SCO is made, it imposes certain obligations upon the Health Service Executive and confers a limited discretion as how to provide care services for the child. The immediate effect of the SCO is to commit the child to the care of the applicant Health Service Executive (s.23B(2)) which authorises the Health Service Executive to provide appropriate care, education and treatment for the child. As seen in *Koniarska v UK*, unreported, October 12, 2000 (cited in *Re K (Secure Accommodation Order: Right to Liberty)* [2001] 1 F.L.R. 526) the concept of educational supervision has been broadly and loosely interpreted and embraces many aspects of the exercise of parental rights by a local authority for the benefit and protection of the child concerned. The Health Service Executive is primarily obliged to care for the child in a SCU but s.23B(7)(*a*) authorises the Health Service Executive as part of the child's care, education or treatment and only on a temporary basis, to provide accommodation for a child in accordance with s.36 (foster, residential and care with relatives). In addition, the Health Service Executive may for reasons of health, education or compassion, facilitate temporary release from a SCU with appropriate control and supervision (s.23B(7)(*b*)).

While in a child is the subject of an SCO, the Health Service Executive may take reasonable measures to prevent the child from causing injury to himself or others or absconding from the unit (s.23B(3)).

An SCO remains valid for a maximum period of six months and can be extended provided the court is satisfied that the grounds for an SCO continue to exist (s.23B(4)(*b*)). No limit is placed on the number of applications that can be made for an extension of the SCO. An SCO ceases to have effect when a child reaches the age of 18 or is married if that is before 18 (s.23B(6)). Where the child's circumstances or behaviour no longer warrant the existence of an order (s.23B(5)), the Health Service Executive is obliged to bring an application to discharge the order to the same court that made the original order.

The obligation to bring the application to discharge the order would appear to be strict and should be brought without delay notwithstanding the fact that the duration of the SCO has not yet expired. This obligation mirrors the decision of *LM v Essex C.C.* [1999] 1 F.L.R. 928 which indicated that where a decision was taken by the County Council that a secure accommodation order was no longer appropriate but no action was taken to discharge the order, the appropriate application to court was for a writ of habeas corpus. The court also indicated that where there was disagreement as to whether the circumstances warranted continued secure accommodation, then the appropriate application by the child in question should be by way of judicial review.

A number of the provisions of s.18 of this Act are applied by this section in the case of an SCO, with any necessary modifications, as follows; s.18(3), which permits parental control to be exercised by the Health Service Executive, s.18(4) which gives a power to the Health Service Executive to consent to medical or psychiatric examination, assessment or treatment, s.18(6) under which the court can give directions as it sees fit in the time between the application and the making of the order, s.18(7) which provides for payment to the Health Service Executive by the parents and s.18(8) which permits the discharge or variation of an order by the parents to pay monies to the Health Service Executive.

Section 23C

This provides the criteria for the making of an interim special care order (ISCO), its duration and effect. The court must be satisfied that a family welfare conference has been arranged in accordance with s.23A(2). Section 23C provides the same criteria for the making of an ISCO as s.23B provides for the making of an SCO save that the standard of proof required for an ISCO is lesser than that of an SCO, namely that the judge be satisfied that there is reasonable cause to believe that the grounds exist rather than be satisfied that the threshold criteria exist.

The effect of the order is to place the child in a special care unit but the section does not expressly commit the child to the care of Health Service Executive, however such must be inferred from the section. An application for an ISCO or an extension thereof must be on notice to the parent having custody, a person acting *in loco parentis*, or where appropriate, the Health Service Executive. The obligation to give notice of the application to the persons concerned is subject to the judge directing otherwise where such is not in the interests of the child's welfare. It is presumed that District Court Rules will provide for notice periods similar to those for care and interim care orders of seven days prior to the hearing of the application. The importance of clear and precise time periods for applications was stressed in *DK v Crowley* [2002] 2 I.R. 744 albeit in relation to the Domestic Violence Act 1996. Reference should be had to *Re C (Secure Accommodation Order: Representation)* [2001] 2 F.L.R. 169 where the Court of Appeal indicated that where a court dispenses with notice requirements for the hearing of secure accommodation applications in circumstances where the child objects to detention, the court should make an interim secure accommodation order.

Section 23C(4) makes applicable s.13(3)–(7) to the operation of this section. Those subsections respectively provide for: the issue of a warrant authorising the gardaí to effect an ISCO by entry to specified premises and removal of the child; applications to a judge in an area where the child does not reside and if need be by ex parte applications, which can be heard otherwise than in public; an appeal of an ISCO does not stay its operation; not naming a child in the application where such is not known; and the making of directions relating to withholding the whereabouts of the child, access, medical or psychiatric examination, treatment or assessment of the child and discharge or variation of any such directions (see General Note to s.13).

The duration of an ISCO is primarily for an initial period of 28 days (s.23C(2)(*a*)) and an extension to the ISCO may be for a period in excess of 28 days (s.23C(2)(*b*)) provided the relevant parties (the Health Service Executive, parent with custody or person acting *in loco parentis*) consent to the period exceeding 28 days. The court must be satisfied that the criteria for an extension of the ISCO continue to exist. The section does not provide for an upper time limit on the duration of an extension to the ISCO.

Section 23D

This section confers emergency powers upon the gardaí in relation to a child to whom the criteria applicable for an ISCO or SCO exist. In addition, the member in question need only have reasonable grounds to believe the threshold criteria exist and that the awaiting of an application for an ISCO, either by notice or ex parte, would be insufficient to protect the child.

Where such circumstances exist, the member is obliged to attempt to deliver the child to the Health Service Executive where the child normally resides. In addition and by contrast with s.13, the member must inform the Health Service Executive of the circumstances in which the child came to the attention of the gardaí.

Once the Health Service Executive is satisfied that the child meets the threshold criteria for an order under Pt IVA, the Health Service Executive must institute an application for an SCO or more likely an ISCO by ex parte application.

This section is silent as to how the Health Service Executive may accommodate the child once delivered by the gardaí in this fashion. It is suggested that the only form of accommodation that the Health Service Executive can provide is residential, foster care or with relatives as provided for in s.36. It would appear to be unlawful to detain a child in a SCU in the absence of an order to that effect even though the only practical means of providing for a child that meets the criteria is by way of care in a SCU.

The Health Service Executive seems not to be obliged to inform the parent having custody or person acting *in loco parentis* of the fact that the child has been delivered to the Health Service Executive and the Health Service Executive need only give such notification once an ISCO has committed the child to a SCU.

This section is not yet effective (S.I. No.548 of 2004, Children Act 2001 (Commencement) (No.2) Order 2004).

Section 23E

This imposes an obligation to inform a parent having custody or a person acting *in loco parentis* of the fact that a child has been placed in a SCU on foot of an ISCO unless the relevant person is missing or cannot be found.

The relevant person can be deemed to have notice of the placing of the child in a SCU when either present at the court sitting at which the order was made or is given or shown a copy of the order. Parents are entitled to information concerning significant events occurring to the child and, in particular, where restraint of the child is necessary or the need for single separation (arts 16(3), 17(5) and 18(5) respectively of S.I. No.550 of 2004, Child Care (Special Care) Regulations 2004). The Health Service Executive would be advised to adopt a proactive role in involving parents in all aspects of a child's care at all stages of the decision-making process regarding care proceedings and, in particular, to consult with parents regarding a care plan or alteration of such (see *Re G (Care: Challenge to Local Authority's Decision)* [2003] 2 F.L.R. 42, *B v UK* (1988) 10 E.H.R.R. 87 and *W v UK* (1988) 10 E.H.R.R. 29 dealing with parental involvement in care proceedings).

Section 23F

This section provides for the variation, discharge and, where appropriate, substitution of an SCO. Either the court of its own motion or any person may apply to vary or discharge an SCO. The discharge of the SCO is subject to the court motion or Health Service Executive application to substitute the SCO with either a supervision order (s.19) or a care order (s.18) provided the court is satisfied that the child can only receive the care and protection needed by remaining in the care of the Health Service Executive or that the return of the child to a parent or other person (parent, person acting *in loco parentis*, foster parent or relative) is not in the interests of the child. Article 31 of S.I. No.550 of 2004, Child Care (Special Care) Regulations 2004 details the discharge of a child from a SCU which precludes discharge save in accordance with art.31.

Section 23G

This section applies the provisions of s.21 to any appeal from the making of an ISCO or an SCO. Either the court making the ISCO or SCO, or the court to which the appeal is made can stay the operation of the order on such terms, if any, as the relevant court decides to impose. Section 23G also provides that the order cannot be stayed other than as outlined.

Section 23H

This section applies the provisions of s.23 to SCOs which has the effect of preserving the status quo of the child where an SCO is found to be invalid. The practical effect is to enable the Health Service Executive to lawfully maintain a child notwithstanding the fact that the original order is invalid. The section operates by way of court finding of invalidity and direction not to return a child to a parent or person acting *in loco parentis* where such is considered not to be in the child's best interests. The court may make an order to this effect of its own motion or application by any person. Section 23 sets out four orders that can be made where the original order is invalid. Where an SCO is found to be invalid, that order can be deemed valid or alternatively the court may make a care order.

Section 23I

This makes applicable to ISCOs and SCOs Pt V of the 1991 Act which provides for the jurisdiction and procedures governing care proceedings. The relevant provisions are ss.24–35 (see Note to Pt V). Broadly those provisions relate to the following matters: the principle of the child's welfare being of paramount importance in the court's consideration (s.24); joining the child as a party to the proceedings by court order and appointment of a solicitor to represent the child and payment of costs (s.25); the appointment of a guardian ad litem for the child (s.26); directing the procurement of a welfare report of the child (s.27); jurisdiction of the District and Circuit Court on appeal (s.28); the hearing of proceedings in camera (s.29); the hearing of proceedings in the absence of the child (s.30); publication and broadcasting restrictions on identifying a child the subject of proceedings (s.31); power of the court to deem or presume the age of the child for the purpose of a hearing (s.32); rules providing for the expeditious service of documents and rules of court (s.33); penalties for failing to deliver up a child on foot of an order under Pts III, IV and IVA (s.34) and the issue of a warrant to effect an order under Pts IV and IVA (s.35).

Section 23J

This makes applicable the following sections of Pt VI of the 1991 Act (see General Notes to relevant sections):

Section 37 provides for access to a child in care under Pts III, IV or IVA by parents, a person acting *in loco parentis* or any other person in the Health Service Executive's opinion who has a bona fide interest in the child. Section 37(1) authorises the Health Service Executive to allow a child to reside temporarily with a specified person but it is difficult to imagine how this provision can operate in the context of an SCO or an ISCO. Section 37 also provides for applications to court to resolve disputes relating to access and to refuse access if need be.

Section 42 obliges the Minister to make regulations for the review of the cases of children in special care units.

Section 45 relates to the provision of aftercare to children who have exceeded the age of 18 but not the age of 21. Section 45 specifies the types of assistance that can be provided by the Health Service Executive.

Section 47 enables the District Court to make directions relating to the child's welfare whilst in care.

Section 23K

This provides for the provision, maintenance, operation and regulation of SCUs. The Health Service Executive is primarily responsible for the provision and maintenance of SCUs but only with the approval of the Minister (s.23K(1)(*a*)). The Health Service Executive may, however, delegate the provision and operation of SCUs to voluntary bodies or other persons (s.23K(1)(*b*)). No SCU can be provided, maintained or operated unless approved by the Minister. Ministerial approval is contingent upon the unit being inspected and a satisfactory report to the Minister that regulations governing the provision and maintenance of a SCU will be complied with (s.23K(2)(*a*) and (*b*)). Any approval granted by the Minister has a maximum duration of three years and can be renewed for further periods of no more than three years (s.23K(3)). Once a SCU is approved, the Minister is obliged to issue a certificate which is presumed to be statutory proof of Ministerial approval of the unit (s.23K(4)). Any such certificate can be cancelled where, in the Minister's opinion, the unit is no longer suitable as a unit or is no longer required for that purpose (s.23K(5)).

The Minister is statutorily obliged to make regulations governing the operation of SCUs (s.23K(6)) which may prescribe requirements as to: the maintenance, care and welfare of children detained in the unit; staffing; physical standards of the unit including adequate and suitable accommodation and facilities; the periodic review of the cases of children's in the unit and such matters to be considered in such reviews; the keeping of, examination of and copying of records of the unit and inspection of units by authorised persons on behalf of the Minister (s.23K(1)–(*e*)). Where a voluntary body or other person provides the unit, the Health Service Executive inspects the unit. Where the Health Service Executive provides the unit, the inspection is conducted in accordance with s.69, which authorises the Minister to appoint an inspector to inspect and examine any service provided and premises maintained by the Health Service Executive (s.23K(*f*)(i) and (ii)). S.I. No.550 of 2004, Child Care (Special Care) Regulations 2004 governs the operation, maintenance and inspection of special care units. S.I. No.550 of 2004 took effect as of September 24, 2004.

S.I. No.550 of 2004 also contains very detailed regulations governing the management and operation of SCUs. In particular children are provided with a number of rights which the Health Service Executive/manager of the SCU is obliged to respect save where circumstances otherwise warrant. A child can make a complaint concerning detention in a SCU (art.19), the right to have a parent, guardian, guardian ad litem or legal representative informed of significant events (art.16(3)); of restraint (art.17(5)); and single separation (art.18(5)). A child is specifically not to be subjected to corporal punishment or other physical violence, deprived of food or drink, subjected to physical, psychological or emotional ill-treatment or inhuman and degrading treatment but is obliged to abide by the rules of the unit (art.15). The child is ordinarily not to be restrained (art.17) nor confined to single separation (art.16) save where otherwise necessary. A child or other stated person may request a special case review (art.29) and must be the subject of a review at least once a month from the date of detention and within a month of the court making the order (art.28). The Health Service Executive must ensure that appropriate arrangements are in place to facilitate reasonable access between the child and parent, guardian, guardian *ad litem* or legal representative (art.11).

S.I. No.550 of 2004 contains detailed provisions concerning records, registers and information concerning children in SCUs. A care record (art.20) must be kept in relation to every child in a SCU which the Health Service Executive is obliged to ensure is kept (art.21) and monitored (art.22) and the details of which are kept in a register (art.24). A case record (art.25) and a care plan (art.26) must be drafted and maintained.

The Health Service Exective may provide financial and other assistance to voluntary bodies or other persons providing and maintaining a SCU (s.23K(8)). The Health Service

Executive is prohibited from delegating its statutory function of applying for an ISCO or an SCO to a voluntary body or any other person (s.23K(9)). Voluntary bodies or any other person providing and maintaining a SCU may, however, take reasonable steps to prevent a child in the unit causing injury to himself or to others and from escaping (s.23K(10)). No child can be placed in a SCU except in accordance with an ISCO or an SCO (s.23K(11)).

Section 23L

This section applies the provisions of s.46 of this Act (provisions in relation to children unlawfully removed) to the case of children who abscond from an SCU. Section 46 enables the Health Service Executive to recover a child either by requesting the gardaí to search for and deliver up the child which can be effected by the gardaí exercising reasonable measures or alternatively by application for a court direction that a person so specified deliver up a child to the custody of the Health Service Executive. Section 46(4) and (5) provides for sanctions for failing to comply with a court direction and notice of the direction. The direction to deliver up can be enforced by warrant authorising the gardaí to enter and search a specified place for a child and deliver the child, if found, to the Health Service Executive. Section 46(7) provides for the making an application for an order to deliver up a child ex parte, section 46(8) provides that an application for an order to deliver up a child, or a warrant to search can be heard other than at a public sitting of the court. Section 46(9) provides that an application to deliver up a child shall be made in the district court district in which the person sought to be ordered to deliver up the child resides, and that an application for a warrant to search a particular specified premises shall be made in the district court district in which the specified premises is located. Article 30 of S.I. No.550 of 2004 provides for children being absent from a SCU without permission and the obligations of the manager in these circumstances. A child recovered, having absconded from a unit may be subjected to a medical examination (art.23) on request to the Health Service Executive.

Section 23M

Section 23M provides that reference to Parts III, IV and VI in s.4 includes reference to this Part IVA. Section 4 concerns the voluntary taking of a child into care. Two provisions of that section in particular, subsections (2) and (4), are expressed to be 'without prejudice' to this Part of the Act. Section 4(2) does not permit the taking of a child into voluntary care against the wishes of his parents, and section 4(4) requires the Health Service Executive to endeavour to reunite a child with its parents where the child is taken into voluntary care on the basis that he is lost, deserted or abandoned.

Section 23N

This expressly prohibits the placing of a child in a SCU who has been found guilty of an offence. This is an important provision especially in light of s.77 of the Children Act 2001 which authorises a court to adjourn proceedings in which a child is charged with a criminal offence and direct the holding of a family welfare conference. The court may also make, on an interim basis, an emergency care order or a supervision order pending the findings of the conference. Section 77 of the Children Act 2001 reverses the effect of *DPP (Murphy) v PT* [1998] 1 I.L.R.M. 344 which held that where a child was the subject of a fit person order and was also before the court charged with offences, the court had no jurisdiction to postpone the hearing of the criminal charges while an investigation was directed to be conducted by the Health Board into the child's circumstances.

The prohibition on placing a convicted child in a SCU should be assessed not from

98   *The Child Care Acts*

the convicted child's perspective but from the perspective of the children occupying the SCUs on foot of an SCO or ISCO. The exclusion of such children is necessary to secure the proper welfare of the children resident in SCUs where it is inappropriate to mix children convicted of criminal offences in a unit intended to provide for the special care and protection of children (see the dissenting judgment of Denham J. in *TD v Minister for Education* [2001] 4 I.R. 259).

[PART IVB

PRIVATE FOSTER CARE

AMENDMENT

Part IVB, ss. 23O to 23X inserted by s.16 of the Children Act 2001, No.24 of 2001, which came into effect on September 23, 2004 (S.I. No.548 of 2004).

[Definitions

[23O.—In this Part—
["authorised officer" means a person appointed by the Health Service Executive under *section 23S*;]
[…];
"private foster care arrangement" means any arrangement or undertaking whereby a child is for more than 14 days in the full-time care, for reward or otherwise, of a person other than his or her parent or guardian, a person cohabiting with a parent or guardian or a relative, except where the child—
  (a) is residing at a boarding school and receiving full-time education,
  (b) is in an institution managed by or on behalf of a Minister of the Government or [the Health Service Executive],
  (c) is in an institution in which the majority of persons being cared for and maintained are being treated for acute illness,
  (d) is in an institution for the care and maintenance of children with a disability,
  (e) is in a mental institution within the meaning of the Mental Treatment Acts, 1945 to 1966,
  (f) is detained in a children detention school or children detention centre within the meaning of the Children Act, 2001,
  (g) is placed for adoption under the Adoption Acts, 1952 to 1998,
  (h) is in the care of [the Health Service Executive],
  (i) is on holidays for a continuous period not exceeding 42 days,
  (j) is placed with a person or body for primarily educational purposes, or
  (k) is placed with a friend of the child's parent or guardian for a period not exceeding 42 days, while the parent or guardian is on holidays;
"relative", in relation to a child, means a grandparent, brother, sister, uncle or aunt, whether of the whole blood, half blood or by affinity, and includes the spouse of any such person and any person cohabiting with any such person.]

AMENDMENT

Section 23O inserted by s.16 of the Children Act 2001, No.24 of 2001, with effect from September 23, 2004 (S.I. No.548 of 2004).

Definition of "authorised officer" substituted, definition of "health board" deleted, definition of "private foster care arrangement" amended by s.75 and Schedule 7 of the Health Act 2004, No.42 of 2004, with effect from January 1, 2005 (S.I. No.887 of 2004).

[Notice of private foster care arrangement

[23P.—(1) A person arranging or undertaking a private foster care arrangement shall give notice to the [Health Service Executive] in the manner specified in section 23Q not less than thirty days before the placement.

(2) Where a child is placed in a private foster care arrangement owing to an unforeseen emergency, both the person making the arrangement and the person undertaking it shall notify the [Health Service Executive] in the manner specified in section 23Q as soon as practicable and not more than 14 days after the placement.

[(3) Any person arranging or undertaking a private foster care arrangement before the establishment day of the Health Service Executive who has submitted to the Health Service Executive before that day the information the health board required in relation to the arrangement or undertaking shall be deemed to have complied with subsection (1).]

AMENDMENT

Section 23P inserted by s.16 of the Children Act 2001, No.24 of 2001, with effect from September 23, 2004 (S.I. No.548 of 2004).

Subsections (1) and (2) amended, and subs.(3) substituted, by s.75 and Schedule 7 of the Health Act 2004, No.42 of 2004, with effect from January 1, 2005 (S.I. No.887 of 2004).

[Information to be submitted to relevant [Health Service Executive]

[23Q.—(1) Any person arranging or undertaking a private foster care arrangement shall submit to [the Health Service Executive] in writing—

(a) the person's name and address,

(b) the name, sex, date and place of birth and address of the child concerned,

(c) the name and address of the parent or guardian of the child,

(d) if the child's residence is changed, the child's new address,

(e) if the private foster care arrangement terminates, the reasons for its termination, and any other information that [the Health Service Executive] may consider necessary in relation to any persons involved in the arrangement.

(2) Any person arranging a private foster care arrangement shall submit to the [Health Service Executive], in writing, the name and address of the person undertaking the arrangement and any other information in respect of that person that [the Executive] may consider necessary.]

AMENDMENT

Section 23Q inserted by s.16 of the Children Act 2001, No.24 of 2001, with effect from September 23, 2004 (S.I. No.548 of 2004).

Subsections (1) and (2) amended by s.75 and Schedule 7 of the Health Act 2004, No.42 of 2004, with effect from January 1, 2005 (S.I. No.887 of 2004).

[Duty in respect of children in private foster care

[23R.—(1) Any person arranging or undertaking a private foster care arrangement in respect of a child shall regard the child's welfare as the first and paramount consideration.

(2) Any person undertaking such an arrangement shall take all reasonable measures to safeguard the health, safety and welfare of the child concerned.

(3) Any person arranging such an arrangement shall make all reasonable enquiries to ensure that the person undertaking it is in a position to comply with subsection (2).]

AMENDMENT

Section 23R inserted by s.16 of the Children Act 2001, No.24 of 2001, with effect from September 23, 2004 (S.I. No.548 of 2004).

[Authorised officers

[23S.—(1) [The Health Service Executive shall appoint such and so many of its employees] as it thinks fit to be authorised officers for the purposes of this Part.

(2) Each authorised officer shall be given a warrant of his or her appointment and, when exercising any power conferred by this Part, shall, on request by any person affected, produce the warrant or a copy thereof, together with a form of personal identification.]

AMENDMENT

Section 23S inserted by s.16 of the Children Act 2001, No24 of 2001, with effect from September 23, 2004 (S.I. No.548 of 2004).

Amended by s.75 and Schedule 7 of the Health Act 2004, No. 42 of 2004, with effect from January 1, 2005 (S.I. No.887 of 2004).

[Inspection by authorised persons

[23T.—(1) Where the [Health Service Executive] has received a notice in accordance with section 23P in respect of a private foster care arrangement, an authorised officer may at all reasonable times enter any premises (including a private dwelling) in which the child concerned is residing.

(2) A judge of the District Court may, if satisfied on the sworn information of an authorised officer that there are reasonable grounds for believing that a private foster care arrangement has been arranged or undertaken and that the [Health Service Executive] has not received the requisite notice, issue a warrant authorising an authorised officer, accompanied if necessary by other persons,

to enter, if need by reasonable force, and inspect any premises (including a private dwelling) in which the child may be residing.

(3) An authorised officer, on entering any such premises, shall investigate the care and attention that the child is receiving and the condition of the premises with a view to ensuring that the person undertaking the arrangement is complying with his or her duty to take all reasonable measures to safeguard the child's health, safety and welfare.

(4) An authorised officer may request a member of the Garda Síochána to accompany him or her when carrying out an inspection.]

AMENDMENT

Section 23T inserted by s.16 of the Children Act 2001, No.24 of 2001, with effect from September 23, 2004 (S.I. No.548 of 2004).

Subsections (1) and (2) amended by s.75 and Schedule 7 of the Health Act 2004, No.42 of 2004, with effect from January 1, 2005 (S.I. No.887 of 2004).

[Institution of proceedings by [Health Service Executive]

[**23U.**—If [the Health Service Executive] believes—

 (*a*) that a person who is arranging or undertaking a private foster care arrangement has not notified it under section 23P, or

 (*b*) that such a person is not taking all reasonable measures to safeguard the health, safety and welfare of the child concerned,

it may apply to the District Court for one of the following orders:

 (i) that a supervision order under section 19 be made in respect of the child,

 (ii) that the child be taken into the care of [the Health Service Executive] under section 13, 17 or 18, or

 (iii) that the arrangement be terminated and the child returned to his or her parents or guardian, and the Court may order accordingly.]

AMENDMENT

Section 23U inserted by s.16 of the Children Act 2001, No.24 of 2001, with effect from September 23, 2004 (S.I. No.548 of 2004).

Subsequent amendments by s.75 and Schedule 7 of the Health Act 2004, No.42 of 2004, with effect from January 1, 2005 (S.I. No.887 of 2004).

[Restrictions on private foster care arrangements in certain cases

[**23V.**—(1) A person shall not arrange or undertake a private foster care arrangement for the purpose of adopting a child under the Adoption Acts, 1952 to 1998.

(2) Any person undertaking a private foster care arrangement in respect of a child shall not apply under those Acts to adopt the child unless—

 (*a*) the child is eligible for adoption under the Adoption Acts, 1952 to 1998, and

 (*b*) the [the Health Service Executive] has consented to the continuance of the arrangement pending the completion of an assessment of that person under those Acts.

(3) If [the Health Service Executive] believes that a person who is arranging or undertaking a private foster care arrangement is doing so in contravention of subsection (1) or (2), it may apply to the District Court for an order either—
- (a) that the child be taken into its care under section 13, 17 or 18, or
- (b) that the arrangement be terminated and the child returned to his or her parents or guardian,

and the Court may order accordingly.]

AMENDMENT

Section 23V inserted by s.16 of the Children Act 2001, No.24 of 2001, with effect from September 23, 2004 (S.I. No.548 of 2004).

Subsections (2)(b) and (3) amended by s.75 and Schedule 7 of the Health Act 2004, No.42 of 2004, with effect from January 1, 2005 (S.I. No.887 of 2004).

[Offences

[23W.—(1) Any person—
- (a) who while arranging or undertaking a private foster care arrangement does not notify the [Health Service Executive] under section 23P,
- (b) who contravenes subsection (2) or (3) of section 23R,
- (c) who refuses to allow an authorised officer to enter any premises in accordance with subsection (1) or (2) of section 23T or obstructs or impedes an authorised officer in the exercise of his or her powers under that section,
- (d) who while arranging or undertaking a private foster care arrangement knowingly or wilfully makes or causes or procures any other person to make a false or misleading statement to the [Health Service Executive],
- (e) who contravenes section 23V(1), or
- (f) who does not comply with an order under paragraph (ii) or (iii) of section 23U or under section 23V(3),

is guilty of an offence and liable on summary conviction to a fine not exceeding €1,904.61.

(2) Where a person is convicted of an offence under this section, the District Court may by order prohibit the person from arranging or undertaking a private foster care arrangement for such period as may be specified in the order.]

AMENDMENT

Section 23W inserted by s.16 of the Children Act 2001, No.24 of 2001, with effect from September 23, 2004 (S.I. No.548 of 2004).

Subsections (1)(a) and (d) amended by s.75 and Schedule 7 of the Health Act 2004, No.42 of 2004, with effect from January 1, 2005 (S.I. No.887 of 2004).

[Saver

[23X.—This Part is without prejudice to any other provision of this Act or any provision of the Children Act, 2001, which imposes, in the interests of a child, duties or obligations on [the Health Service Executive] or a member of the Garda Síochána.]

Amendment

Section 23X inserted by s.16 of the Children Act 2001, No.24 of 2001, with effect from September 23, 2004 (S.I. No.548 of 2004).
Subsequently amended by s.75 and Schedule 7 of the Health Act 2004, No.42 of 2004, with effect from January 1, 2005 (S.I. No.887 of 2004).

Definitions

"authorised officer": s.23O.
"health board": s.23O.
"private foster care arrangement": s.23O.
"relative": s.23O.

Note

Part IVB provides for private foster care arrangement. It defines what constitutes private foster care and provides for the regulation and control of such care services by the Health Service Executive. Of particular note is the prohibition on utilising a private foster care service for the purpose of adopting a child (s.23V).
Control of private foster care is achieved through notifying and liasing between the private foster carer and the Health Service Executive. The control is enforced through a number of offences created by this part.

Section 23O
This is the definition section for Pt IVB. The terms "authorised officer" and "health board" are set out above. A "private foster care arrangement" is defined by reference to a number of exclusions but must primarily involve the child being in the full-time care for a period in excess of 14 days with a person other than his parent or guardian, a person co-habiting with a parent or guardian or a relative. The arrangement may be for reward or otherwise. The following scenarios are excluded from the definition of a private foster care arrangement: boarding schools or full-time educational institutions; institutions managed by a Minister or Health Service Executive; institutions maintaining and caring for children with acute illnesses; institutions maintaining and caring for children with disabilities; a mental institution as defined in the Mental Treatment Acts 1945–1966; a children detention school or detention centre within the meaning of the Children Act 2001; an adoption placement under the Adoption Acts 1952–1998, in Health Service Executive care; on holidays for a continuous period not exceeding 42 days; placement with a person for primarily educational purposes or placed with a friend of the child's parent or guardian for a period not exceeding 42 days while the parent or guardian is on holidays.
A "relative" is defined as: a grandparent, brother, sister, uncle or aunt of either half blood or affinity and includes the spouse and person cohabiting with any such person.

Section 23P
This imposes a statutory duty on persons making (i.e. arranging (person 'giving' the child) and undertaking (person 'taking' the child)) a private foster care arrangement to notify the Health Service Executive of certain matters within a specified time. Failure to do so constitutes a criminal offence triable summarily and punishable with a fine not

exceeding €1,904.61 (s.23W(1)) and possible disqualification from arranging or undertaking a private foster care arrangement for such period as the court considers appropriate (s.23W(2)).

The matters that must be notified to the Health Service Executive are set out in s.23Q. A person intending to arrange or undertake a private foster care arrangement must give notice of such to the Health Service Executive (to the Health Service Executive in which area the child resided prior to placement and to the Health Service Executive if the area is a different one after the placement) 30 days prior to a placement (s.23P(1)) unless an emergency situation arises, in which case notification must be given within 14 days after the placement (s.23P(2)).

The information to be notified to the Health Service Executive must be in writing (s.23Q(1)) and includes: the name and address of the person providing the foster care; the name, date and place of birth and address of the child; the name and address of the parent or guardian of the child, any change of address of the child and where the foster care is terminated, the reasons for termination and any other information the Health Service Executive considers necessary relating to the individuals involved in the foster care arrangement.

The information to be notified to the Health Service Executive must be in writing. The information to be given is set out in s.23Q(1)(*a*) to (*e*). The information must be given by either the person arranging or the person undertaking the arrangement. In addition, the person arranging must also submit the name and address of the person undertaking the arrangement, as well as such other information in respect of that person as is required by the Health Service Executive.

Section 23Q
This obliges persons arranging or undertaking private foster care to submit information to the Health Service Executive (see note to s.23P).

Section 23R
Section 23R sets out a number of statutory obligations with regard to private foster care arrangements as follows – both the person arranging (giving the child) and undertaking (taking the child) the arrangement must regard the child's welfare as the first and paramount consideration. Also, the person undertaking the arrangement must take all reasonable steps to ensure the health, safety and welfare of the child. The person arranging the arrangement must take all reasonable steps to ensure that the other person is in a position to take all reasonable steps to safeguard the health, safety and welfare of the child. Failure by either arranger or undertaker to take the "reasonable steps" as outlined is a criminal offence, although interestingly, failure to regard the child's welfare as the first and paramount consideration would not be a criminal offence. Section 23R should not be read as absolving the Health Service Executive of statutory responsibility for children in private foster care but as imposing a duty on those persons arranging and undertaking private foster care. The Health Service Executive is potentially vulnerable for liability in negligence and breach of statutory duty where inadequate vetting procedures are adopted and implemented as evident from a number of English cases involving foster care. Liability can extend to the child that is fostered as well as to the foster parents as evident from *Barrett v Enfield L.B.C.* [1999] 3 All E.R. 193 and *S v Gloucestershire C.C.* [2000] 3 All E.R. 346, [2001] 2 W.L.R. 909, [2000] 1 F.L.R. 825. But the Health Service Executive can take solace from the decision of *L v Tower Hamlets L.B.C.* [2000] 3 All E.R. 346, [2001] 2 W.L.R. 909, [2000] 1 F.L.R. 825 where the defendant local authority was found to have conducted a rigorous and detailed assessment of the foster parents in question so that an action in negligence could not possibly succeed.

Ultimately the issue arising here will be whether the provisions of s.23S and s.23T are adequate to fulfil the Health Service Executive's duty in the circumstances.

Section 23S

The Health Service Executive is positively obliged to appoint "authorised officers" for the visiting of foster children. Authorised officers are entitled to enter any premises in which a child is residing with private foster parents where the Health Service Executive has received a notice in accordance with s.23P (s.23T(1)). Where an "authorised officer" is so appointed by the Health Service Executive, such an officer must be provided with a warrant of appointment. Where an officer attempts to enter premises where a child is residing, the officer is obliged to produce the warrant or a copy thereof to the person affected by the entry along with evidence of personal identification, i.e. must show two separate documents (s.23S(2)).

Section 23T

This enables the Health Service Executive through their "authorised officers" to enter premises and investigate the care and attention children are receiving in private foster care at all reasonable times. The right of entry is subject to the Health Service Executive having received a notice in accordance with s.23P.

Where no notice in respect of s.23P has been received and there are reasonable grounds to believe that a private arrangement has been made, the Health Service Executive may apply to the District Court for a warrant authorising an authorised officer to enter any premises, and, with reasonable force, for the purpose of inspecting the premises in which a child resides. The authorised officer may enter the premises accompanied by other persons and may request a member of the gardaí to accompany the authorised officer during the inspection (s.23T(4)). The issue of the warrant to enter is contingent upon the judge being satisfied that there are reasonable grounds to believe that a private foster care arrangement has been arranged or undertaken and in respect of which the Health Service Executive has not received the s.23P notice. The application for a warrant must be grounded upon the sworn information of the authorised officer.

The authorised officer is positively obliged to investigate the care and attention the child is receiving and the condition of the premises when they enter premises either as of right (s.23T(1)) or by warrant (s.23T(2)). The purpose of the inspection is to be satisfied that the person arranging or undertaking the private foster care arrangement is complying with the statutory duty in s.23R to safeguard the child's health, safety and welfare. Failure to allow an entry for inspection by an authorised officer constitutes a criminal offence under s.23W(1)(*c*).

Section 23U

This provides a number of remedies for the Health Service Executive where there is a failure to comply with s.23P (notice to Health Service Executive) or s.23R (failure to safeguard the child's health, safety or welfare).

The Health Service Executive may apply to the District Court for one of the following orders: a supervision order (s.19); an emergency care order (s.13); an interim care order (s.17); a care order (s.18) or order terminating the private foster care arrangement and the return of the child to his parent or guardian. Where a person arranging or undertaking a private foster care arrangement fails to comply with an order under s.23U(ii) or (iii) such constitutes a criminal offence under s.23W(1)(*f*).

Section 23V

This places a prohibition upon persons arranging or undertaking private foster care from using the arrangement for the purposes of adoption. The person undertaking (taking the child) the private arrangement may apply under the Adoption Acts if the child is eligible, and the Health Service Executive has consented to the continuation of the private arrangement pending the assessment of the 'undertaker' under those Acts. Where the Health Service Executive believes that the private foster care is arranged or undertaken in contravention of subsection (1) or (2), then an application may be brought to the District Court for an emergency care order, an interim care order or a care order in respect of the child. Alternatively an order may be sought terminating the private foster care arrangement and the return of the child to his parent or guardian as the court considers appropriate.

Section 23W

This provides for the creation of offences and penalties in relation to Pt IVB. Upon summary conviction a person is liable to a fine not exceeding €1,904.61 and, at the court's discretion, a prohibition for a specified period on arranging or undertaking a private foster care arrangement. The offences provided for by s.23W are: failure to notify the Health Service Executive in accordance with s.23P; failure to safeguard the health, safety or welfare of a child and failure to make reasonable enquiries to ensure a person is in a position to comply with safeguarding the child's health, safety and welfare (s.23R(2) and (3)); failure to allow an authorised officer entry to premises either as of right or by warrant under s.23T(1) or (2) and obstructing or impeding the inspection of the premises; knowingly or wilfully making or causing or procuring any other person to make a false or misleading statement to the relevant Health Service Executive; arranging or undertaking a private foster care arrangement for the purposes of adopting a child; or failure to deliver up a child on foot of an order under s.23U(ii) or (iii) and s.23V(3).

PART V

JURISDICTION AND PROCEDURE

Welfare of child to be paramount

24.—In any proceedings before a court under this Act in relation to the care and protection of a child, the court, having regard to the rights and duties of parents, whether under the Constitution or otherwise, shall—

    (*a*) regard the welfare of the child as the first and paramount consideration, and

    (*b*) in so far as is practicable, give due consideration, having regard to his age and understanding, to the wishes of the child.

DEFINITIONS

"child": s.2.
"parents": s.2.

COMMENCEMENT

Child Care Act, 1991 (Commencement) Order, 1995 (S.I. No. 258 of 1995) took effect as of October 31, 1995.

Note

This section prescribes two fundamental principles upon which any proceedings under the Act must be conducted. Any court in exercising its jurisdiction must regard both the welfare of the child as the first and paramount consideration and, where practicable, regard the wishes of the child. In considering these two principles the court must also have regard to the rights and duties of parents whether these arise under the Constitution or otherwise (statutory or common law).

The obligation to give due consideration is subject to the court considering the child's age and understanding. The wishes of children arises in custody disputes under s.11 of the Guardianship of Infants Act 1964 (see *NAD v TD* [1985] 5 I.L.R.M. 153, *MK v PK*, unreported, High Court, Finlay P., November 1982, and Shatter, *Family Law in the Republic of Ireland* (4th ed., Butterworths, 1997). Of note in this regard is the position in England and particularly the decision of the House of Lords in *Gillick v West Norfolk Area Health Authority* [1986] A.C. 112 which recognises that mature young people may make decisions about their own lives.

A potential conflict could arise under this section where a child of sufficient age and understanding refuses or objects to a direction given to undergo medical or psychiatric treatment or assessment. In these circumstances the fundamental principle of securing the welfare of the child would have to override the child's wishes where his wishes were contrary to his welfare.

Also a child might express the wish to be present at hearing under s.30 which the court can refuse where such is not in the child's interests.

In addition to these express statutory provisions, courts should be mindful of the emerging ECHR jurisprudence on the litigating of child care cases and the close scrutiny that complaints are subjected to. In particular such cases should be heard within a reasonable period of time (see *EP v Finland* (2001) 31 E.H.R.R. 17 and *H v UK* (1988) 10 E.H.R.R. 95); that fair procedures are adhered to in relation to a parent not being notified of new evidence being submitted on appeal (see *Buchberger v Austria* (2003) 37 E.H.R.R. 13) and the need to ensure that parents or guardians have proper legal representation during a hearing (see *P, C and S v UK* (2002) 35 E.H.R.R. 31).

Power of court to join child as a party and costs of child as a party

25.—(1) If in any proceedings under *Part IV* or *VI* the child to whom the proceedings relate is not already a party, the court may, where it is satisfied having regard to the age, understanding and wishes of the child and the circumstances of the case that it is necessary in the interests of the child and in the interests of justice to do so, order that the child be joined as a party to, or shall have such of the rights of a party as may be specified by the court in, either the entirety of the proceedings or such issues in the proceedings as the court may direct. The making of any such order shall not require the intervention of a next friend in respect of the child.

(2) Where the court makes an order under *subsection (1)* or a child is a party to the proceedings otherwise than by reason of such an order, the court may, if it thinks fit, appoint a solicitor to represent the child in the proceedings and give directions as to the performance of his duties (which may include, if necessary, directions in relation to the instruction of counsel).

(3) The making of an order under *subsection (1)* or the fact that a child is a party to the proceedings otherwise than by reason of such an order shall not prejudice the power of the court under *section 30(2)* to refuse to accede to a

request of a child made thereunder.

(4) Where a solicitor is appointed under *subsection* (2), the costs and expenses incurred on behalf of a child exercising any rights of a party in any proceedings under this Act shall be paid by the [Health Service Executive]. [The Executive] may apply to the court to have the amount of any such costs or expenses measured or taxed.

(5) The court which has made an order under *subsection* (2) may, on the application to it of [the Health Service Executive], order any other party to the proceedings in question to pay to [the Executive] any costs or expenses payable by [the Executive] under *subsection* (4).

AMENDMENT

See s.267(2) of the Children Act 2001, No.24 of 2001 which provides that reference to Part IV shall include reference to Parts IVA and IVB as inserted by the 2001 Act. Section 267(2) came into effect on July, 29 2004 (S.I. No.468 of 2004).

Subsections (4) and (5) amended by s.75 and Schedule 7 of the Health Act 2004, No.42 of 2004, with effect from January 1, 2005 (S.I. No.887 of 2004).

DEFINITIONS

"child": s.2.
"health board": s.2.

COMMENCEMENT

Child Care Act, 1991 (Commencement) Order, 1995 (S.I. No. 258 of 1995) took effect as of October 31, 1995.

NOTE

This enables a child who is the subject of any proceedings under Pt IV (ss.16–23 concerning interim care orders, care orders, supervision orders, certain orders under the Guardianship of Infants Act 1964 and the Judicial Separation and Family Law Reform Act 1989 concerning the hearing of appeals, variations and discharge of any of the aforementioned orders); Pt IVA (see s.23I of the Children Act 2001 making applicable Pt V of the Child Care Act 1991 to proceedings under Pt IVA); and Pt VI (ss.36–48 which concern children in the care of the Health Service Executive) to be joined as a party to the proceedings and to be afforded separate representation at the hearing.

The draft legislation contained no provision for the separate representation of children who are the subject of care proceedings. The section was included in the legislation by amendment and the rationale for the provision was stated to be that an older child could have representation to oppose the plans the Health Service Executive intends for the child (see Minister for State Treacy, 403 *Dáil Debates* Cols 2335–2421). Perhaps the most appropriate circumstances in which to make an order would be where the child's parents are missing or cannot be found or there is no person acting *in loco parentis* to the child.

Subsection (1)

This sets out the requirements that must be satisfied to the court before an order may be made. The requirements of s.24 must be first regarded. The order is a discretionary one and it must be necessary in both the interests of the child and the interests of justice that the child be joined as a party to the proceedings. Where it is found to be in the child's interests to be joined in the proceedings, it should reasonably follow that it is thus necessary in the interests of justice that the child be joined and represented. The need for separate representation will probably arise only in the case of older children who have a level and degree of understanding of their circumstances. *Re S* (*Independent Representation*) [1993] Fam. 263 stresses that emphasis should be placed on the child's sufficiency of understanding rather than age in determining the extent of involvement in proceedings. Here the emotionally complex and highly fraught character of the proceedings warranted the child not participating. Where a child's views are at variance with the proposals the Health Service Executive has for the child, then the need for separate representation should arise. The court in determining these requirements must have regard to the age, understanding and wishes of the child and the circumstances of the case. Where an order is made making the child a party to the proceedings then any order already made appointing a guardian *ad litem* ceases automatically on the making of the child a party to the proceedings (see s.26(4)).

Where these requirements are satisfied the court has a discretion in defining the extent of the child's involvement in the proceedings. A child can be made a party to the proceedings or have such rights of a party to the proceedings as the court specifies. The child can be involved as a party to the entire proceedings or his involvement can be limited to such issues as the court directs.

Of particular effect of the order for making the child a party to the proceedings, is the fact that a next friend shall not be required. Usually a parent acts as "next friend" where a minor becomes party to proceedings. This is a desirable exclusion of parental authority over a child particularly where for example a child has been brought into care owing to physical or sexual abuse by a parent.

Subsection (2)

Where an order is made making the child a party to the proceedings, either by order under s.25(1) or otherwise, the court has a discretion in both appointing a solicitor to represent the child and giving directions to the solicitor on behalf of the child. The rationale for the court being empowered to direct a solicitor is that the child may not be capable of understanding the nature or significance of the proceedings or be capable of instructing counsel (see 129 *Seanad Debates* Col.608, Minister of State Treacy).

Subsection (3)

This provides that making a child a party to the proceedings shall not prejudice the operation of s.30(2) which provides that a court shall accede to the request of a child to be present at the hearing of proceedings, unless having regard to the age of the child or the nature of the proceedings, it is not in the child's interests to grant the request.

Subsection (4)

This provides that the costs and expenses incurred by a solicitor appointed by the court to represent a child in any proceedings under the Act shall be paid by the Health Service Executive concerned. The Health Service Executive may apply to the court to have any costs and expenses measured or taxed.

Subsection (5)

This enables the Health Service Executive to recoup the cost and expense of legal representation paid in accordance with s.25(4). The costs or expenses are ordered by the court and levied against any other party to the proceedings. Whilst the Health Service Executive may make an application for such an order, the court has a discretion in whether to make the order sought.

Appointment of guardian ad litem for a child

26.—(1) If in any proceedings under *Part IV* or *VI* the child to whom the proceedings relate is not a party, the court may, if it is satisfied that it is necessary in the interests of the child and in the interests of justice to do so, appoint a guardian ad litem for the child.

(2) Any costs incurred by a person in acting as a guardian ad litem under this section shall be paid by the [Health Service Executive]. The [Health Service Executive] may apply to the court to have the amount of any such costs or expenses measured or taxed.

(3) The court which has made an order under *subsection (1)* may, on the application to it of [the Health Service Executive], order any other party to the proceedings in question to pay to [the Executive] any costs or expenses payable by [the Executive] under *subsection (2)*.

(4) Where a child in respect of whom an order has been made under *subsection (1)* becomes a party to the proceedings in question (whether by virtue of an order under *section 25(1)* or otherwise) then that order shall cease to have effect.

AMENDMENT

See s.267(2) of the Children Act 2001, No.24 of 2001 which provides that reference to Part IV shall include reference to Parts IVA and IVB as inserted by the 2001 Act. Section 267(2) came into effect on July 29, 2004 (S.I. No.468 of 2004).

Subsections (2) and (3) amended by s.75 and Schedule 7 of the Health Act 2004, No.42 of 2004, with effect from January 1, 2005 (S.I. No.887 of 2004).

DEFINITIONS

"child": s.2.
"health board": s.2.

COMMENCEMENT

Child Care Act, 1991 (Commencement) Order, 1995 (S.I. No. 258 of 1995) took effect as of October 31, 1995.

NOTE

This section provides for the appointment of a guardian *ad litem* for a child. The costs of the guardian ad litem are provided for and the consequences of the appointment where a child is also made a party to the proceedings are set out. The role of the guardian ad litem is an independent one to safeguard the child's interests and ensure the most positive outcome possible for the child. Costello J. remarked in *Re M.H. & J.H., Oxfordshire C.C. v JH and VH*, unreported, High Court, May 19, 1988 on the role of a guardian ad litem in proceedings, that it was significant that a person is appointed who is independent of parents and local authorities (the Health Service Executive in this jurisdiction) and acts to advise the court on the infant's behalf of what is to happen. Any confidential information that a guardian ad litem acquires in preparation of a report to the court belongs to the court and not the guardian ad litem. In *Oxfordshire C.C. v P* [1995] Fam. 161 the court held that an admission of harm made by a mother to the guardian ad litem should not have been disclosed to a social worker who in turn informed the police. The court noted that disclosure of such information was confidential and should only be disclosed upon prior leave of the court granting permission to disclose. For an extensive discussion of the role and duties of a guardian ad litem under the equivalent English legislation on care proceedings, the Children Act 1989, see Timms, *Children's Representation, A Practitioner's Guide* (Sweet and Maxwell, London, 1995).

Subsection (1)

This sets out the requirements for the appointment of a guardian *ad litem*. First, the child to whom the proceedings relate must not already be a party to those proceedings. Where a guardian ad litem is appointed and subsequently the child is made a party to the proceedings, presumably with legal representation by an order under s.25(2), then the order appointing the guardian ad litem ceases to have effect (see s.26(4)). Where a child has been made a party to the proceedings but has no legal representation, the guardian *ad litem* ought to continue to represent the child until such time as the child has legal representation (see *Re H (A Minor) (Guardian As Litem: Requirement)* [1994] Fam. 11 on the factors surrounding the discharge of a guardian ad litem). A guardian ad litem may be appointed only in proceedings under Pt IV which relate to interim care orders (s.17), care orders (s.18), supervision orders (s.19), Pt IVA (see s.23I of the Children Act 2001 making applicable Pt V of the Child Care Act 1991 to proceedings under Pt IVA), related family law proceedings under s.20 and applications to vary or discharge orders made under these sections or directions made thereunder under s.22 and Pt VI which relates to children in the care of the Health Service Executive. In addition the requirements of s.24 must be regarded.

Secondly the court must be satisfied that the appointment of a guardian *ad litem* is both in the interests of the child and in the interests of justice. What the court must be satisfied of under this section contrasts with the requirements for making a child a party to the proceedings under s.25. Where these two requirements are satisfied the court has a discretion in the appointment of a guardian *ad litem*.

Subsection (2)

This provides for the costs incurred by a guardian *ad litem* to be paid for by the relevant Health Service Executive which may in turn apply to the court to have the costs measured or taxed.

Subsection (3)

This enables the Health Service Executive to apply to the court for an order directing any other party to the proceedings to pay any costs payable by the Health Service Executive.

Subsection (4)

This provision relates to a situation where a guardian *ad litem* has been appointed and subsequently an order is made making the child to whom the proceedings relate a party to the proceedings. Where this arises the order appointing the guardian ad litem ceases to have effect.

Power to procure reports on children

27.—(1) In any proceedings under *Part IV* or *VI* the court may, of its own motion or on the application of any party to the proceedings, by an order under this section give such directions as it thinks proper to procure a report from such person as it may nominate on any question affecting the welfare of the child.

(2) In deciding whether or not to request a report under *subsection* (*1*) the court shall have regard to the wishes of the parties before the court where ascertainable but shall not be bound by the said wishes.

(3) A copy of any report prepared under *subsection* (*1*) shall be made available to the counsel or solicitor, if any, representing each party in the proceedings or, if any party is not so represented, to that party and may be received in evidence in the proceedings.

(4) Where any person prepares a report pursuant to a request under subsection (1), the fees and expenses of that person shall be paid by such party or parties to the proceedings as the court shall order.

(5) The court, if it thinks fit, or any party to the proceedings, may call the person making the report as a witness.

AMENDMENT

See s.267(2) of the Children Act 2001, No.24 of 2001 which provides that reference to Part IV shall include reference to Parts IVA and IVB as inserted by the 2001 Act. Section 267(2) came into effect on July 29, 2004 (S.I. No.468 of 2004).

DEFINITIONS

"child": s.2.

COMMENCEMENT

Child Care Act, 1991 (Commencement) Order, 1995 (S.I. No. 258 of 1995) took effect as of October 31, 1995.

NOTE

This section enables the ordering of a direction for the procuring of a report (welfare report) concerning any aspect of the welfare of a child. The section requires the court to consider the wishes of the parties to the proceedings and where a report is prepared such must be made available to the parties concerned. Any person making a report may be called as a witness and the cost incurred in its preparation may be ordered to be paid by such party as the court orders.

Subsection (1)

Either the court of its own motion or any party to the proceedings may apply for a direction to procure a welfare report. Where an application for a direction to procure a report is made it must be on notice to the other parties and served at least two days prior to the date fixed for the application (see Ord.84, r.22(1) of S.I. No.93 of 1997, District Court Rules 1997). The report must be lodged with the district court clerk and copies made available to legal representatives of each party or to the party personally (Ord.84, r.22(2) of S.I. No.93 of 1997, District Court Rules 1997).

An application for a direction to procure a report may only be sought in the proceedings set out in Pt IV, which concern interim care orders, care orders, supervision orders and orders under related family proceedings, Pt IVA (see s.23I of the Children Act 2001 making applicable Pt V of the Child Care Act 1991 to proceedings under Pt IVA) and Pt VI, concerning children in the care of the Health Service Executive.

A report may concern any aspect of the welfare of the child ranging from medical and psychiatric to behavioural.

Whilst the making of a direction is discretionary, it may be necessary to procure a report in contested cases.

Subsection (2)

This obliges the court, in addition to the requirements set out in s.24, to have regard to the wishes of the parties before the court before making an order directing the procurement of a report. The wishes need only be regarded where ascertainable and thus in the case of a child whose parents are missing or cannot be found, the court can order a report on the welfare of the child without having obtained the views of such parents. Any wishes expressed by any of the parties are clearly stated not to be binding upon the court.

Subsection (3)

This imposes an obligation to make available a copy of a report to the legal representatives of the parties (either to counsel or the solicitor). Where the parties are not represented the report must be made available to the parties themselves. Order 84, r.22(2) of S.I. No.93 of 1997, District Court Rules 1997 requires the applicant to furnish the report to the parties or their legal representatives concerned.

Rule 22(2) further requires the report to be lodged with the clerk of the court. The report, when prepared, may also be received in evidence.

Subsection (4)

The fee or expense of the person who has prepared the report may be ordered to be paid, at the court's discretion, by such party or parties to the proceedings.

Subsection (5)

Where a person has prepared a report, the court at its discretion, or any other party to the proceedings, may call that person as a witness. On the preference for oral testimony rather than submission of reports see *Thompson v Thompson* (1975) [1986] 1 F.L.R. 212 at 217, *per* Buckley L.J.: "Where a judge has to arrive at crucial findings of fact he should found them upon sworn evidence rather than unsworn report". See also the Supreme Court decision in *Southern Health Board v CH and CH* [1996] 2 I.L.R.M. 142 on the role of expert witnesses in cases concerning children in care arising from allegations of child sexual abuse, and *Re MS and W (infants)* [1996] 1 I.L.R.M. 370, Costello J.

Jurisdiction

28.—(1) The District Court and the Circuit Court on appeal from the District Court shall have jurisdiction to hear and determine proceedings under Part III, IV or VI.

(2) Proceedings under *Part III, IV* or *VI* may be brought, heard and determined before and by a justice of the District Court for the time being assigned to the district court district where the child resides or is for the time being.

AMENDMENT

See s.267(2) of the Children Act 2001, No.24 of 2001 which provides that reference to Part IV shall include reference to Parts IVA and IVB as inserted by the 2001 Act. Section 267(2) came into effect on July 29, 2004 (S.I. No.468 of 2004).

COMMENCEMENT

Child Care Act, 1991 (Commencement) Order, 1995 (S.I. No. 258 of 1995) took effect as of October 31, 1995.

NOTE

This section confers upon the District Court and the Circuit Court on appeal, the jurisdiction to hear and determine proceedings under Pts III, IV, IVA (see s.23I of the Children Act 2001 making applicable Pt V of the Child Care Act 1991 to proceedings under Pt IVA) and Pt IV of the Act. Part III concerns the protection of children in emergencies. Part IV concerns care proceedings and Pt VI provides for orders concerning children in the care of the Health Service Executive (see generally S.I. No.93 of 1997, District (Child Care) Rules 1997).

Section 71 of the Children Act 2001 now refers to applications brought under Pts III, IV, IVA (see s.23I of the Children Act 2001 making applicable Pt V of the Child Care Act 1991 to proceedings under Pt IVA) or Pt V to the District Court as the Children's Court. When sitting as the Children's Court for the purposes of the Child Care Act 1991, the Children's Court, as far as practicable, should sit in a different building or room or at a different time or day to the Children Court exercising jurisdiction in other matters (s.71(1)(*b*) of the Children Act 2001). Where children are attending the Children Court for the purposes of the 1991 Act s.71(2) of the Children Act 2001 provides that they should not come into contact with individuals attending the court in the exercise of some other jurisdiction.

Subsection (2)

This provides an alternative jurisdictional basis for the hearing of applications under Pts III, IV, IVA (see s.23I of the Children Act 2001 making applicable Pt V of the Child Care Act 1991 to proceedings under Pt IVA) and Pt VI. Ordinarily the child must reside in the area of the District Court to which any of the above applications are made. Where an application is made to a District Court in a district court area in which the child does not reside, but is for the time being, the District Court has jurisdiction to hear and determine any application made. This provision is particularly relevant to applications where the child is in the care of or is sought to be brought in to the care of the Health Service Executive in a district court area different to the place of residence of the child (see generally S.I. No.93 of 1997, District Court Rules 1997).

Hearing of proceedings

29.—(1) Proceedings under *Part III, IV* or *VI* shall be heard otherwise than in public.

(2) The provisions of *sections 33(1)* of the Judicial Separation and Family Law Reform Act, 1989, shall apply to proceedings under Part III, IV or VI as they apply to proceedings to which those provisions relate.

(3) The District Court and the Circuit Court on appeal from the District Court shall sit to hear and determine proceedings under *Part III, IV* or *VI* at a different place or at different times or on different days from those at or on which the ordinary sittings of the Court are held.

(4) Proceedings before the High Court in relation to proceedings under *Part III, IV* or *VI* shall be as informal as is practicable and consistent with the administration of justice.

AMENDMENT

See s.267(2) of the Children Act 2001, No.24 of 2001 which provides that reference to Part IV shall include reference to Parts IVA and IVB as inserted by the 2001 Act. Section 267(2) came into effect on July 29, 2004 (S.I. No.468 of 2004).

COMMENCEMENT

Child Care Act, 1991 (Commencement) Order, 1995 (S.I. No. 258 of 1995) took effect as of October 31, 1995.

NOTE

This section provides for the manner in which proceedings are to be heard under Pts III, IV, IVA (see s.23I of the Children Act 2001 making applicable Pt V of the Child Care Act 1991 to proceedings under Pt IVA) and Pt VI of the Act. S.I. No.93 of 1997, District Court Rules 1997, is of relevance to this section.

Subsection (1)

This provides that proceedings under Pt III, protection of children in emergencies; Pt IV, care proceedings; Pt IVA (see s.23I of the Children Act 2001 making applicable Pt V of the Child Care Act 1991 to proceedings under Pt IVA); and Pt VI, children in care shall be held in camera (see r.2(1) of S.I. No.93 of 1997, District Court Rules 1997). The privacy of the hearing is necessary to safeguard the general welfare of the child by not making known to the public the identity of a child who is the subject of care proceedings.

Subsection (2)

This renders applicable four provisions of the Judicial Separation and Family Law Reform Act 1989 (the 1989 Act) as they apply under Pts III, IV, IVA (see s.23I of the Children Act 2001 making applicable Pt V of the Child Care Act 1991 to proceedings under Pt IVA) and Pt VI of the Act. The provisions of the 1989 Act are s.33(1) which relates to proceedings in the Circuit Court which are required to be as informal as practicable and consistent with the administration of justice.

Section 33(2) of the 1989 Act relates to the prohibition of judges, barristers and solicitors appearing in wigs and gowns before the Circuit Court. This is consistent with the conduct of proceedings before the District Court (see r.2(3) of S.I. No.93 of 1997, District Court Rules 1997).

Section 45(1) of the 1989 Act relates to the conducting before the District Court, in as informal a manner as practicable and consistent with the administration of justice, of proceedings under the following Acts: the Guardianship of Infants Act 1964; the Family Law (Maintenance of Spouses and Children) Act 1976; the Family Home Protection Act 1976; s.9 of the Family Law Act 1981, the Family Law (Protection of Spouses and Children) Act 1981; and the Status of Children Act 1987.

Section 45(2) of the 1989 Act relates to the above-mentioned proceedings and the prohibition of judges, barristers and solicitors wearing wigs and gowns.

Subsection (3)

This provides that proceedings in both the District Court and Circuit Court on appeal must hear and determine proceedings under Pts III, IV, IVA (see s.23I of the Children Act 2001 making applicable Pt V of the Child Care Act 1991 to proceedings under Pt IVA) and Pt VI separate from the ordinary sittings of the court. The separate hearing of these proceedings can be by the court sitting in a different place, at different times or on different days to the ordinary sittings of the court.

Subsection (4)

This provision concerns the hearing of proceedings under Pts III, IV, IVA (see s.23I of the Children Act 2001 making applicable Pt V of the Child Care Act 1991 to proceedings under Pt IVA) and Pt VI in the High Court. The only requirement set out in this provision is that the proceedings be as informal as practicable and consistent with the administration of justice.

Power to proceed in absence of child

30.—(1) It shall not be necessary in proceedings under *Part III, IV* or *VI* for the child to whom the proceedings relate to be brought before the court or to be present for all or any part of the hearing unless the court, either of its own motion or at the request of any of the parties to the case, is satisfied that this is necessary for the proper disposal of the case.

(2) Where the child requests to be present during the hearing or a particular part of the hearing of the proceedings the court shall grant the request unless it appears to the court that, having regard to the age of the child or the nature of the proceedings, it would not be in the child's interests to accede to the request.

Amendment

See s.267(2) of the Children Act 2001, No.24 of 2001 which provides that reference to Part IV shall include reference to Parts IVA and IVB as inserted by the 2001 Act. Section 267(2) came into effect on July 29, 2004 (S.I. No.468 of 2004).

DEFINITIONS

"child": s.2.

COMMENCEMENT

Child Care Act, 1991 (Commencement) Order, 1995 (S.I. No. 258 of 1995) took effect as of October 31, 1995.

NOTE

This sections deals with the need or request of the presence of the child at the hearing of the proceedings. The section clearly states that proceedings may be conducted without the presence of the child at the hearing. Generally, it is undesirable to have the child involved in the judicial process. Where a child is too young to appreciate the nature of the proceedings or the proceedings are likely to disturb the child, it would not be appropriate for the child to be present. The presence of a child may be necessary where for example, the wishes of that child have to be ascertained in accordance with s.24 or where perhaps the child is directed to undergo a medical or psychiatric examination and the child objects to this.

Subsection (1)

This sets out as a general principle that the attendance of the child at the hearing of any or part of proceedings under Pts III, IV, IVA (see s.23I of the Children Act 2001 making applicable Pt V of the Child Care Act 1991 to proceedings under Pt IVA) and Pt VI shall not be necessary. This is, however, subject to the proviso, that, for the proper disposal of the case, the child's presence at the hearing is necessary. Where the child's presence is so necessary, the section implies in its wording that this may be achieved by either an order directing the child to be present or by the child being "brought" before the court. Order 84, r.21 of S.I. No.93 of 1997, District Court Rules 1997 provides that the request for bringing a child before the court should be in writing addressed to the court and lodged with the clerk prior to or during the hearing. Additionally a request may be made orally to the court at the commencement of or during the hearing. An application to have the child present may be made by the court of its own motion or on the request of any of the parties.

Subsection (2)

This provision relates to a request by the child to whom the proceedings relate to be present at the hearing. There is an obligation upon the court to accede to such a request except where the court, having regard to age of the child or the nature of the proceedings, decides that it would not be in the interests of the child. Obviously very young children are unlikely to assist the judicial process and only older children may express a wish to be present at the hearing. Where, also, the nature of the proceedings concerns allegations of sexual or physical abuse, it would clearly not be in the child's interests to be present in court for the giving of such evidence, particularly if the allegations relate to a parent.

Where a child makes a request to be present at the hearing of the proceedings that request is to be made in writing by a letter addressed to the court and lodged with the clerk either prior to or during the hearing. A request may also be made orally to the court either at the commencement or during the hearing (see Ord.84, r.21 of S.I. No.93 of 1997, District Court Rules 1997).

Prohibition on publication or broadcast of certain matters

31.—(1) No matter likely to lead members of the public to identify a child who is or has been the subject of proceedings under Part III, IV or VI shall be published in a written publication available to the public or be broadcast.

(2) Without prejudice to subsection (1), the court may, in any case if satisfied that it is appropriate to do so in the interests of the child, by order dispense with the prohibitions of that subsection in relation to him to such extent as may be specified in the order.

(3) If any matter is published or broadcast in contravention of subsection (1), each of the following persons, namely—

(*a*) in the case of publication in a newspaper or periodical, any proprietor, any editor and any publisher of the newspaper or periodical,

(*b*) in the case of any other publication, the person who publishes it, and

(*c*) in the case of a broadcast, any body corporate who transmits or provides the programme in which the broadcast is made and any person having functions in relation to the programme corresponding to those of an editor of a newspaper,

shall be guilty of an offence and shall be liable on summary conviction to a fine not exceeding €1,269.74 or to imprisonment for a term not exceeding 12 months or both.

(4) Nothing in this section shall affect the law as to contempt of court.

(5) In this section—

"broadcast" means the transmission, relaying or distribution by wireless telegraphy of communications, sounds, signs, visual images or signals, intended for direct reception by the general public whether such communications, sounds, signs, visual images or signals are actually received or not;

"written publication" includes a film, a sound track and any other record in permanent form (including a record that is not in a legible form but which is capable of being reproduced in a legible form) but does not include an indictment or other document prepared for use in particular legal proceedings.

AMENDMENT

See s.267(2) of the Children Act 2001, No.24 of 2001 which provides that reference to Part IV shall include reference to Parts IVA and IVB as inserted by the 2001 Act. Section 267(2) came into effect on July 29 2004 (S.I. No.468 of 2004).

DEFINITIONS

"broadcast": s.31.
"child": s.2.
"written publication": s.31.

COMMENCEMENT

Child Care Act, 1991 (Commencement) Order, 1995 (S.I. No. 258 of 1995) took effect as of October 31, 1995.

NOTE

This section concerns restrictions upon publishing matter likely to identify a child who is or has been the subject of proceedings under Pts III, IV, IVA (see s.23I of the Children Act 2001 making applicable Pt V of the Child Care Act 1991 to proceedings under Pt IVA) or Pt VI of the Act. The prohibition is broadly defined by use of the phrase "no matter likely to lead members of the public to identify a child". Thus actual or potential identification of a child is prohibited.

Publication can be in written form, either visual or aural, which is defined as: "... film, a sound track and any other record in permanent form (including a record that is not in a legible form but which is capable of being reproduced in a legible form)". Specifically excluded from this definition is an indictment or other document prepared for use in legal proceedings.

Publication by broadcast is defined as the "transmission, relaying or distribution by wireless telegraphy of communications, sounds, signs, visual images or signals, intended for direct reception by the general public whether such communications, sounds, signs, visual images or signals are actually received or not".

Subsection (2)

This provides for an exception to the prohibition on publication of the identity of a child in proceedings under Pts III, IV, IVA (see s.23I of the Children Act 2001 making applicable Pt V of the Child Care Act 1991 to proceedings under Pt IVA) or Pt VI of the Act. The court has a discretion in dispensing with the ban on publication where it is satisfied that such is in the interests of the child. The court may also determine the extent of such publication concerning the child.

Subsection (3)

This specifies the penalties and those persons (natural or legal) who may be liable for a breach of the prohibition. On summary conviction, the persons concerned shall be liable to a fine not exceeding €1,269.74 or a term of imprisonment not exceeding 12 months or both.

Those who shall be liable for the above fines are, in the case of publication in a newspaper or periodical, the proprietor, editor and publisher. In the case of any other publication, the person who publishes shall be liable for the above penalties.

In the case of publication by broadcast, the body corporate who transmits or provides the programme in which the broadcast is made and any person having functions in relation to the programme which correspond to those of an editor of a newspaper.

Subsection (4)

This provides that in addition to the above sanctions, a person (natural or legal) may be subject to the law as to contempt of court. (See McGonagle, *A Textbook on Media Law* (Gill & McMillan), chap.6, p.137 on contempt of court.)

Presumption and determination of age

32.—In any application for an order under *Part III, IV* or *VI*, the court shall make due inquiry as to the age of the person to whom the application relates and the age presumed or declared by the court to be the age of that person shall, until the contrary is proved, for the purposes of this Act, be deemed to be the true age of that person.

AMENDMENT

See s.267(2) of the Children Act 2001, No.24 of 2001 which provides that reference to Part IV shall include reference to Parts IVA and IVB as inserted by the 2001 Act. Section 267(2) came into effect on July 29, 2004 (S.I. No.468 of 2004).

COMMENCEMENT

Child Care Act, 1991 (Commencement) Order, 1995 (S.I. No. 258 of 1995) took effect as of October 31, 1995.

NOTE

This section provides for a presumption as to the age of a child. The provisions of the Act apply only to "a child" who is a person under the age of 18 who is not or has not been married.

Rules of court

33.—(1) For the purpose of ensuring the expeditious hearing of applications under *Part III, IV* or *VI*, rules of court may make provision for the service of documents otherwise than under section 7 of the Courts Act, 1964 (as amended by *section 22* of the Courts Act, 1971) in circumstances to which the said *section 7* relates.

(2) Rules of court may make provision for the furnishing of information and documents by parties to proceedings under *Part III, IV* or *VI* to each other or to solicitors acting for them.

(3) This section is without prejudice to *section 17* of the Interpretation Act, 1937, which provides for rules of court.

AMENDMENT

See s.267(2) of the Children Act 2001, No.24 of 2001 which provides that reference to Part IV shall include reference to Parts IVA and IVB as inserted by the 2001 Act. Section 267(2) came into effect on July 29, 2004 (S.I. No.468 of 2004).

COMMENCEMENT

Child Care Act, 1991 (Commencement) Order, 1995 (S.I. No. 258 of 1995) took effect as of October 31, 1995.

NOTE

This section enables the making of rules of court, in relation to the service of documents, to ensure the expeditious hearing of applications under the Act, other than as already provided in s.7 of the Courts Act 1964. In short, it provides for the non-application of s.7 of the 1964 Act as amended, in the circumstances outlined in the section.

Subsection (2)
This provides for Rules of Court to prescribe the furnishing of information and documents by parties to the proceedings to each other or to solicitors acting for them. The information and documents may be furnished in this fashion where they relate to proceedings under Pts III, IV, IVA (see s.23I of the Children Act 2001 making applicable Pt V of the Child Care Act 1991 to proceedings under Pt IVA) and Pt VI.

Subsection (3)
This provides that this section is unaffected by s.17 of the Interpretation Act 1937 which provides for the making of rules of court for proceedings under Pts III, IV, IVA (see s.23I of the Children Act 2001 making applicable Pt V of the Child Care Act 1991 to proceedings under Pt IVA) and Pt VI. Section 17 of the Interpretation Act 1937 enables the making of rules of court in relation to the conferring of a new jurisdiction upon the courts or the extension or variation of an existing jurisdiction.

Failure or refusal to deliver up a child

34.—(1) Without prejudice to the law as to contempt of court, where the District Court has made an order under *Part III* or *IV* directing that a child be placed or maintained in the care of [the Health Service Executive], any person having the actual custody of the child who, having been given or shown a copy of the order and having been required, by or on behalf of [the Executive], to give up the child to [the Executive], fails or refuses to comply with the requirement shall be guilty of an offence and shall be liable on summary conviction to a fine not exceeding €634.87 or, at the discretion of the court, to imprisonment for a term not exceeding 6 months or both such fine and such imprisonment.

(2) For the purposes of this section, a person shall be deemed to have been given or shown a copy of an order made under *Part III* or *IV* if that person was present at the sitting of the court at which such an order was made.

Amendment

See s.267(2) of the Children Act 2001, No.24 of 2001 which provides that reference to Part IV shall include reference to Parts IVA and IVB as inserted by the 2001 Act. Section 267(2) came into effect on July 29, 2004 (S.I. No.468 of 2004).

Subsection (1) amended by s.75 and Schedule 7 of the Health Act 2004, No.42 of 2004, with effect from January 1, 2005 (S.I. No.887 of 2004).

Commencement

Child Care Act, 1991 (Commencement) Order, 1995 (S.I. No. 258 of 1995) took effect as of October 31, 1995.

Definitions

"child": s.2.
"health board": s.2.

Note

This section provides for the penalties on summary conviction for failing to comply with an order under Pts III, IV or IVA (see s.23I of the Children Act 2001 making applicable Pt V of the Child Care Act 1991 to proceedings under Pt IVA) to deliver up a child to the Health Service Executive. The maximum fine is €634.87 or, at the court's discretion, six months imprisonment or both.

The person liable on conviction is the individual who had actual custody of the child. That person must be given or shown a copy of the order directing the delivery up of the child. The giving or showing of the order to the person having custody will be deemed where that person was present at the sitting of the court at which the order was made.

Orders for the delivery up of a child arise under a s.13 emergency care order, a s.17 interim care order and a s.18 care order.

A prosecution under this section does not affect the law as to contempt of court, of which an individual who has failed to comply with an order may be subject to. On contempt of court, see McGonagle, *A Textbook on Media Law* (Gill & McMillan), chap.6, p.137.

Warrant to search for and deliver up a child

35.—Where a justice has made an order under *Part IV* directing that a child be placed or maintained in the care of [the Health Service Executive], a justice may for the purpose of executing that order issue a warrant authorising a member of the Garda Síochána, accompanied by such other members of the Garda Síochána or such other persons as may be necessary, to enter (if need be by force) any house or other place specified in the warrant (including any building or part of a building, tent, caravan, or other temporary or moveable structure, vehicle, vessel, aircraft or hovercraft) where the child is or where there are reasonable grounds for believing that he is and to deliver the child into the custody of [the Health Service Executive].

Amendment

See s.267(2) of the Children Act 2001, No.24 of 2001 which provides that reference to Part IV shall include reference to Parts IVA and IVB as inserted by the 2001 Act. Section 267(2) came into effect on July 29, 2004 (S.I. No.468 of 2004).

Amended by s.75 and Schedule 7 of the Health Act 2004, No.42 of 2004, with effect from January 1, 2005 (S.I. No.887 of 2004).

COMMENCEMENT

Child Care Act, 1991 (Commencement) Order, 1995 (S.I. No. 258 of 1995) took effect as of October 31, 1995.

DEFINITIONS

"child": s.2.
"health board": s.2.

NOTE

This is a provision facilitating the enforcement of an order directing the placement or maintenance of a child with the Health Service Executive by the issue of a warrant to effect the order. It enables a member of the gardaí to enter premises, with force if necessary, either where the child is, or where there are reasonable grounds to believe the child is. Any number or type of premises may be entered once they are specified in the warrant.

A warrant issued under this section may only relate to proceedings under Pts IV and IVA (see s.23I of the Children Act 2001 making applicable Pt V of the Child Care Act 1991 to proceedings under Pt IVA) and concern a s.17 interim care order and a s.18 care order. (See also Note to s.13(3) (Issue of warrant) and s.18 and Ord.84, r.24 of S.I. No.93 of 1997, District Court Rules 1997.)

PART VI

CHILDREN IN THE CARE OF HEALTH BOARDS

Accommodation and maintenance of children in care

36.—(1) Where a child is in the [care of the Health Service Executive], [the Executive shall]provide such care for him, subject to its control and supervision, in such of the following ways as it considers to be in his best interests—

(*a*) by placing him with a foster parent, or

(*b*) by placing him in residential care (whether in a children's residential centre registered under *Part VIII*, in a residential home maintained [by the Executive]or in a school or other suitable place of residence), or

(*c*) in the case of a child who may be eligible for adoption under the Adoption Acts, 1952 to 1988, by placing him with a suitable person with a view to his adoption, or

(*d*) by making such other suitable arrangements (which may include placing the child with a relative) [as the Executive]thinks proper.

(2) In this Act, "foster parent means a person other than a relative of a child who is taking care of the child on behalf of [the Health Service Executive] in accordance with regulations made under section 39 and "foster care" shall be

construed accordingly.

(3) Nothing in this section shall prevent [the Health Service Executive] sending a child in its care to any hospital or to any institution which provides nursing or care for children suffering from physical or mental disability.

AMENDMENT

Amendments by s.75 and Schedule 7 of the Health Act 2004, No. 42 of 2004, with effect from January 1, 2005 (S.I. No.887 of 2004).

COMMENCEMENT

Child Care Act, 1991 (Commencement) Order, 1995 (S.I. No. 258 of 1995) took effect as of October 31, 1995.

DEFINITIONS

"centre": s.59.
"child": s.2.
"foster parent": s.36(2).
"health board": s.2.
"children's residential centre": s.59 of the 1991 Act and rule 3 of the District Court (Child Care) Rules, 1995.

NOTE

This section concerns the obligation imposed upon the Health Service Executive towards children in their care. The Health Service Executive is obliged to care for children in one of four ways set out in the section. The care can be provided by the Health Service Executive itself or by voluntary bodies. In the latter case, the child remains under the care and supervision of the Health Service Executive on foot of the order made. The manner of the care to be provided for the child is a matter for the Health Service Executive which is determined according to what is in the child's best interests.

In *Western Health Board v KM* [2002] 2 I.R. 493 the Supreme Court held that on the direction of the District Court, the Health Board could place a child with relatives or foster parents resident outside the jurisdiction. Likewise in *East Coast Area Health Board v MM*, unreported, High Court, February 5, 2002, Finnegan P. held that the Health Board by direction of the District Court could place a child in a residential unit situate outside the jurisdiction.

The first option for the Health Service Executive in providing care is to place the child with foster parents. "Foster Parent" is defined in s.36(2) as "a person other than a relative of a child who is taking care of the child on behalf of the Health Service Executive in accordance with section 39 and the regulations made thereunder" (see S.I. No.260 of 1995, Child Care (Placement of Children in Foster Care) Regulations 1995 and art.16 on the duties of foster parents).

The second option for the Health Service Executive is to place the child in residential care. Residential care may be in a registered residential centre under Pt VIII or a residential home maintained by the Health Service Executive, a school or other suitable place of residence.

The Health Service Executive may decide what form of residential care to afford the child where residential care is opted for (see S.I. No.259 of 1995, Child Care (Placement of Children in Residential Care) Regulations 1995).

The third option that arises for the Health Service Executive is to place a child for adoption, where the child is eligible for adoption under the Adoption Acts, 1952–1988.

The final option gives the Health Service Executive a wide discretion in making such other arrangements as the Health Service Executive considers proper. Placement with relatives is mentioned as an option under this provision and governed by S.I. No.261 of 1995, Child Care (Placement of Children with Relatives) Regulations 1995).

Subsection (3)

This specifically confers upon Health Service Executive the authority to care for children by sending a child to hospital or institutions where nursing is provided. The Health Service Executive may also send a child to an institution providing care for children suffering from physical or mental disability. Where the Health Service Executive has a care order under s.18, it falls within the Health Service Executive's authority to send a child to any of the above institutions.. Where, however, the Health Service Executive has an interim care order or emergency care order, an application for a direction (under ss.13(7)(*a*)(iii) and 17(4) respectively) from the court would appear necessary.

Access to children in care

37.—(1) Where a child is in the care of [the Health Service Executive] whether by virtue of an order under *Part III* or *IV* or otherwise, [the Executive] shall, subject to the provisions of this Act, facilitate reasonable access to the child by his parents, any person acting *in loco parentis*, or any other person who, in the opinion of [the Executive], has a bona fide interest in the child and such access may include allowing the child to reside temporarily with any such person.

(2) Any person who is dissatisfied with arrangements made [by the Health Service Executive under *subsection (1)* or by the Health Service Executive under that subsection before the amendment of the subsection by the Health Act 2004] may apply to the court, and the court may—

    (*a*) make such order as it thinks proper regarding access to the child by that person, and

    (*b*) vary or discharge that order on the application of any person.

(3) The court, on the application of [the Health Service Executive], and if it considers that it is necessary to do so in order to safeguard or promote the child's welfare, may—

    (*a*) make an order authorising [the Executive] to refuse to allow a named person access to a child in its care, and

    (*b*) vary or discharge that order on the application of any person.

(4) This section is without prejudice to *section 4(2).*

Amendment

Subsections (1), (2) and (3) amended by s.75 and Schedule 7 of the Health Act 2004, No.42 of 2004, with effect from January 1, 2005 (S.I. No.887 of 2004).

Child Care Act, 1991 (Commencement) Order, 1995 (S.I. No. 258 of 1995) took effect as of October 31, 1995.

DEFINITIONS

"child": s.2.
"health board": s.2.

NOTE

This provision concerns the access to children in care by their parents and other persons. There is an obligation on the Health Service Executive to facilitate access but the nature of the access is a matter for the Health Service Executive to determine. Where a dispute as to access arises, either party must apply to the court for an order either to obtain more favourable access or prohibit access as the case may be. It does not fall within the competence of the Health Service Executive to unilaterally deny access to a parent or other person and such may only denied by obtaining a court order to that effect.

Access to a child by his parents, in the context of custody disputes between parents, is generally considered to be of benefit to the child. The maintenance of a parent-child relationship is important to the child's general welfare. Access has been considered to be a right of the child rather than that of the parent. In *M v M* [1973] 2 All E.R. 81, Wrangham J. stated that access by a parent should not be denied to the child except where the interests of the child so require.

Irrespective of whether a child has been brought into care in an emergency situation under Pt III or by virtue of an interim care order or care order under Pt IV, or otherwise, the Health Service Executive is obliged to provide reasonable access to the child. The section specifically provides for parents and persons acting *in loco parentis* to be allowed access. In addition the Health Service Executive, under the broad terms of the section, may allow access to any other person with a bona fide interest in the child. This may include members of the child's immediate and extended family.

ECHR case law on access to children in care is both clear and abundant. In *K and T v Finland* (2001) 31 E.H.R.R. 18, the Court reiterated that States enjoy a wide margin of appreciation in assessing the need to take a child into public care. However, all decisions relating to the restriction or termination of parental rights of access or contact with children in care will be rigorously scrutinised. Care proceedings must be considered as temporary measures involving the ultimate objective of re-uniting a family. In this regard access and contact with children in care is fundamental to achieving the overall objective. In *K and T v Finland* (2001) 31 E.H.R.R. 18 the taking into care of a newborn child where the parents were denied access in the first days of birth was a breach of Art.8 of the Convention. In *W v UK* (1988) 10 E.H.R.R. 29 a decision to restrict and terminate parental access to a child in care with a view to adoption was a breach of Art.8 where the local authority failed to involve the parent in the decision-making process relating to the termination of access (see also *B v UK* (1988) 10 E.H.R.R. 87). Where restricting or terminating access is necessary, the making of such a decision and the institution of proceedings must be done expeditiously as such can constitute a breach of Art.8. In *H v UK* (1988) 10 E.H.R.R. 95 even though the child was to be adopted, thus terminating the parent-child relationship, the local authority in question was found to be in breach of Art.8 by taking some two years and seven months to resolve the legal issues (see also *EP v Italy* (2001) 31 E.H.R.R. 17 on delay).

Not every restriction or denial of access or contact will amount to a breach of the right to respect for family life under Art.8 of the Convention. Where the best interests of the child so require, the access or contact that a parent enjoys can be legitimately restricted (see *L v Finland* (2001) 31 E.H.R.R. 30 and *Gnahore v France* (2001) 31 E.H.R.R. 38).

The Health Service Executive may facilitate access at the place where the child is being maintained or allow access, in the form of temporary residence to the child at the place of residence of the person seeking access.

Subsection (2)

This provides that where a parent or other person mentioned in s.37(1) is dissatisfied with the access arrangements provided by the Health Service Executive, that person may apply to the District Court. The District Court may then make any order that it considers proper regarding access to the child. Such an application must be on notice to the Health Service Executive and served two days prior to the date fixed for the hearing (see Ord.84, r.25(1) of S.I. No.93 of 1997, District Court Rules 1997).

Where an order has been made under s.37(2)(*a*), an application by any person to vary or discharge that order must be in accordance with Ord.84, r.25(2) of S.I. No.93 of 1997, District Court Rules 1997.

There is no express entitlement of a child to initiate an application for access under the section. This, however, may be possible if the phrase "any person with a bona fide interest in the child" is interpreted to include the child's legal representative or guardian ad litem to whom the child can express his wishes.

Subsection (3)

This enables the Health Service Executive to apply for an order refusing any named person access to a child. The requirement of this section is in contrast to the above application by a parent or other person in that the court must consider the refusal of access necessary to safeguard or promote the child's welfare. This provision is in keeping with the general principle of the section that access to the child must be afforded to the parents or other person, and that it is only in circumstances where access would not be in the interests of the child that an order refusing that access be granted. The authority to refuse access lies with the court and can only arise where an application is made. Any application to refuse access must be on notice to the person concerned and served two days prior to the hearing of the application (see Ord.84, r.26(1) of S.I. No.93 of 1997, District Court Rules 1997).

An application to vary or discharge an order made refusing access may be made and in accordance with Ord.84, r.26(2) of S.I. No.93 of 1997, District Court Rules 1997.

Subsection (4)

This provides that s.37 is to operate without prejudice to s.4(2) which concerns the maintenance of children placed voluntarily in care by parents or a person acting *in loco parentis*. Such persons may not have their rights to access interfered with and should the Health Service Executive wish to curtail access, the appropriate procedures of obtaining the necessary care order and other orders must first be complied with.

Provision of residential care by [the Health Service Executive]

38.—(1) [The Health Service Executive] shall make arrangements with the registered proprietors of children's residential centres or with other suitable persons to ensure the provision of an adequate number of residential places for children in its care.

(2) [The Health Service Executive] may, with the approval of the Minister, provide and maintain a residential centre or other premises for the provision of residential care for children in care.

(3) The Minister shall make regulations with respect to the conduct of homes or other premises provided by [the Health Service Executive] under this section and for securing the welfare of children maintained therein.

(4) Without prejudice to the generality of *subsection (3)*, regulations under this section may—

(*a*) prescribe requirements as to the maintenance, care and welfare of children while being maintained in centres,

(*b*) prescribe requirements as to the numbers, qualifications and availability of members of the staffs of centres,

(*c*) prescribe requirements as to the design, maintenance, repair, cleaning and cleanliness, ventilation, heating and lighting of centres,

(*d*) prescribe requirements as to the accommodation (including the amount of space in bedrooms, the washing facilities and the sanitary conveniences) provided in centres,

(*e*) prescribe requirements as to the food provided for children while being maintained in centres,

(*f*) prescribe requirements as to the records to be kept in centres and for the examination and copying of any such records or of extracts therefrom by officers of the Minister.

AMENDMENT

Subsections (1), (2) and (3) amended by s.75 and Schedule 7 of the Health Act 2004, No.42 of 2004, with effect from January 1, 2005 (S.I. No.887 of 2004).

COMMENCEMENT

Child Care Act, 1991 (Commencement) Order, 1995 (S.I. No. 258 of 1995) took effect as of October 31, 1995.

DEFINITIONS

"centre": s.59.
"certified school": s.44 of the Children Act, 1908.
"children's residential centre": s.59.
"health board": s.2.
"mental institution": s.3 of the Mental Health Act, 1945.
"prescribed": s.2.
"registered proprietor": s.59.
"the Minister": s.2.

NOTE

This section imposes upon the Health Service Executive the obligation to provide an adequate number of places in residential centres for children in care. This must be achieved by arrangement with registered proprietors of residential centres or other suitable persons. The Health Service Executive may itself, with Ministerial approval, provide and maintain residential centres for children. The section also provides for the making of regulations governing the maintenance of children in residential centres which regulations may prescribe certain requirements as set out in s.38(4).

Subsection (1)
This obliges the Health Service Executive to make arrangements with registered proprietors of children's residential centres or other suitable persons. All children's residential centres must be registered (ss.60 and 61) and only a registered proprietor may operate a children's residential centre. The registered proprietor is the person whose name is entered on the register as the person carrying on the centre.

Residential centres are defined in s.59 as "any home or other institution for the residential care of children in the care of the Health Service Executive or other children who are not receiving adequate care and protection". Five categories of institution are specifically excluded from the definition of children's residential centre, the effect of which is to exclude them from having to comply with either the registration requirements or any regulations governing the operation of such centres. The rationale for excluding state-run institutions from the effect of registration and regulation was explained by Minister of State Treacy in the Seanad. The excluded institutions are already governed by regulation and the imposition of additional regulations might conflict with the existing roles of the particular institution. In addition it would be illogical to require a state-run institution to register and inspect itself. The reason for the regulations was to ensure that privately operated children's residential centres would be notified of the standards expected for the operation of such centres (see 129 *Seanad Debates* Cols 810–812 and 817–818, Minister for State Treacy, and generally on the debated issue, Cols 806–820). Minister for State Treacy assured the Seanad that every institution providing residential care of children would be subject to the same standards (see 129 *Seanad Debates* Col.189).

The five types of state-run institutions excluded are: first, an institution managed by or on behalf of a Minister of the Government or the Health Service Executive; secondly, an institution in which a majority of the children being maintained are being treated for acute illnesses; thirdly, an institution for the care and maintenance of physically or mentally handicapped children; fourthly, a mental institution within the meaning of Mental Treatment Acts 1945–1966, which is defined in s.3 of the 1945 Act; fifthly, an institution which is a "certified school" within the meaning of Pt IV of the Children Act 1908. A "certified school" is defined in s.44 of the Children Act 1908 as a reformatory or industrial school.

In addition to maintaining children in care in children's residential centres, the Health Service Executive may make arrangements with other suitable persons.

Subsection (2)
This subsection authorises Health Service Executive to themselves, with Ministerial approval, provide and maintain children's residential centres or other premises for children in care.

Subsection (3)
This obliges the Minister to make regulations governing the operation of children residential centres, homes or other premises. The regulations governing children in residential care are S.I. No.259 of 1995, Child Care (Placement of Children in Residential Care) Regulations 1995 and S.I. No.397 of 1996, Child Care (Standards in Children's Residential Centres) Regulations 1996.

Subsection (4)
The regulations may deal with the matters set out in sub-paras (*a*)– (*f*). These concern, first, general requirements as to the maintenance, care and welfare of children in

residential centres. Article 5 of S.I. No.259 of 1995, Child Care (Placement of Children in Residential Care) Regulations 1995, requires the Health Service Executive to satisfy themselves that appropriate and suitable care practices and operational policies are in place in residential care centres. (See also art.5 of S.I. No.397 of 1996, Child Care (Standards in Children's Residential Centres) Regulations 1996.)

Secondly, regulations may prescribe the numbers, qualifications and availability of staff of centres (see art.6 of S.I. No.259 of 1995, Child Care (Placement of Children in Residential Care) Regulations 1995 and art.7 of S.I. No.397 of 1996, Child Care (Standards in Children's Residential Centres) Regulations 1996).

Thirdly, standards as to the design, maintenance, repair, cleaning and cleanliness, ventilation, heating and lighting may be prescribed (see art.7 of S.I. No.259 of 1995, Child Care (Placement of Children in Residential Care) Regulations 1995 and art.8 of S.I. No.397 of 1996, Child Care (Standards in Children's Residential Centres) Regulations 1996).

Fourthly, standards as to accommodation, including matters such as bedroom space, washing facilities and sanitary conveniences may be prescribed (see art.7 of S.I. No.259 of 1995, Child Care (Placement of Children in Residential Care) Regulations 1995 and art.8 of S.I. No.397 of 1996, Child Care (Standards in Children's Residential Centres) Regulations 1996).

Fifthly, standards as to the food provided may be prescribed (see art.11 of S.I. No.259 of 1995, Child Care (Placement of Children in Residential Care) Regulations 1995 and art.12 of S.I. No.397 of 1996, Child Care (Standards in Children's Residential Centres) Regulations 1996).

Sixthly, standards for the keeping of records which may be inspected and copied by officers of the Minister (see arts 21, 22 and 31 of S.I. No.259 of 1995, Child Care (Placement of Children in Residential Care) Regulations 1995 and arts 17 and 18 of S.I. No.397 of 1996, Child Care (Standards in Children's Residential Centres) Regulations 1996).

Regulations as to foster care

39.—(1) The Minister shall make regulations in relation to the placing of children in foster care by [the Health Service Executive] under *section 36* and for securing generally the welfare of such children.

(2) Without prejudice to the generality of *subsection (1)*, regulations under this section may—

(*a*) fix the conditions under which children may be placed in foster care;

(*b*) prescribe the form of contract to be entered into by [the Health Service Executive] with foster parents;

(*c*) provide for the supervision and visiting by [the Health Service Executive] of children in foster care.

AMENDMENT

Subsections (1), (2)(*b*) and (2)(*c*) amended by s.75 and Schedule 7 of the Health Act 2004, No.42 of 2004, with effect from January 1, 2005 (S.I. No.887 of 2004).

COMMENCEMENT

Child Care Act, 1991 (Commencement) Order, 1995 (S.I. No. 258 of 1995) took effect as of October 31, 1995.

DEFINITIONS

"child[ren]": s.2.
"foster parent": s.36(2).
"health board": s.2.
"prescribe": s.2.
"the Minister": s.2.

NOTE

This obliges the Minister for Health to make regulations governing both the placement of children in foster care and for securing, generally, the welfare of children in foster care. The section identifies three aspects of foster care that the regulations may concern. The regulations governing foster care placements are S.I. No.260 of 1995, Child Care (Placement of Children in Foster Care) Regulations 1995.

Regulations may fix the conditions under which children may be placed in foster care. Part III of S.I. No.260 of 1995, Child Care (Placement of Children in Foster Care) Regulations 1995 deals with the requirements to be fulfilled before a child is placed with foster parents. Article 6 of S.I. No.260 of 1995, Child Care (Placement of Children in Foster Care) Regulations 1995 requires an assessment of the child's circumstances. Article 7 of S.I. No.260 of 1995, Child Care (Placement of Children in Foster Care) Regulations 1995 requires the Health Service Executive to satisfy itself that the foster parents selected have the capacity to meet the needs of the child. The wishes of the guardian of a child should, where possible, be respected concerning the religious upbringing of the child and the religion of the persons with whom the child is to be placed (S.I. No.260 of 1995, Child Care (Placement of Children in Foster Care) Regulations 1995.). Articles 10 and 11 of S.I. No.260 of 1995, Child Care (Placement of Children in Foster Care) Regulations 1995, concern the giving of certain information (see the Second Schedule) on the child and the preparation of a care plan respectively. *W v Essex C.C.* [1998] 3 All E.R. 111, [1998] 3 W.L.R. 534, [1998] 2 F.L.R. 278 held that the contract entered into between foster parents and the County Council was an enforceable one. Further, the court held that a social worker owed a common law duty of care to provide to the foster parents, before and during the placement, such information about the child as a reasonable social worker would provide in all the circumstances, and a local authority was vicariously liable for the social worker. The failure to disclose the fact that the child to be placed was a known child sexual abuser was actionable as a negligent misstatement and damages for nervous shock recoverable.

Regulations may also govern the form of contract to be entered into between the Health Service Executive and the foster parents which is governed by art.9 and the form of contract is set out in the First Schedule of S.I. No.260 of 1995, Child Care (Placement of Children in Foster Care) Regulations 1995.

Regulations may govern the supervision and visiting of children in foster care. Article 17 of S.I. No.260 of 1995, Child Care (Placement of Children in Foster Care) Regulations 1995 sets the requirements for the supervising and visiting of children in foster care. The intervals between visits vary between three and six months depending on the type of placement and when that placement was made.

Regulations as to residential care

40.—(1) The Minister shall make regulations in relation to the placing of children in residential care (whether in children's residential centres or in other institutions) by [the Health Service Executive] under *section 36* and for securing generally the welfare of such children.

(2) Without prejudice to the generality of *subsection (1)*, regulations under this section may—

(a) fix the conditions under which children may be placed in residential care;

(b) prescribe the form of contract to be entered into by [the Health Service Executive] with persons providing residential care;

(c) provide for the supervision and visiting by [the Health Service Executive]of children in residential care.

AMENDMENT

Subsections (1), (2)(*b*) and (2)(*c*) amended by s.75 and Schedule 7 of the Health Act 2004, No.42 of 2004, with effect from January 1, 2005 (S.I. No.887 of 2004).

DEFINITIONS

"child[ren]": s.2.
"children's residential centres": s.59.
"health board": s.2.
"the Minister": s.2.

COMMENCEMENT

Child Care Act, 1991 (Commencement) Order, 1995 (S.I. No. 258 of 1995) took effect as of October 31, 1995.

NOTE

This section obliges the Minister for Health to make regulations governing the placing of children in residential care by the Health Service Executive under s.36. Residential care includes care in registered children's residential centres or other institutions. The relevant regulations are S.I. No.259 of 1995, Child Care (Placement of Children in Residential Care) Regulations 1995.

Regulations under this section may govern the conditions under which children may be placed in residential care. The form of contract between the Health Service Executive and the person providing the residential care may be prescribed. Provision by way of regulation may also be made governing the supervising and visiting of children in residential care (see art.24 of S.I. No.259 of 1995, Child Care (Placement of Children in Residential Care) Regulations 1995).

Regulations as to placement with relatives

41.—(1) The Minister shall make regulations in relation to the making of arrangements by [the Health Service Executive] under section *36(1)(d)* for the care of children and for securing generally the welfare of such children.

(2) Without prejudice to the generality of *subsection (1)*, regulations under this section may—

(a) fix the conditions under which children may be placed by [the Health Service Executive] with relatives;

(b) prescribe the form of contract to be entered into by [the Health Service Executive] with relatives;

(c) provide for the supervision and visiting by [the Health Service

Executive] of children placed with relatives.

AMENDMENT

Amendments by s.75 and Schedule 7 of the Health Act 2004, No.42 of 2004, with effect from January 1, 2005 (S.I. No.887 of 2004).

DEFINITIONS

"child[ren]": s.2.
"health board": s.2.
"the Minister": s.2.
"relative": art.3 of the Child Care (Placement of Children with Relatives) Regulations 1995 (S.I. No. 261 of 1995).

COMMENCEMENT

Child Care Act 1991 (Commencement) Order, 1995 (S.I. No. 258 of 1995) took effect as of October 31, 1995.

NOTE

This obliges the Minister for Health to make regulations governing the arrangements by the Health Service Executive in the placing of children under s.36(1)(*d*), the making of 'other suitable arrangements', including placing the child with a relative, with regard to children in the care of the Health Service Executive. A relative is defined in art.3 of S.I. No.261 of 1995, Child Care (Placement of Children with Relatives) Regulations 1995 as including "the spouse of a relative of that child and a person who has acted *in loco parentis*". The duties of relatives where a child is placed with them are set out in art.16 and generally require that all reasonable measures be taken to promote the child's health, development and welfare. In particular relatives must permit a visit by the Health Service Executive of the child in their home, co-operate with the person visiting and furnish such information as is reasonably requested by that person, ensure that information given to them (i.e. the relevant relative) is treated confidentially, seek appropriate medical care for the child, inform the Health Service Executive of any significant event affecting the child, inform the Health Service Executive of any significant change in their circumstances which might affect their ability to care for the child, co-operate with the Health Service Executive in facilitating access to the child by his parents, give 28 days notice of any intended change in their normal place of residence, make good and proper arrangements for the care of the child in case of absence of the child or both of the relatives from the home and give the Health Service Executive prior notice of any such absence which is likely to exceed 72 hours.

Regulations made under this section may govern the conditions under which children may be placed by the Health Service Executive with relatives.

Save for in emergency situations, the Health Service Executive must satisfy a number of requirements before placing a child with relatives. Article 5 of S.I. No.261 of 1995, Child Care (Placement of Children with Relatives) Regulations 1995 requires an assessment of relatives to be conducted. This involves the relatives furnishing the Health Service Executive with a registered medical practitioner's written report on their state of health, the names and addresses of two referees who are not related to the relatives with whom the Health Service Executive may consult concerning their suitability to take care of a child, authorisation to obtain a garda statement as to convictions of the relative or of relevant members of the household and such other information as the

Health Service Executive may require. The Health Service Executive must conduct an assessment as to the suitability of the relative and their home. A report of a committee established to assess the relatives must be obtained. This report must be in writing. The Health Service Executive must ensure that the relative has received appropriate advice, guidance and training. A care plan must also be prepared for the child prior to placing with relatives (see art.11 of S.I. No.261 of 1995, Child Care (Placement of Children with Relatives) Regulations 1995).

Prior to placement the child must be assessed as to his circumstances, including a medical examination where necessary (art.7 of S.I. No.261 of 1995, Child Care (Placement of Children with Relatives) Regulations 1995). Regard must also be had as to the child's religious upbringing and the wishes of parents in this regard (see art.8 of S.I. No.261 of 1995, Child Care (Placement of Children with Relatives) Regulations 1995).

The form of contract to be entered into between the relatives and the Health Service Executive is set out in the First Schedule to S.I. No.261 of 1995, Child Care (Placement of Children with Relatives) Regulations 1995.

The supervising and visiting of children placed with relatives may also be prescribed by regulations. Articles 12 and 13 of S.I. No.261 of 1995, Child Care (Placement of Children with Relatives) Regulations 1995 requires the establishment and maintenance of a register containing particulars of the child and the compiling of a case record on the child. Article 17 of S.I. No.261 of 1995, Child Care (Placement of Children with Relatives) Regulations 1995, obliges the Health Service Executive concerned to have the child visited by an authorised person as often as the Executive considers necessary. The visits must be at least once every three months in the first two years and thereafter at least every six months. The first visit is to take place within one month of the child being placed and a note of every visit must be entered into the child's case record.

Review of cases of children in care

42.—(1) The Minister shall make regulations requiring the case of each child in the care of [the Health Service Executive] to be reviewed in accordance with the provisions of the regulations.

(2) Without prejudice to the generality of *subsection (1)*, regulations under this section may make provision—

(*a*) as to the manner in which each case is to be reviewed,

(*b*) as to the frequency of reviews, and

(*c*) requiring the [Health Service Executive] to consider whether it would be in the best interests of the child to be given into the custody of his parents.

AMENDMENT

Amendments by s.75 and Schedule 7 of the Health Act 2004, No.42 of 2004, with effect from January 1, 2005 (S.I. No.887 of 2004).

DEFINITIONS

"child": s.2.
"health board": s.2.
"the Minister": s.2.

Child Care Act, 1991 (Commencement) Order, 1995 (S.I. No. 258 of 1995) took effect as of October 31, 1995.

NOTE

This section obliges the Minister for Health to make regulations governing the case of every child in the care of the Health Service Executive to be reviewed. The relevant articles of the various regulations governing the review of cases of children in the care of the Health Service Executive is art.25 of S.I. No.259 of 1995, Child Care (Placement of Children in Residential Care) Regulations 1995, art.18 of S.I. No.260 of 1995, Child Care (Placement of Children in Foster Care) Regulations 1995 and art.18 of S.I. No.261 of 1995, Child Care (Placement of Children with Relatives) Regulations 1995.

Subsection (2)(a)
This concerns the various regulations which prescribe the manner of each review. S.I. No.259 of 1995, Child Care (Placement of Children in Residential Care) Regulations 1995 provides in art.25(4) for the Health Service Executive to inform the manager of the children's residential centre, the child and every guardian of the child of the review and afford those persons an opportunity to be heard at the review or otherwise consulted. Article 25(5) requires the Health Service Executive to have regard to: the views or information given by the child, the parents of the child, the manager and any other person the Executive has consulted; a report from the residential centre in which the child resides; a report of a visit to the child under art.24 of the Regulations and any other information which in the opinion of the Executive is relevant. The Health Service Executive has to further consider: whether all reasonable measures are being taken to promote the welfare of the child; whether the care being provided for the child continues to be suitable for the child's needs; whether the circumstances of the parents of the child have changed; whether it would be in the best interests of the child to be given into the custody of his parents and in the case of a child who is due to leave the care of the Health Service Executive in the following two years, the child's need for assistance under s.45 of the Act (aftercare).

Article 25(6) requires the Health Service Executive making a decision following a review to make it known to the manager of the children's residential centre, the child where practicable, any guardian of the child or any other person whom the Executive considers ought to be informed. All reviews must be noted and entered into the child's case record along with any action taken on foot of the review (see art.25(7)).

Under S.I. No.260 of 1995, Child Care (Placement of Children in Foster Care) Regulations 1995 and S.I. No 261 of 1995 (Placement of Children with Relatives) Regulations 1995 the exact same requirements are set out in art.18 of both Instruments, save for the substitution of foster parents and relative for manager of a children's residential centre.

Subsection (2)(b)
This provides that the regulations made under this section may provide for the frequency of reviews. In the case of S.I. No.259 of 1995, Child Care (Placement of Children in Residential Care) Regulations 1995, art.24 provides for reviews at intervals not exceeding three months in the first two years and thereafter at intervals not exceeding six months. The first review is to take place one month after the placement. Article 17 of S.I. No.261 of 1995, Child Care (Placement of Children with Relatives) Regulations 1995 provides for the same timescales for review for placements with relatives.

In the case of S.I. No.260 of 1995, Child Care (Placement of Children in Foster

Care) Regulations 1995, art.18 provides for a review at intervals not exceeding six months in the first two years and thereafter not less than once a year. The first review is to take place within two months of placement.

Subsection (2)(c)
This provides that regulations made under this section may oblige the Health Service Executive to consider whether it would be in the best interests of the child to be given to the custody of his parents. This is reflected in art.25(5)(iv) of S.I. No.259 of 1995, Child Care (Placement of Children in Residential Care) Regulations 1995, art.18(5)(iv) of S.I. No.260 of 1995, Child Care (Placement of Children in Foster Care) Regulations 1995 and art.18(5)(*d*) of S.I. No.261 of 1995, Child Care (Placement of Children with Relatives) Regulations 1995.

Removal from placement

43.—[(1) The Health Service Executive may, in accordance with any regulations made by the Minister, remove a child in its care from the custody of any person with whom the child has been placed under section 36 before or after the amendment of that section by the Health Act 2004.]

(2) Where a person refuses or neglects to comply with a request of [the Health Service Executive] to deliver up a child in accordance with regulations made under *subsection (1)*, [the Executive] may apply to the District Court for an order directing that person to deliver up the child to the custody of [the Executive] and the justice may, if he considers that it is in the best interests of the child so to do, make such an order.

(3) Without prejudice to the law as to contempt of court, where the District Court has made an order under *subsection (2)* (requiring that a child be delivered up to the custody of [the Health Service Executive]), any person having the actual custody of the child who, having been given or shown a copy of the order and having been required, by or on behalf of [the Executive], to give up the child to [the Executive], fails or refuses to comply with the requirement shall be guilty of an offence and shall be liable on summary conviction to a fine not exceeding €634.87 or, at the discretion of the court, to imprisonment for a term not exceeding 6 months or both such fine and such imprisonment.

(4) For the purposes of this section, a person shall be deemed to have been given or shown a copy of an order made under *subsection (2)* if that person was present at the sitting of the court at which such an order was made.

(5) Where a child is removed from the custody of a person in pursuance of this section, any contract between [the Health Service Executive] and that person in respect of the child shall terminate immediately upon the removal.

(6) The provisions of this section are without prejudice to the power of [the Health Service Executive] to apply for an order under *Part III* or *IV*.

AMENDMENT

Subsection (1) substituted and subss.(2), (3), (5) and (6) amended by s.75 and Schedule 7 of the Health Act 2004, No.42 of 2004, with effect from January 1, 2005 (S.I. No.887 of 2004).

DEFINITIONS

"child": s.2.
"health board": s.2.
"the Minister": s.2.

COMMENCEMENT

Child Care Act, 1991 (Commencement) Order, 1995 (S.I. No. 258 of 1995) took effect as of October 31, 1995.

NOTE

This section provides for the removal from the custody of persons with whom the children have been placed under s.36. Any removal must be in accordance with regulations made by the Minister for Health. In uncontested removals by the Health Service Executive, there is a one-step procedure of notification of the intention to remove in accordance with art.28(1) of S.I. No.259 of 1995, Child Care (Placement of Children in Residential Care) Regulations 1995, art.22(1) of S.I. No.260 of 1995, Child Care (Placement of Children in Foster Care) Regulations 1995 and art.22 of S.I. No.261 of 1995, Child Care (Placement of Children with Relatives) Regulations 1995.

Where there is an objection to the removal of the child from residential or foster care or from relatives, then the Health Service Executive concerned must afford the person with custody of the child an opportunity to make representations. Where the Executive decides to proceed with the removal of the child, the Health Service Executive must inform the relevant person with custody of that decision and the reasons. The Health Service Executive must then request the relevant person to deliver up the child at a specified time and place (see art.28(2) of S.I. No.259 of 1995, Child Care (Placement of Children in Residential Care) Regulations 1995, arts 22(2) of S.I. No.260 of 1995, Child Care (Placement of Children in Foster Care) Regulations 1995 and S.I. No.261 of 1996, Child Care (Placement of Children with Relatives) Regulations 1996).

Where the relevant person refuses or neglects to comply with the request to deliver up the child, the Health Service Executive may apply to the District Court for an order directing that person to deliver up the child to the Health Service Executive.

This procedure for the removal of children was introduced at Report Stage in the Dáil. The primary reason for the insertion was to allay the fears of foster parents who were concerned that children placed in their custody under s.36 could be arbitrarily removed by the Health Service Executive. Where there is an objection to the removal of a child, that removal can only be effected by the intervention of the Court in the matter and by the making of an order directing the delivery up of the child (see 403 *Dáil Debates* Cols 2445–2452).

Subsection (2)

This provides for the procedure to be followed where a person who has been given custody of a child in the care of the Health Service Executive under s.36, refuses or neglects to comply with the Health Service Executive request to deliver up the child. The request to deliver up may only be made once the relevant provision of the governing regulations have been complied with (see above). The Health Service Executive may apply to the District Court for an order directing the delivery up of the child and the District Judge may so order where he considers such to be in the best interests of the child. An application under this section must be on notice to the respondent and served two days prior to the hearing of the application. Where an order is made it must be served upon the respondent (see Ord.84, r.27 of S.I. No.93 of 1997, District Court Rules 1997).

Subsection (3)

This provides the penalties on summary conviction for failing or refusing to comply with an order under s.43(2). The person with custody of the child to whom the order directing delivery up of the child relates, who is required by or on behalf of the Health Service Executive to deliver up the child, must be given or shown a copy of the order. The penalties on summary conviction are a fine not exceeding €634.87 and, at the discretion of the court, a term of imprisonment not exceeding six months or both a fine and imprisonment.

The penalties as prescribed do not affect the law as to contempt of court. (See McGonagle, *A Textbook on Media Law* (Gill & McMillan), chap.6, p.137.)

Subsection (4)

This provides that where a person is present at the sitting of the court at which an order under this section is made, that person is deemed to have been given or shown a copy of the order for the purposes of this section.

Subsection (5)

This provides for the automatic termination of a contract entered into by the Health Service Executive with a person who has been ordered to deliver up a child under this section.

Subsection (6)

This provides that, although the child has been voluntarily placed by the Health Service Executive with a person under s.36 and there is a contract in existence with that person to that effect, the Health Service Executive retains the power to apply for an order under Pts III, IV or IVA to apply for a different type of order.

Children who become adopted

44.—[(1) Where a child becomes adopted under the Adoption Acts 1952 to 1998 and the child was immediately before the adoption being maintained in foster care by the Health Service Executive or the Health Service Executive with the adopter or adopters, the Health Service Executive may, subject to any general directions given by the Minister and subject to such conditions as the Executive sees fit, contribute to the child's maintenance as if the child continued to be in foster care.]

(2) Where a child becomes adopted under [the Adoption Acts, 1952 to 1998], any care order in force in respect of the child shall cease to have effect.

AMENDMENT

Subsection (1) substituted and subs.(2) amended by s.75 and Schedule 7 of the Health Act 2004, No.42 of 2004, with effect from January 1, 2005 (S.I. No.887 of 2004).

DEFINITIONS

"child": s.2.
"health board": s.2.
"the Minister": s.2.

COMMENCEMENT

Child Care Act, 1991 (Commencement) Order, 1995 (S.I. No. 258 of 1995) took effect as of October 31, 1995.

NOTE

This provides for the continuation of payments of foster parent allowances to persons who formerly were foster parents of a child placed by the Health Service Executive in their custody and who subsequently adopt that child under the Adoption Acts 1952–1988. The discretion of the Health Service Executive to continue to make payments is subject to any general directions given by the Minister and such conditions as the Health Service Executive sees fit.

Subsection (2)
This provides that the making of an adoption order terminates the effect of any care order in existence.

Aftercare

45.—(1)(*a*) Where a child leaves the care of [the Health Service Executive], [the Executive] may, in accordance with *subsection (2)*, assist him for so long as [the Executive] is satisfied as to his need for assistance and, subject to *paragraph (b)*, he has not attained the age of 21 years.

(*b*) Where [the Health Service Executive] is assisting a person in accordance with *subsection (2)(b)*, and that person attains the age of 21 years, [the Executive] may continue to provide such assistance until the completion of the course of education in which he is engaged.

(2) [The Health Service Executive] may assist a person under this section in one or more of the following ways—

(*a*) by causing him to be visited or assisted;

(*b*) by arranging for the completion of his education and by contributing towards his maintenance while he is completing his education;

(*c*) by placing him in a suitable trade, calling or business and paying such fee or sum as may be requisite for that purpose;

(*d*) by arranging hostel or other forms of accommodation for him;

(*e*) by co-operating with housing authorities in planning accommodation for children leaving care on reaching the age of 18 years.

(3) Any arrangement made by [the Health Service Executive] under *section 55(4)* or *(5)* of the Health Act, 1953, in force immediately before the commencement of this section shall continue in force as if made under this section.

(4) In providing assistance under this section, [the Health Service Executive] shall comply with any general directions given by the Minister.

AMENDMENT

Amendments by s.75 and Schedule 7 of the Health Act 2004, No.42 of 2004, with effect from January 1, 2005 (S.I. No.887 of 2004).

DEFINITIONS
"child": s.2.
"health board": s.2.
"the Minister": s.2.

COMMENCEMENT

Child Care Act, 1991 (Commencement) Order, 1995 (S.I. No. 258 of 1995) took effect as of October 31, 1995.

NOTE

This provision concerns the aftercare which may be given to a child leaving the care of the Health Service Executive. The general age limit is 21 years beyond which the Health Service Executive has a discretion to provide assistance. There is an exception to the 21-year age limit where a child is in the process of completing a course of education, then the assistance may continue to be given until that course of education is completed (s.45(1)(*b*) and (2)(*b*)). The assessment of whether a child is in need of assistance is carried out by the Health Service Executive. The section outlines the type of assistance that the Health Service Executive may provide. The assistance that may be provided relates to children returning to their families or leaving home. There is also provision for assisting the homeless. The forms of assistance vary from the general to visiting, educating and setting up the child in a career and the provision of accommodation.

Subsection (2)
This provides five ways in which the Health Service Executive may assist a child under this section. The provision of assistance is subject to the age of the child not exceeding 21. One or more of the following five types of assistance may be given. First, the Health Service Executive may cause the child to be visited or assisted. This is broad in its interpretation and may include any assistance, financial or otherwise. Secondly the Health Service Executive may both arrange for a child formerly in care to complete his education, which may involve the payment of fees, and to contribute to the maintenance of the child whilst completing his education. In these circumstances the 21-year age limit does not apply. Thirdly, the Health Service Executive may place a child in a suitable trade, calling or business. Where this involves the payment of a fee, the Health Service Executive may discharge such. Fourthly, the Health Service Executive may arrange hostel or other forms of accommodation. Fifthly, the Health Service Executive may co-operate with housing authorities in planning accommodation for children leaving care or reaching the age of 18.

Subsection (3)
This provides that arrangements made under s.55(4) and (5) of the Health Act 1953 shall continue in force as if made under this section. Section 55(4) and (5) of the Health Act 1953 concern the placing of a child in a suitable trade, calling or business which the Health Service Executive may pay the fees for and contribute to the maintenance of the child, which may continue after the child has reached the age of 16. The latter provision relates to the boarding out or sending to school of a child and for the completion of the child's education and maintenance where the child has reached the age of 16.

Subsection (4)

This obliges the Health Service Executive in the provision of assistance under this section to comply with any general directions given by the Minister for Health.

Recovery of children removed from care etc.

46.—(1) The provisions of this section shall apply to any child who is in the care of [the Health Service Executive] and who is, without lawful authority, removed from the custody of [the Executive] or from the custody of any person who is taking care of him on behalf of [the Executive] or prevented from returning to such custody at the end of any period of leave.

(2) The [Health Service Executive] may request the Garda Síochána to search for the child and to deliver him up to the custody of the [Executive] and the Garda Síochána may take all reasonable measures to comply with such a request.

[(2A) A request made by the Health Service Executive to the Garda Siochana under *subsection* (2) before the amendment of that subsection by the Health Act 2004 shall be deemed to have been made by the Health Service Executive if the child in respect of whom the request was made is not delivered up to the Health Service Executive before the establishment day of the Executive.]

(3) A justice of the District Court may, if satisfied by information on oath that there are reasonable grounds for believing that a person specified in the information can produce the child named in the application, make an order directing that person to deliver up the child to the custody of the [Health Service Executive].

(4) Without prejudice to the law as to contempt of court where the District Court has made an order under *subsection* (3) directing that a child be delivered up to the care of [the Health Service Executive], any person having the actual custody of the child who, having been given or shown a copy of the order and having been required, by or on behalf of [the Executive], to give up the child to [the Executive], fails or refuses to comply with the requirement shall be guilty of an offence and shall be liable on summary conviction to a fine not exceeding €634.87 or, at the discretion of the court, to imprisonment for a term not exceeding 6 months or both such fine and such imprisonment.

(5) For the purposes of this section, a person shall be deemed to have been given or shown a copy of an order made under *subsection* (3) if that person was present at the sitting of the court at which such an order was made.

(6) A justice of the District Court may, if satisfied by information on oath that there are reasonable grounds for believing that the child named in the application is in any house or other place (including any building or part of a building, tent, caravan or other temporary or moveable structure, vehicle, vessel, aircraft or hovercraft) specified in the information, issue a warrant authorising a member of the Garda Síochána, accompanied by such other members of the Garda Síochána or such other persons as may be necessary to enter (if need be by force) and to search the house or other place for the child; and if the child is found he shall be returned to the custody of [the Health Service Executive].

(7) An application for an order under *subsection* (3) may, if the justice is satisfied that the urgency of the matter so requires, be made ex parte.

(8) An application for an order under subsection (3) or for a warrant under

subsection (6) may, if the justice is satisfied that the urgency of the matter so requires, be heard and an order made thereon elsewhere than at a public sitting of the District Court.

(9) Without prejudice to *section 28*—

(*a*) an order under *subsection (3)* may be made by a justice of the District Court for the time being assigned to the district court district where the person specified in the information resides or is for the lime being, and

(*b*) a warrant under *subsection (6)* may be issued by a justice for the time being assigned to the district where the house or other place specified in the information is situated,

and, in either case, where such justice is not immediately available the order may be made, or the warrant issued, by any justice of the District Court.

AMENDMENT

Subsection (2A) inserted, and subss.(1), (2), (3), (4) and (6) amended by s.75 and Schedule 7 of the Health Act 2004, No.42 of 2004, with effect from January 1, 2005 (S.I. No.887 of 2004).

DEFINITIONS

"child": s.2.
"health board": s.2.

COMMENCEMENT

Child Care Act, 1991 (Commencement) Order, 1995 (S.I. No. 258 of 1995) took effect as of October 31, 1995.

NOTE

This section concerns the recovery of children unlawfully removed from the care of the Health Service Executive. A number of procedures governing the recovery of children unlawfully removed are set out.

The unlawful removal may arise where the child is taken from the care and custody of the Health Service Executive or a person with whom the Health Service Executive has placed a child and who is caring for the child on behalf of the Health Service Executive. This will arise where a child is removed from foster parents, children's residential centre or relatives of the child. A wrongful removal may also arise where a child is prevented from being returned to the custody of the Health Service Executive or person who has been given custody by the Health Service Executive. This might arise where a parent or guardian has been given residential access under s.37(1) to a child and the parent or guardian fails to return the child at the end of the access period. The removal will only be unlawful where the Health Service Executive has a care order in relation to the child.

Subsection (2)

This facilitates the recovery of a child unlawfully removed. The Health Service Executive may request a member of the gardaí to search and deliver up the child to the Health Service Executive.

In complying with a request by the Health Service Executive, the gardaí may take all reasonable steps in recovering the child.

Subsection (3)

This provides a means of obtaining an order from the District Court directing a specified person to deliver up the child to the Health Service Executive. The application for an order directing the delivery up of the child is made by the issue of a summons based upon information on oath. The District Judge must be satisfied that there are reasonable grounds to believe that the person specified in the information can produce the child. The application is governed by Ord.84, r.28 of S.I. No.93 of 1997, District Court Rules 1997 which must be by information on oath and in writing. Where a District Judge issues a summons under this section, it must be served upon the respondent two days prior to the date fixed for the hearing. Where the urgency of the matter so requires, however, an application may be made *ex parte* for an order directing the delivery up of the child, and the order must be served upon the respondent (see s.46(7) and Ord.84, r.28 of S.I. No.93 of 1997, District Court Rules 1997). In appropriate circumstances and where the urgency of the matter so requires and it is established to the satisfaction of the District Judge, both the granting of an order under subs.3 and a warrant under subs.6 may be made otherwise than at a public sitting of the District Court (s.46(8)). Further an application for an order under subs.3 and a warrant to enforce that order may be made to a Judge of the District Court in that district court area in which the person specified in the information, and, in relation to a warrant, the area in which the premises sworn in the information is situated. Where the District Court Judge for the district in which the person specified in the information is unavailable, then an application may be made to any Judge of the District Court (s.46(9)(*a*) and (*b*)).

An order granted under s.46(3) or (7) may be enforced by the issue of a warrant under s.46(6) authorising a member of the gardaí to enter premises and search for a child. The issue of a warrant under this subsection is dependent upon the District Judge being satisfied that there are reasonable grounds for believing that the child named is located in the place or premises sworn in the information. On foot of a warrant a member of the gardaí may enter, with force if necessary, and search the premises and may be accompanied by such persons as are necessary. Where a child is found, the gardaí must return the child to the custody of the Health Service Executive.

Subsection (4)

This provides for the penalties on summary conviction for failing or refusing to comply with an order directing the delivery up of a child named in the order. The person liable to prosecution is the person with actual custody of the child who has been shown or given a copy of the order and required to give up the child. This will be deemed to have occurred where the person with actual custody is present at the sitting of the court where the order is made (s.46(5)). The penalties that may be imposed on conviction are a fine not exceeding €632.90 or, at the discretion of the court, a term of imprisonment not exceeding six months or both a fine and a term of imprisonment. The penalties as set out are in addition to any penalty imposed by the court for contempt of court.

Subsection (5)

This provides for the circumstances in which the respondent of an order under s.46(3) will be deemed to have been served with such. Where the respondent is present at the sitting of the court at which an order is made, that person is deemed to have been given or shown a copy of the order for the purposes of being directed to deliver up the child to the Health Service Executive.

Subsection (6)
This provides for the issuing of a warrant to execute an order authorises an entry and search of any premises where the child is as specified in the information (see General Note to s.46(3)). Order 84, r.29 of S.I. No.93 of 1997, District Court Rules 1997 provides that the information grounding the application for the warrant shall be on oath and in writing in accordance with Form 84.57 of Sch.C of S.I. No.93 of 1997, District Court Rules 1997. The warrant when issued must be comply with Form 84.58 of Sch.C of S.I. No.93 of 1997, District Court Rules 1997.

Subsection (7)
This provides for making an application for an order under s.46(3) on an ex parte basis (see Note to s.46(3)).

Subsection (8)
This provides that, where the urgency of the matter so requires, an order under s.46(3) may be applied for otherwise than at a public sitting of the District Court.

Subsection (9)
This provides that an order under s.46(3) should be sought from the District Judge in the district in which the person specified in the information resides, and a warrant under s.46(6) should be sought from the District Judge in the district in which the premises is located, but in either case, if the relevant District Judge is not immediately available, then the order or warrant may be sought from a District Judge in any district.
The exercise of this jurisdiction by any District Judge is stated not to prejudice s.28 (jurisdiction of the courts).

Application for directions.

47.—Where a child is in the care of [the Health Service Executive], the District Court may, of its own motion or on the application of any person, give such directions and make such order on any question affecting the welfare of the child as it thinks proper and may vary or discharge any such direction or order.

AMENDMENT

Amended by s.75 and Schedule 7 of the Health Act 2004, No.42 of 2004, with effect from January 1, 2005 (S.I. No.887 of 2004).

DEFINITIONS

"child": s.2.
"health board": s.2.

COMMENCEMENT

Child Care Act, 1991 (Commencement) Order, 1995 (S.I. No. 258 of 1995) took effect as of October 31, 1995.

NOTE

This provision relates to the application for directions whilst a child is in the care of the Health Service Executive. The court of its own motion or any other person may apply for a direction concerning the welfare of the child. Central to an application for a direction is the welfare of the child. This is a very broad term and includes all aspects of the child's upbringing, health development or care. The court determines the application as it thinks proper. This section was extensively considered in *Eastern Health Board v McDonnell* [1999] 1 I.R 174, [1999] 2 I.L.R.M 382 where McCracken J. upheld the authority of the court to make an order for directions where the child in question was the subject of a care order as opposed to an interim care order. The Health Board had claimed the District Judge had acted *ultra vires* in making the order for directions.

McCracken J. held that on the interpretation of ss.24 and 27, the District Court was obliged to consider the child's welfare as the first and paramount consideration which, in turn, obliged the court to make the directions in question. In addition, s.47 was interpreted as obliging the court to retain overall control of a child even where a care order had been made. The nature of the directions made in this were highly specific and imposed a number of obligations on the Health Board pending the adjourned hearing.

In *Western Health Board v KM* [2002] 2 I.R. 493, the Supreme Court upheld a High Court decision which authorised the District Court under s.47 to permit or direct the placement of a child with relatives or foster parents outside the jurisdiction provided there was evidence before the court indicating that such a placement was truly in the child's best interests. The court stressed that such an order should be made rarely and with considerable caution. In this regard the Supreme Court stated the following non-exhaustive list of factors: (i) the constitutional rights of both the child and his/her parents; (ii) the parameters of law regarding children in the jurisdiction in which it was proposed the child should live including principles of the paramouncy of the child's welfare, the comity of the courts and whether the order of the court was capable of recognition and enforcement; (iii) whether the jurisdiction was a signatory to the Hague and/or Luxembourg Convention on Child Abduction; (iv) whether a system of co-operation existed between the Health Board and the care authorities in the relevant jurisdiction or whether such could be easily established; (v) whether access by the parents to the child was a realistic practicality in terms of distance and expense; and (vi) whether there was a reasonable possibility of using either undertakings or mirror orders to make the position of the child and the Health Board more secure. In addition, where a care order under s.18 was in existence, this enabled the court to consent to a removal of the child from the jurisdiction for the purposes of s.40 of the Adoption Act 1952. See also, *East Coast Area Health Board v M(M) v P(M)*, unreported, High Court, Finnegan P., February 5, 2002, on a similar issue regarding the placement of a child in a residential unit in the UK reiterated that the position concerning placement in a residential unit was indistinguishable from placement with relatives or foster parents but did stress that only a court could permit or direct such a placement and that the Health Board could not place a child in any such type of care without court approval.

Any application must be on notice to each of the parties or any other person affected by the direction. Two days notice of the hearing of the application must be given to the respondent and the notice must be served (see r.30(1) of S.I. No.93 of 1997, District Court Rules 1997).

An order making a direction may be varied or discharged and an application to do so must be on notice and served in accordance with Ord.84, r.30(2) of S.I. No.93 of 1997, District Court Rules 1997. Where an order is made varying or discharging a direction, it must be served upon the parties and any other person affected by the order.

Transitional provisions

48.—(1) On the commencement of *Part IV* any child who is in the care of the Health Service Executive pursuant to an order made under *Part II* or *IV* of the Children Act, 1908 shall be deemed to be the subject of a care order committing him to the care of that Health Service Executive and the provisions of *Part IV* shall apply with the necessary modifications.

(2) Where, on the commencement of *Part IV*, a child is in the care of the Health Service Executive pursuant to an order made under section 21 or 24 of the Children Act, 1908 in respect of the commission of an offence against him and the person charged with the commission of the offence is acquitted of the charge or the charge is dismissed for want of prosecution, any care order to which the child is deemed to be subject under *subsection (1)* shall forthwith be void, but without prejudice to anything that may have been lawfully done under it.

(3) Nothing in this Act shall affect an order made under *Part II* or *IV* of the Children Act, 1908 committing a child to the care of a relative or fit person other than the Health Service Executive.

(4) On the commencement of *Part III*, any child who is being detained in a place of safety under any provision of the Children Act, 1908 shall be deemed to have been received into that place pursuant to an emergency care order on the date of such commencement.

(5) Where, on the commencement of *Part II*, a child is in the care of the Health Service Executive otherwise than by virtue of a court order, he shall be deemed to have been taken into care under *section 4* on the date of such commencement.

(6) Where, on the commencement of *Part VI*, a child is boarded-out by the Health Service Executive, he shall be deemed to have been placed by the Health Service Executive in foster care under an arrangement made under section 36.

(7) Where, on the commencement of *Part VI*, the Health Service Executive is contributing towards the maintenance of a child in accordance with section 55(9)(*c*) of the Health Act, 1953, the board may, subject to such conditions as it sees fit, continue to contribute to the maintenance of the child as if he were in foster care.

(8) Where, on the commencement of *Part VI*, a child is being maintained by the Health Service Executive in a home or school approved by the Minister for the purposes of section 55 of the Health Act, 1953, he shall be deemed to have been placed in residential care by the Health Service Executive under an arrangement made under *section 36*.

(9) Nothing in *section 67* shall affect the operation of an order committing a child to a certified industrial school to which that section applies.

DEFINITIONS

"child": s.2.
"health board": s.2.

COMMENCEMENT

Child Care Act, 1991 (Commencement) Order, 1995 (S.I. No. 258 of 1995) took effect as of October 31, 1995.

NOTE

This section provides for a number of existing orders under the Children Act 1908 to continue to take effect as if they were orders made under this Act and as to the boarding out and placements of children under the 1908 Act. In addition there is provision for the continued maintenance of children received into care under the Health Act 1953. Section 79 of this Act repeals the relevant sections of both the Children Act 1908 and the Health Act 1953 affected by these transitional provisions. S.I. No.258 of 1995, Child Care (Commencement) Order 1995, brought into operation this section.

Subsection (1)

This provides that on the commencement of Pt IV (care and supervision orders) of the Act any orders made under Pts II or IV of the Children Act 1908 are deemed to be care orders under Pt IV of this Act, the effect of which is to commit any child to the care of the relevant Health Service Executive. The provisions of the 1991 Act relevant to Pt IV shall apply to such children in the care of the Health Service Executive under Pt IV.

Part II of the 1908 Act concerned the prevention of cruelty to children and young persons. Part IV of the 1908 Act concerns the sending of children to industrial or reformatory schools. The relevant sections of Pt II are s.20 (removal by a member of the gardaí to a place of safety) and s.24 (place of safety order). Section 58 authorised a District Judge to send a child to a certified school and to make a fit person order giving custody of a child to the Health Service Executive or other individual.

Subsection (2)

This provision relates to the situation where under s.21 or s.24 of the Children Act 1908, a child against whom one of specified offences was allegedly committed, is brought into care pending the prosecution of the individual for those alleged offences and at the trial of that individual, either the charges were dismissed for want of prosecution or the individual was acquitted, then any order deemed to have taken effect on the commencement of this section is void.

The voiding of a care order under this section is subject, however, to s.23 which confers certain powers upon the court where a care order is found to be invalid (see Note to s.23).

Subsection (3)

This provides that any fit person order made under Pts II or IV of the Children Act 1908 committing a child to the custody of a relative or fit person shall not be affected by any provision of this Act.

Subsection (4)

This provides that any child who was the subject of a place of safety order under the 1908 Act, the order authorising the detention of the child shall be deemed to be an emergency care order under s.13 of Pt III of the Act. As the maximum duration of an emergency care order is eight days, this transitional provision is of a very temporary nature.

Subsection (5)
This provides that where the Health Service Executive has a child in its care in the absence of a court order to that effect on the coming into operation of Pt II, the child will be deemed to be in the care of the Health Service Executive in accordance with s.4 of the Act. Section 4 of the Act concerns the voluntary placing of children in the care of the Health Service Executive by their parents or guardian.

Subsection (6)
This provision concerns children who are boarded out at the commencement of Pt VI of the 1991 Act. Boarding out of children is governed by s.55 of the Health Act 1953. Where children are boarded out at the commencement of the Act they are deemed to have been placed in foster care by the Health Service Executive under s.36(1)(*a*).

Subsection (7)
This relates to s.55(9)(*c*) of the Health Act 1953 which authorises the Health Service Executive to continue to contribute to the maintenance of a child, who was formerly boarded out to persons and who subsequently adopt the child as if the child was being maintained as a boarded-out child by the adopters. The adopters under this section will be considered to be fostering the child for the purpose of the Health Service Executive continuing to maintain the child. The authority to continue to maintain the child is subject to any conditions the Health Service Executive sees fit and any general directions given by the Minister for Health to the Health Service Executive in this regard (see s.44).

Subsection (8)
This provides that, at the commencement of Pt VI, where a child was being maintained by the Health Service Executive in a school or home approved by the Minister under s.55 of the Health Act 1953, the child will be deemed to have been placed in residential care by the Health Service Executive in accordance with s.36(1)(*b*).

Subsection (9)
This provides that the effect of s.67 (cessation of certified schools under the Children Act 1908 and conversion to registered children's residential centres for the purposes of Part IV of the Act) shall not affect any order committing a child to a certified industrial school.

PART VII

SUPERVISION OF PRE-SCHOOL SERVICES

Definitions for *Part VII*

49.—In this Part—
"authorised person" means a person appointed under *section 54* to be an authorised person for the purposes of this Part;
"national school" has the meaning assigned to it in the School Attendance Act, 1926;
"pre-school child" means a child who has not attained the age of six years and who is not attending a national school or a school providing an educational programme similar to a national school;

"pre-school service" means any pre-school, play group, day nursery, créche, day-care or other similar service which caters for pre-school children, including those grant-aided by [the Health Service Executive]; [...].

AMENDMENT

Definition of 'pre-school service' amended, and definition of 'relevant Health Service Executive' deleted by s.75 and Schedule 7 of the Health Act 2004, No.42 of 2004, with effect from January 1, 2005 (S.I. No.887 of 2004).

DEFINITIONS

"authorised person": s.49.
"national school": s.49.
"pre-school child": s.49.
"pre-school service": s.49.
"relevant health board": s.49.

COMMENCEMENT

S.I. No. 399 of 1996, Child Care Act, 1991 (Commencement) Order, 1996, took effect as of December 18, 1996.

NOTE

This is the definition section for this Part of the Act which governs the provision of pre-school services (crèches, child-minding services, play-groups, etc.). Part VII authorises the making of regulations to govern the carrying on of pre-school services.

There is an obligation on persons providing such services to notify the relevant Health Service Executive of the service. In addition, a statutory obligation is imposed upon such persons to safeguard the health, safety and welfare of children attending the service. The Health Service Executive, in addition to carrying on pre-school services, may supervise such services by visiting and inspecting the premises where the service is being provided. Penalties on summary conviction for a breach of any of the provisions of this Part are detailed. There are specified activities which are specifically excluded from the effect of this Part of the Act.

Crèches and pre-school services are now subject to the provisions of the Equal Status Act 2000 (see s.7(1)).

Regulations as to pre-school services

50.—(1) The Minister shall, after consultation with the Minister for Education and the Minister for the Environment, make regulations for the purpose of securing the health, safety and welfare and promoting the development of pre-school children attending pre-school services.

(2) Without prejudice to the generality of *subsection (1)*, regulations may—

  (*a*) prescribe requirements as to the heating, lighting, ventilation, cleanliness, repair and maintenance of premises in which pre-school services are carried on and as to the equipment and facilities to be provided;

  (*b*) provide for the enforcement and execution of the regulations by [the

Health Service Executive];
(*c*) prescribe the annual fees to be paid to [the Health Service Executive] by persons carrying on pre-school services towards the cost of inspections under this Part.

(3) Regulations under this section may—
(*a*) make different provision for different classes of pre-school services;
(*b*) prescribe different requirements for different classes of pre-school services;
(*c*) provide for exemptions from any provision or provisions of the regulations for a specified class or classes of pre-school services.

(4) The Public Offices Fees Act, 1879, shall not apply in respect of any fees paid under regulations under this section.

AMENDMENT

Subsections (2)(*b*) and (*c*) amended by s.75 and Schedule 7 of the Health Act 2004, No.42 of 2004, with effect from January 1, 2005 (S.I. No.887 of 2004).

DEFINITIONS

"health board": s.2.
"premises": art.3 of the Child Care (Pre-school Services) Regulations, 1996 (S.I. No. 398 of 1996).
"pre-school child": s.49.
"pre-school service": s.49.
"the Minister": s.2.

COMMENCEMENT

S.I. No. 399 of 1996, Child Care Act, 1991 (Commencement) Order, 1996, took effect as of December 18, 1996.

NOTE

This authorises the Minister for Health, after consultation with the Minister for Education and the Minister for the Environment, to make regulations governing the provision of pre-school services. The regulations are to secure the health, safety, welfare and promote the development of pre-school children attending pre-school services.

The regulations made under this Part are S.I. No.398 of 1996, Child Care (Pre-School Services) Regulations 1996.

A pre-school service is defined in s.49 as "any pre-school, play-group, day nursery, crèche, day-care or other similar service which cares for pre-school children, including those grant aided by the Health Service Executive". A pre-school child is defined in s.49 as "a child who has not attained the age of six years and who is not attending a national school or a school providing an educational programme similar to a national school". A national school is defined in s.1 of the School Attendance Act 1926 as a "public elementary day school for the time-being recognised by the Minister as a national school".

In terms of promoting the development of children, art.4 of S.I. No.398 of 1996, Child Care (Pre-school Services) Regulations 1996 obliges persons carrying on the service to ensure that children attending the service have suitable means of expression and development through the use of books, toys, games and other play materials, having regard to his age or development. This requires that materials must be provided as appropriate for the varying ages and development of pre-school children attending the service. The effect of this, in practical terms, is to require only basic means of promoting the development of children. There is no specific requirement that there be professionally trained and educated staff skilled in the education and development of pre-school children. On the assumption that this is a correct interpretation and not a drafting error, the nature of the duty imposed upon persons carrying on pre-school services relates more to the provision of proper and adequate premises, facilities and equipment rather than also imposing standards as to the development of pre-school children. Development here must be broadly interpreted and must include both physical and educational development as well as emotional and social. Nowhere in the regulations are there requirements as to this aspect of child care. The emphasis, in this regard, appears to be on child minding and the appropriate standard to achieve that rather than on the educational and other development of pre-school children.

There is also a requirement in art.7 that there be a sufficient number of competent adults supervising pre-school children at all times. There is no stipulation as to educational or training qualifications for individuals supervising pre-school children. The person carrying on the service, on giving notice in accordance with s.51(1), must state their qualification and the body awarding that qualification and other relevant experience with children (see Schedule to S.I. No.398 of 1996, Child Care (Pre-School Services) Regulations 1996).

In terms of securing the health, safety and welfare of children, S.I. No.398 of 1996, Child Care (Pre-School Services) Regulations 1996 requires the provision of a number of measures. Articles 5 and 6 require that there be a suitably equipped first aid box and adequate arrangements to summon medical assistance in an emergency. In this regard provision should be made for obtaining the consent of a parent or guardian to medical treatment in an emergency situation or authorisation given to the person carrying on the service to give a consent on behalf of the child where the parent or guardian is not available to do so. Article 8 of the 1996 Regulations prohibits the infliction of corporal punishment on pre-school children attending a pre-school service. Article 27 requires that pre-school services conform to the safety measures prescribed in relation to fire, fire drill, fire retardant materials, heating, secure doors, gates and fencing, hazardous objects and the temperature of hot running water. There is also the obligation to provide nourishing and varied food and adequate and suitable facilities for the storage, preparation, cooking, serving and consumption of food.

In securing the general welfare of pre-school children, art.13 imposes upon the person carrying out a pre-school service to maintain a register for each child which must contain a number of particular personal details of each child. In addition there is an obligation to maintain a record concerning the provision of the service containing information on the day-to-day running of the service (see art.14 of S.I. No.398 of 1996, Child Care (Pre-school Services) Regulations 1996).

Of particular importance in regard to the general duty to safeguard the health, safety and welfare of children is the authority of the Health Service Executive in art.12 to regulate the maximum number of children that may be catered for in the premises.

Subsection (2)

This identifies what may be prescribed in regulations made under s.50(1) (the relevant provisions of S.I. No.398 of 1996, Child Care (Pre-school Services) Regulations 1996 appear in brackets). Firstly, there are requirements as to heating (art.19); lighting (art.21); ventilation (art.20); cleanliness (arts 22 and 23); repair and maintenance (art.18); and equipment and facilities (art.25).

Secondly, regulations may provide for the enforcement and execution of the regulations. This is primarily achieved by the notice requirements set out in arts 9–11

and the obligation to furnish to the Health Service Executive information in art.29 of
S.I. No.398 of 1996, Child Care (Pre-school Services) Regulations 1996. The Health
Service Executive has specific powers of inspection (art.32) and to enforce and execute
these regulations by any steps necessary. Section 57 prescribes the penalties on summary
conviction for a breach of the provisions of Pt VII and any regulations made thereunder.
A person may be liable to a fine not exceeding €1,269.74 or at the discretion of the
court and in substitution of or in relation to a fine, be prohibited from carrying on a
pre-school service (s.57(2)).

Thirdly, there is provision for the charging of fees payable to the Health Service
Executive by persons carrying on pre-school services which fees are specified to
discharge the cost of inspections. Article 31 of S.I. No.398 of 1996, Child Care (Pre-
School Services) Regulations 1996 imposes a levy of £25 where the service does not
exceed 3.5 hours per day and £50 in all other cases. There is provision to waive a fee
where the service is not provided for profit (art.31(4)). S.I. No.268 of 1997, (Child
Care) (Pre-School Services) (Amendment) Regulations 1997 require the notice and
fee/request for waiver to be sent together to the Health Service Executive. The Health
Service Executive must annually notify the service provider of the fee which must be
paid within 28 days of notification (art.31(2) and (3) of S.I. No.398 of 1996, Child
Care (Pre-school Services) Regulations 1996).

Subsection (3)
This provides for the making of regulations for different classes of pre-school service.
As the definition of a pre-school service is very broad, almost all forms of child care or
minding activity is covered by the Act save for those types expressly excluded by s.58.
A "drop in centre" is the only pre-school service with separate provision made for it in
S.I. No.398 of 1996, Child Care (Pre-School Services) Regulations 1996. A "drop in
centre" is defined as "a premises in which a pre-school service is used exclusively on
an intermittent basis". An example of which is perhaps crèche facilities attached to
supermarkets or shopping centres or other venues which are used on a temporary and
irregular basis.

Requirements different to those of pre-school services are prescribed, though the
difference is negligible. Drop in centres are obliged to comply with the regulations set
out in S.I. No.398 of 1996, Child Care (Pre-school Services) Regulations 1996 save
for art.13(1)(*b*), (*c*) and (*h*) which relate to recording in a register the date on which the
pre-school child first attended the service, the date on which the pre-school child ceased
to attend the service and recording immunisations received by the pre-school child.
Section 50(3)(*c*) provides for the exemption from any regulations of a class or classes
of pre-school service.

Subsection (4)
This excludes the operation of the Public Offices Fees Act 1897 from application to
any fees paid under art.31(1) of S.I. No.398 of 1996, Child Care (Pre-School Services)
Regulations 1996 made under s.50.

[Notice to Health Service Executive

[51.—(1) A person who proposes to carry on a pre-school service shall
give notice to the Health Service Executive in the prescribed manner.

(2) A person who, before the amendment of this section by the Health Act
2004, gave notice to the Health Service Executive in the prescribed manner
shall be deemed for the purposes of this Part to have given notice to the Health
Service Executive.]

AMENDMENT

Section 51 substituted by s.75 and Schedule 7 of the Health Act 2004, No.42 of 2004, with effect from January 1, 2005 (S.I. No.887 of 2004).

DEFINITIONS

"relevant health board": s.49.
"pre-school service": s.49.

COMMENCEMENT

S.I. No. 399 of 1996, Child Care Act, 1991 (Commencement) Order, 1996, took effect as of December 18, 1996.

NOTE

This provides for notice requirements for both persons who are carrying on a pre-school service at the commencement of Pt VII of the Act and those who, after the commencement of Pt VII of the Act, propose to carry on a pre-school service.

Notice must be given to the relevant Health Service Executive which is the Health Service Executive for the area in which a pre-school service is being or is proposed to be carried on.

Where a person is carrying on a pre-school service art.9 of S.I. No.398 of 1996, Child Care (Pre-School Services) Regulations 1996 requires notice of the service to be given to the relevant Health Service Executive within six months of the date of commencement of Pt VII (S.I. No.399 of 1996 brought Pt VII into operation on December 18, 1996).

The notice must be in writing and in the form prescribed, a copy of which is annexed to S.I. No.398 of 1996, Child Care (Pre-school Services) Regulations 1996. All the particulars requested must be submitted along with the requisite fee.

Where a person proposes to carry on a pre-school service, then art.11 of S.I. No.398 of 1996, Child Care (Pre-school Services) Regulations 1996 applies which requires 28 days notice of the intention to commence the service. The notice must be in writing in the prescribed form and accompanied by the requisite fee.

Where any change in circumstances arises since the commencement of the pre-school service relevant to the notification given to the Health Service Executive, the person carrying on the pre-school service must inform the Health Service Executive of that change within 28 days.

The notification of change must be in writing in like manner to the notification requirement. Where a person ceases to carry on a pre-school service, notice, in writing, of that cessation must be given within 14 days.

Failure to comply with the requirements of this section or the regulations made thereunder may result in the penalties set out in s.57 on summary conviction.

It is important to note here that this is a notification of a carrying on of a service as opposed to a register of pre-school services. This is in contrast to the position with regard to children's residential centres, in Part VIII of this Act, s.61 makes provision for the maintenance by the Health Service Executive of a register of such centres. It would appear that the Health Service Executive would not be civilly liable for any harm resulting to a child in a pre-school service that had been notified to the Health Service Executive. This notification procedure should be contrasted with the registration process for child minders in England and the case of *T v Surrey C.C.* [1994] 4 All E.R. 577. Further, s.52, imposes a statutory obligation upon the person carrying on the pre-school service to safeguard the health, safety and welfare of children attending the service.

Duty of person carrying on pre-school service

52.—It shall be the duty of every person carrying on a pre-school service to take all reasonable measures to safeguard the health, safety and welfare of pre-school children attending the service and to comply with regulations made by the Minister under this Part.

DEFINITIONS

"pre-school service": s.49.
"the Minister": s.2.

COMMENCEMENT

Child Care Act, 1991 (Commencement) Order, 1996 (S.I. No. 399 of 1996) took effect as of December 18, 1996.

NOTE

This imposes upon persons carrying on a pre-school service a statutory obligation to safeguard the health, safety and welfare of pre-school children attending the service. Further, it is explicitly stated that the conduct of such services must be in accordance with regulations made by the Minister for Health under this part (S.I. No.398 of 1996, Child Care (Pre-school Services) Regulations 1996).

The statutory obligation is to take all reasonable measures. The minimum reasonable measures expected can be said to be those prescribed by the regulations (S.I. No.398 of 1996, Child Care (Pre-school Services) Regulations 1996).

Supervision of pre-school services

53.—[The Health Service Executive]shall cause to be visited from time to time each pre-school service [...] in order to ensure that the person carrying on the service is fulfilling the duties imposed on him under *section 52.*

AMENDMENT

Amendments by s.75 and Schedule 7 of the Health Act 2004, No.42 of 2004, with effect from January 1, 2005 (S.I. No.887 of 2004).

DEFINITIONS

"health board": s.2.
"pre-school service": s.49.

COMMENCEMENT

Child Care Act, 1991 (Commencement) Order, 1996 (S.I. No. 399 of 1996) took effect as of December 18, 1996.

NOTE

This obliges the Health Service Executive to visit pre-school services in its functional area to ensure that the person carrying on the service is fulfilling the duties imposed upon that person under s.52.

Article 32 of S.I. No.398 of 1996, Child Care (Pre-school Services) Regulations 1996, obliges the authorised person (s.55) conducting the inspection to furnish a report to the person carrying on the service of the outcome of the inspection. Article 32(2) provides that once an inspection and report thereof has been made, the Health Service Executive must take such steps as are reasonably necessary to enforce the Regulations. The most effective means of securing compliance with the Act and the regulations made thereunder is to prosecute a person carrying on a pre-school service for a breach of the provisions of the Act or regulations with the possibility of the person being prohibited from carrying on a pre-school service by order of the court under s.57(2).

Authorised persons

54.—(1) [The Health Service Executive shall appoint such and so many of its employees] as it thinks fit to be authorised persons for the purposes of this Part.

(2) [The Health Service Executive] may, with the consent of the Minister for Education, appoint an officer of that Minister to be an authorised person for the purposes of this Part.

(3) Every authorised person shall be furnished with a warrant of his appointment as an authorised person, and, when exercising any power conferred on an authorised person under this Part, shall, if requested by any person affected, produce the warrant to that person.

Amendment

Subsections (1) and (2) amended by s.75 and Schedule 7 of the Health Act 2004, No.42 of 2004, with effect from January 1, 2005 (S.I. No.887 of 2004).

DEFINITIONS

"authorised person": s.49 of the 1991 Act and article 3 of S.I. 398 of 1996, Child Care (Pre-School Services) Regulations, 1996.
"health board": s.2.

COMMENCEMENT

Child Care Act, 1991 (Commencement) Order, 1996 (S.I. No. 399 of 1996) took effect as of December 18, 1996.

NOTE

This provides for the appointment of authorised persons to inspect premises under s.55 where pre-school services are being carried out.

An authorised person is defined in s.54 as "a person appointed under section 54 of the Act to be an authorised person for the purposes of Part VII of the Act". The appointment of an authorised person is made by the Health Service Executive, which it is statutorily obliged to do, and the Health Service Executive determines the number of such authorised persons. Authorised persons are appointed from the officers of the Health Service Executive. An authorised person may be an appointment made by the Health Service Executive of an officer of the Minister for Education, provided the Minister for Education consents to the appointment of the officer as an authorised person (s.54(2)).

Subsection (3)

This requires that every authorised person must be furnished with a warrant of appointment as an authorised person. An authorised person must, if requested, produce his warrant to any person affected by the authorised person's exercise of powers under Pt VII (entering premises with a warrant issued under s.55(2) and inspection and examination of pre-school service premises).

Inspection by authorised persons

55.—(1) Where the [Health Service Executive] has received notification in accordance with *section 51* in respect of a pre-school service, an authorised person shall be entitled at all reasonable times to enter any premises (including a private dwelling) in which the service is being carried on.

(2) A justice of the District Court may, if satisfied on information on oath that there are reasonable grounds for believing that a pre-school service is being carried on in any premises (including a private dwelling) in respect of which notice has not been received by the [Health Service Executive] in accordance with *section 51*, issue a warrant authorising a person appointed by the [Executive] in accordance with section 54 to enter and inspect the premises.

(3) An authorised person who enters any premises in accordance with *subsection (1)* or (2) may make such examination into the condition of the premises and the care and attention which the pre-school children are receiving as may be necessary for the purposes of this Part.

(4) A warrant under *subsection (2)* may be issued by a justice of the District Court for the time being assigned to the district court district where the premises are situated.

AMENDMENT

Subsections (1) and (2) amended by s.75 and Schedule 7 of the Health Act 2004, No.42 of 2004, with effect from January 1, 2005 (S.I. No.887 of 2004).

DEFINITIONS

"authorised person": s.49.

"premises": art.3 of the Child Care (Pre-School Services) Regulations, 1996 (S.I. 398 of 1996).

"pre-school service": s.49.

"relevant health board": s.49.

COMMENCEMENT

Child Care Act, 1991 (Commencement) Order, 1996 (S.I. No. 399 of 1996) took effect as of December 18, 1996.

NOTE

Section 55 confers a statutory right of entry by an authorised person to inspect and examine premises in which a pre-school service is being carried on. The section provides for the issue of warrants for the purpose of entering and inspecting premises which have not been notified to the relevant Health Service Executive under s.51. There is also provision for the nature of the examination of premises entered by an authorised person.

Premises is not defined in s.49 of the Act but it is in Art.3 of the Child Care (Pre-School Services) Regulations 1996 as "a premises, building or part of a building, and any outoffices, yard, garden or land appurtenant thereto or usually enjoyed therewith in which a preschool service is being or is proposed to be carried on".

Subsection (1)

Section 55(1) provides an authorised person with a statutory right to enter any premises, including a private dwelling, in which a pre-school service is being carried on. The entry may be at all reasonable times. The right to enter is, however, subject to the premises in question having been notified to the Health Service Executive in accordance with s.51. Where premises in which a pre-school service is being carried on have not been notified, then the right of entry to inspect must be by warrant issued to that effect under s.55(2).

Subsection (2)

Section 55(2) provides for an inspection and examination of pre-school service premises and the service being therein provided, where notice of the pre-school service has not been notified to the relevant Health Service Executive. In these circumstances a warrant from the District Court in the district in which the premises are situated must be obtained. The application for a warrant to enter and inspect must be on application in writing and information on oath (see r.33(2) of the District Court (Child Care) Rules 1995). The District Court judge in question must be satisfied that there are reasonable grounds for believing that a pre-school service is being carried on in the premises in question, which may include a private dwelling. The issue of a warrant under this section authorises the entry and inspection of the condition of the premises and the care and attention which the pre-school children are receiving.

Where the pre-school service is being carried on in a private dwelling, the extent of the inspection, whether as of right or by warrant, may only be in relation to those areas of the private dwelling in which the pre-school service is being carried on.

The penalties on summary conviction for failing to allow an authorised person entry, either as of right or by warrant, are a fine not exceeding €1,269.74 (s.57(1)).

Subsection (3)

Section 55(3) provides for the nature and extent of an inspection by an authorised person either as of right under s.55(1) or by warrant to that effect under s.55(2). An authorised person is entitled to inspect both the condition of the premises (state of repair, facilities etc.) and the care and attention that the pre-school children are receiving.

Subsection (4)

Section 55(4) provides that an application for a warrant under s.55(2) to enter and inspect a premises may be issued by a District Court judge in the district in which the premises in question are situated.

COMMENCEMENT

Child Care Act, 1991 (Commencement) Order, 1996 (S.I. No.399 of 1996) took effect as of December 18, 1996.

Provision by [the Health Service Executive] of pre-school services and information

56.—(1) [The Health Service Executive] may, subject to any general directions given by the Minister, provide pre-school services [...] and provide and maintain premises for that purpose.

(2) The Minister may, after consultation with the Minister for Education and the Minister for the Environment, make regulations for the purpose of securing the health, safety and welfare and promoting the development of children attending pre-school services provided by [the Health Service Executive].

[(3) The Health Service Executive shall make available to any interested person information on pre-school services in any of its functional areas, whether those services are provided by the Executive or otherwise.]

AMENDMENT

Subsections (1) and (2) amended, and subs.(3) substituted, by s.75 and Schedule 7 of the Health Act 2004, No.42 of 2004, with effect from January 1, 2005 (S.I. No.887 of 2004).

DEFINITIONS

"area": s.2.
"health board": s.2.
"pre-school service": s.49.
"the Minister": s.2.

COMMENCEMENT

Child Care Act, 1991 (Commencement) Order, 1996 (S.I. No.399 of 1996) took effect as of December 18, 1996.

NOTE

This section provides for the carrying out of pre-school services by the Health Service Executive and the manner in which this may be done.

Subsection (1)
This confers upon the Health Service Executive the statutory authority, subject only to general direction given by the Minister for Health, to provide pre-school services in their functional areas and to provide and maintain premises for that purpose.

Subsection (2)
This authorises the Minister for Health, after consultation with both the Minister for Education and the Minister for the Environment, to make regulations securing the health, safety and welfare and promoting the development of children attending pre-school services provided by the Health Service Executive. This latter obligation is not required of persons carrying on pre-school services.

Subsection (3)
This obliges the Health Service Executive to make available information on pre-school services in its area, to any interested person. The information so provided may be that of the Health Service Executive or other persons or bodies.

Offences under *Part VII*

57.—(1) A person who—
   (*a*) refuses to allow an authorised person to enter any premises in accordance with *subsection (1)* or *(2)* of *section 55* or who obstructs or impedes an authorised person in the exercise of any of his powers under *subsection (3)* of that section, or
   (*b*) contravenes the requirements of this Part or of any regulations made thereunder,
shall be guilty of an offence and shall be liable on summary conviction to a fine not exceeding €1,269.74.

(2) Where a person is convicted of an offence under this Part the court may, either in addition to or in substitution for the imposition of a fine, by order declare that the person shall be prohibited for such period as may be specified in the order from carrying on a pre-school 5 service.

(3) A person who contravenes an order made under *subsection (2)* shall be guilty of an offence and shall be liable on summary conviction to a fine not exceeding €1,269.74 or to imprisonment for a term not exceeding 12 months or both.

DEFINITIONS

   "authorised person": s.49 and art.3 of the Child Care (Pre-School Services) Regulations, 1996 (S.I. 398 of 1996).

COMMENCEMENT

   Child Care Act, 1991 (Commencement) Order, 1996 (S.I. No. 399 of 1996) took effect as of December 18, 1996.

NOTE

   This provides for certain specified offences for breach of the provisions of Pt VII and the regulations made thereunder (S.I. No.398 of 1996, Child Care (Pre-school Services) Regulations 1996). The penalties on summary conviction vary from a fine not exceeding €1,269.74 and/or a term of imprisonment to a prohibition from carrying on a pre-school service for a stated period.

Subsection (1)
   This makes it an offence to refuse to allow an authorised person to enter any premises as of right under s.55(1), where the premises in which the pre-school service have been notified to the relevant Health Service Executive under s.51, or on foot of a warrant issued under s.55(2), where the premises in question have not been notified to the relevant Health Service Executive. In addition, it is an offence to either impede or obstruct an examination of the condition of the premises and the care and attention which the pre-school children are receiving.
   A further offence under subs.(1)(*b*) may be committed where a person fails to comply with the provisions of Pt VII or the regulations made thereunder. The relevant section which may be contravened is s.51 which obliges those persons who are carrying on or who propose to carry on a pre-school service to notify the relevant Health Service Executive of the service. This is the simplest contravention of Pt VII to establish in a prosecution.

Section 52 is also capable of contravention by a person carrying on a pre-school service. It may be more difficult to establish that a person has failed to take all reasonable measures to safeguard the health, safety and welfare of children attending a pre-school service.

To the extent that there is a continued failure to comply with the provisions of the Regulations governing this Part (S.I. No.398 of 1996, Child Care (Pre-school Services) Regulations 1996), that is where the Health Service Executive has requested the taking of certain measures after an inspection under s.54 and in reliance upon art.32 of S.I. No.398 of 1996, Child Care (Pre-school Services) Regulations 1996), then a person may be liable for prosecution for contravention of any of the articles imposing an obligation upon them.

The maximum fine that may be imposed for any of the above offences is €1,269.74 on summary conviction.

Subsection (2)

This provides an alternative and/or additional sanction for an offence committed under this Part, be it a breach of the provisions of Pt VII or the Regulations (S.I. No.398 of 1996, Child Care (Pre-school Services) Regulations 1996). The sanction is the prohibition from carrying on a pre-school service for such period as specified by the court. This may be in substitution for, or in addition to, a fine. In terms of attempting to obtain compliance with the provisions of Pt VII and S.I. No.398 of 1996, Child Care (Pre-school Services) Regulations 1996 this is probably the most effective, particularly where the pre-school service is run on a commercial basis and for profit.

Subsection (3) This provides the penalty on summary conviction for carrying on a pre-school service where a court has prohibited such under s.57(2). A maximum fine of €1,269.74 or a term of imprisonment not exceeding 12 months or both may be imposed, in addition to a prohibition under s.57(2).

Exemptions from provisions of this Part

58.—For the avoidance of doubt it is hereby declared that the provisions of this Part shall not apply to—

(a) the care of one or more pre-school children undertaken by a relative of the child or children or the spouse of such relative,

(b) a person taking care of one or more pre-school children of the same family and no other such children (other than that person's own such children) in that person's home,

(c) a person taking care of not more than 3 pre-school children of different families (other than that person's own such children) in that person's home.

DEFINITIONS

"pre-school child": s.49.

COMMENCEMENT

Child Care Act, 1991 (Commencement) Order, 1996 (S.I. No. 399 of 1996) took effect as of December 18, 1996.

NOTE

This provides for the exemption from the provisions of this Part of certain forms of care, for example where such care is given to a limited number of children only, or where such care is given by relatives.

Paragraph (a)

This provides that where one or more pre-school children are cared for by a relative, or the spouse of a relative of that child or children, then the provisions of Pt VII will not apply.

Paragraph (b)

This provides that a person taking care of one or more pre-school children of the same family in that person's home is exempt from the provisions of Pt VII.

Paragraph (c)

This provides that this Part of the Act shall not apply to a person taking care of not more than three pre-school children of different families in that persons own home.

PART VIII

CHILDREN'S RESIDENTIAL CENTRES

Definitions for *Part VIII*

59.—In this Part—

"children's residential centre" means any home or other institution for the residential care of children [in the care of the Health Service Executive] or other children who are not receiving adequate care and protection excluding—

(*a*) an institution managed by or on behalf of a Minister of the Government or [the Health Service Executive],

(*b*) an institution in which a majority of the children being maintained are being treated for acute illnesses,

(*c*) [...],

(*d*) a mental institution within the meaning of the Mental Treatment Acts, 1945 to 1966,

(*e*) an institution which is a "certified school" within the meaning of *Part IV* of the Children Act 1908, functions in relation to which stand vested in the Minister for Education;

"centre" means a children's residential centre;

["register" means a register of children's residential centres that is established or deemed to have been established by the Health Service Executive under *section 61*, and cognate words shall be construed accordingly;]

"registered proprietor", in relation to a registered children's residential centre, means the person whose name is entered in the register as the person carrying on the centre;

"the regulations" means the regulations under *section 63*.

AMENDMENT

Paragraph (*c*) of definition of "children's residential centre" deleted by s.267 of the Children Act 2001, No.24 of 2001, which came into effect on May 1, 2002 (S.I. No.151 of 2002).

Definition of "children's residential centre" amended and definition of "register" substituted by s.75 and Schedule 7 of the Health Act 2004, No.42 of 2004, with effect from January 1, 2005 (S.I. No.887 of 2004).

DEFINITIONS

"children's residential centre": s.59.
"centre": s.59.
"register": s.59.
"registered proprietor": s.59.
"the regulations": s.59.

COMMENCEMENT

Child Care Act, 1991 (Commencement) Order, 1996 (S.I. No. 399 of 1996) took effect as of December 18, 1996.

NOTE

This is the definition section for Pt VIII which governs children's residential centres and the registration, regulation and discontinuance of them. There is provision for appeals from the refusal of the Health Service Executive to register a children's residential centre and the prescribing of offences under this Part.

The definition of "children's residential centre" requires some explanation as to the exclusion of a number of institutions from the definition. Only a children's residential centre is subject to the provisions of the Act and more particularly regulations made thereunder governing standards in such centres. As the institutions listed in s.59(*a*)–(*e*) are either state or Health Service Executive owned or maintained there would be little point in these institutions being the subject of review and supervision by themselves. The other institutions provide predominantly medical care and treatment and to impose upon such "hospital" like institutions obligations in relation to the care of children may frustrate the primary objective of such institutions.

Section 101 of the Children Act 2001 enables a court to direct a child to reside in a children's residential centre whilst remanded on bail pending the preparation of a report on the child prior to taking a decision as to whether or not to convict the child of an offence.

Section 267(1)(*b*) of the Children Act 2001 deleted para.(*c*) of s.59 (an institution for the care and maintenance of physically or mentally handicapped children) from the exclusion from the definition of a children's residential centre.

Of note also is the effect of s.67 which converts the institution specified therein into residential children's centres. (See the speech of Minister for State Treacy, 129 *Seanad Debates* Cols 810–812 and 817–819, and 403 *Dáil Debates* Cols 2602–2604.) This Part of the Act was extensively amended at Report and Final Stage in the Dáil (see 403 *Dáil Debates* Cols 2601–2634).

Prohibition of unregistered children's residential centres

60.—(1) A person shall not carry on a children's residential centre unless the centre is registered and the person is the registered proprietor thereof.

(2) A person shall not be in charge of a centre unless the centre is registered.

(3) Any person who contravenes a provision of this section shall be guilty of an offence.

DEFINITIONS
"children's residential centre": s.59.
"centre": s.59.
"registered proprietor": s.59.

COMMENCEMENT
Child Care Act, 1991 (Commencement) Order, 1996 (S.I. No. 399 of 1996) took effect as of December 18, 1996.

NOTE

This prohibits a person carrying on an unregistered children's residential centre (centre). Where the centre is registered, a person is prohibited from carrying on that centre unless registered as the registered proprietor in accordance with s.61.

A "children's residential centre" is defined in s.59 as "any home or other institution for the residential care of children in the care of the Health Service Executive or other children who are not receiving adequate care and protection". Excluded from this definition are a number of state-owned and other institutions which are as follows: an institution managed by or on behalf of a Minister of the Government or the Health Service Executive; an institution in which a majority of the children being maintained are being treated for acute illnesses; a mental institution within the meaning of the Mental Treatment Acts 1945–1966; and an institution which is a "certified school" within the meaning of Pt IV of the Children Act 1908, functions in relation to which stand vested in the Minister for Education (see General Note to s.36(1)).

A "registered proprietor" is defined as in s.59, in relation to children's residential centres as "the person whose name is entered in the register as the person carrying on the centre".

The "register" for the purpose of this section is defined as "a register of children's residential centres established under section 61 and, in relation to a particular Health Service Executive, means the register established by that Executive".

Subsection (2)
This prohibits a person being in charge of a centre unless the centre is registered in accordance with s.61. This effectively precludes the carrying on of a centre unless the centre is registered as a centre. A centre cannot be registered unless there is a registered proprietor registered to carry on the centre.

Subsection (3)
This provides that contravention of the registration requirements in relation both to centres and registered proprietors is an offence. The penalties on summary conviction are set out in s.64, where a person may be liable to a fine not exceeding €1,269.74 or to a term of imprisonment not exceeding 12 months or to both a fine and a term of imprisonment.

Registration of children's residential centres

61.—[(1) The Health Service Executive shall establish and maintain a register of children's residential services in each functional area of the Executive.]

[(1A) For the purpose of *subsection* (*1*), each register of children's residential centres established by the Health Service Executive before the amendment of this section by the Health Act 2004 shall be deemed to have been established by the Health Service Executive and shall be maintained by the Executive.]

(2)(*a*) There shall be entered in a register in respect of each centre registered therein the name of the person by whom it is carried on, the name of the person who is in charge of it, the address of the premises in which it is carried on, a statement of the number of children who can be accommodated in the centre, the date on which the registration is to take effect (referred to subsequently in this section as "the date of registration") and such other (if any) particulars as may be prescribed.

(*b*) A register maintained under this section shall be made available for inspection free of charge by members of the public at all reasonable times.

(3)(*a*) [The Health Service Executive] may, on application to it in that behalf by a person who proposes to carry on a centre […], register or refuse to register the centre.

(*b*) Subject to the provisions of this section, the period of a registration shall be 3 years from the date of registration.

[(*c*) An application for registration made to the Health Service Executive before the amendment of this subsection by the Health Act 2004 shall be deemed to have been made to the Health Service Executive if the health board has not, before the establishment day of the Executive, registered or refused to register the centre in relation to which the application was made.]

(4) [The Health Service Executive] may remove a centre from the register.

(5) [The Health Service Executive] shall not—

(*a*) refuse to register a centre in relation to which an application for its registration has been duly made, or

(*b*) remove a centre from the register,

unless—

(i) it is of opinion that—

(I) the premises to which the application or, as the case may be, the registration relates do not comply with the regulations, or

(II) the carrying on of the centre will not be or is not in compliance with the regulations, or

(ii) the applicant or the registered proprietor, as the case may be, or the person in charge or, as the case may be, proposed to be in charge of the centre has been convicted of an offence under this Part or of any other offence that is such as to render the person unfit to carry on or, as the case may be, to be in charge of the centre, or

(iii) the applicant or the registered proprietor, as the case may be, has

failed or refused to furnish the [Health Service Executive] with
information requested by it pursuant to *subsection (8)* or has furnished
the [Health Service Executive] with information that is false or
misleading in a material particular, or
(iv) the registered proprietor has, not more than one year before the date
from which the registration or removal from the register would take
effect, contravened a condition under *subsection (6)*.
(6)(*a*) [The Health Service Executive] may—
(i) at the time of registration or subsequently attach to the
registration conditions in relation to the carrying on of the centre
concerned and such other matters as it considers appropriate
having regard to its functions under this Part,
(ii) attach different conditions to the registration of different
centres, and
(iii) amend or revoke a condition of registration.
(*b*) Conditions imposed under this subsection or amendments and
revocations under this subsection shall be notified in writing to the
registered proprietor of the centre concerned.
[(6A) Conditions imposed, amended or revoked by the Health Service
Executive before the amendment of this subsection by the Health Act 2004
shall be deemed to have been imposed, amended or revoked by the Health
Service Executive.]
(7) An application for registration shall be in the prescribed form or in a
form to the like effect.
(8)(*a*) [The Health Service Executive] may request an applicant for
registration or, as the case may be, a registered proprietor to furnish
it with such information as it considers necessary for the purposes
of its functions under this Part.
(*b*) A person who, whether in pursuance of a request or otherwise,
furnishes information to [the Health Service Executive] for the
purposes of this Part that is false or misleading in a material particular
shall be guilty of an offence unless he shows that, at the time the
information was furnished [to the Executive], he was not aware that
it was false or misleading in a material particular.
(9) The registered proprietor of a centre who proposes to carry on the centre
immediately after the expiration of the period of registration of the centre may
apply under *subsection (3)* to the [Health Service Executive] not less than 2
months before such expiration for the registration of the centre and, [if the
Executive] does not notify him before such expiration that it proposes to refuse
to register the centre, it shall register the centre and its date of registration
shall be the day following the day of such expiration.
(10)(*a*) Where a registered children's residential centre commences to be
carried on by a person other than the registered proprietor—
(i) the centre shall thereupon cease to be registered,
(ii) the person shall (if he has not done so before such
commencement) apply not later than 4 weeks after it to [the
Health Service Executive] for the registration of the centre,
and, if the application is granted, the date of registration of

the centre shall be that of the day following the day of the cesser aforesaid,

(iii) if the application aforesaid is duly made, and is not refused then, during the period from the commencement aforesaid until the centre is registered, it shall be deemed, for the purposes of *section 60* to be registered and there shall be deemed to be attached to the registration any conditions attached to the previous registration.

(*b*) A person who contravenes *paragraph* (*a*)(ii) shall be guilty of an offence.

(11)(*a*) Where [the Health Service Executive] proposes to refuse to register a children's residential centre, to remove a centre from the register, to attach a condition to, or amend or revoke a condition attached to, a registration, it shall notify in writing the applicant or the registered proprietor, as the case may be, of its proposal and of the reasons for it.

(*b*) A person who has been notified of a proposal under *paragraph* (*a*) may, within 21 days of the receipt of the notification, make representations in writing to the [Health Service Executive] [and the Executive] shall—

(i) before deciding the matter, take into consideration any representations duly made to it under this paragraph in relation to the proposal, and

(ii) notify the person in writing of its decision and of the reasons for it.

(12) A notification of a proposal of [the Health Service Executive] under *subsection (11)* shall include a statement that the person concerned may make representations to [the Health Service Executive] within 21 days of the receipt by him of the notification and a notification of a decision of [the Health Service Executive] under *subsection (11)* shall include a statement that the person concerned may appeal to the District Court under *section 62* against the decision within 21 days from the receipt by him of the notification.

(13) Where, in relation to a children's residential centre, there is a contravention of a condition of registration, the registered proprietor and the person in charge of the centre shall be guilty of an offence.

AMENDMENT

Subsection (1) substituted, subss.(1A), (3)(*c*) and (6A) inserted, subss.(3), (4), (5), (6), (8), (9), (10), (11) and (12) amended by s.75 and Schedule 7 of the Health Act 2004, No.42 of 2004, with effect from January 1, 2005 (S.I. No.887 of 2004).

DEFINITIONS

"area": s.2.
"children's residential centre": s.59.
"centre": s.59.
"health board": s.2.

"person in charge": art.3 of Child Care (Standards in Children's Residential Centres) Regulations 1996 (S.I. 397 of 1996).
"register": s.59.
"registered proprietor": s.59.

COMMENCEMENT

Child Care Act, 1991 (Commencement) Order, 1996 (S.I. No. 399 of 1996) took effect as of December 18, 1996.

NOTE

This imposes upon each Health Service Executive the statutory obligation to both establish and maintain a register of children's residential centres in its functional area (a register).

The duties and powers of the Health Service Executive in relation to registration of centres are set out in this section which include an obligation to register all applications to register centres save in accordance with s.61(5), remove a registration and prescribe conditions for the carrying on of a centre. The duration of a registration is specified.

Subsection (2)
This provides for requiring certain details to be entered in the register and for public inspection of the register.

The register, where a centre is being registered, must contain the following: the name of the person carrying on the register: the name of the person who is in charge of the centre: the address of the premises in which the centre operates; a statement concerning the number of children that can be accommodated in the centre; the date on which the registration is to take effect; and such other particulars as may be prescribed.

A register of children's residential centres must be available for public inspection at all reasonable times.

Subsection (3)
This authorises the Health Service Executive to register or refuse to register a children's residential centre. Where the Health Service Executive registers a centre it may attach conditions to be complied with in the carrying on of the centre at the time of registration or subsequently (s.61(a)(i).

Where the Health Service Executive refuses to register a centre then that refusal may only be on the basis of the grounds set out in s.61(5)(a) and (b)(i)–(iv) and the Health Service Executive must notify the applicant of the proposal to refuse registration in accordance with s.61(11) who is entitled to make representations to the Health Service Executive in respect of that proposal.

The duration of a registration of a centre is three years from the date of registration (the date on which the registration is to take effect as contained in the register). The three-year period of registration is subject to that registration being removed in accordance with s.61(4), (5) or (11).

Subsection (4)
This authorises the removal of a registration of a children's residential centre. The removal must be on the basis of one of the grounds set out in s.61(5)(b)(i)–(iv) and in compliance with s.61(11) and (12).

Subsection (5)
This provides that the Health Service Executive is obliged to register a centre for

which an application for registration has been duly made unless the matter set out in s.61(5)(i)–(iv) arises. Section 61(7) provides for the form of application. The basis for a refusal or removal of a registration relates either to the premises or the carrying on of the centre and offences committed under this Part by the applicant, the registered proprietor or person in charge.

A refusal to register or a proposal to remove a registration must be in accordance with the provisions of this section. The Health Service Executive must refuse or remove a registration in the following circumstances. The wording of the section would appear not to afford the Health Service Executive a discretion in the matter.

Firstly, that, in the opinion of the Health Service Executive, the premises to which the application or registration relates does not comply with the regulations (S.I. No.397 of 1996, Child Care (Standards in Children's Residential Centres) Regulations 1996).

Secondly, that, in the opinion of the Health Service Executive, the carrying on of the centre will not be or is not be in compliance with the regulations.

Thirdly, the applicant or the registered proprietor or person in charge of the centre has been convicted of an offence under this Part or of any other offence that is such as to render the person unfit to carry on, or as the case may be, be in charge of the centre. The relevant offences under this Part are s.60, the carrying on of a children's residential centre that has not been registered. Section 61(10)(1) makes it an offence for a person other than the registered proprietor to carry on a centre. Section 61(13) makes it an offence for a registered proprietor to contravene a condition of registration. Section 63(3) concerns a failure or refusal by the registered proprietor or person in charge to comply with a provision of the regulations and s.63(5) concerns the wilful obstruction or interference with the Health Service Executive or its officer in the performance of functions under regulations or the failure or refusal to comply with a requirement of the Health Service Executive or its officer under regulations. Section 63(4)(*c*) makes it an offence to carry on a centre where a person has been disqualified by a court from so doing.

Fourthly, the applicant or registered proprietor has failed to furnish to the Executive with information requested by it pursuant to s.61(8) or has furnished false or misleading information in a material particular.

Fifthly, where the registered proprietor has contravened a condition imposed by the Health Service Executive under s.61(6) in a period not exceeding one year prior to the date on which the registration or removal would take place.

The refusal to register must be notified to the applicant and be in accordance with s.61(11) (right to make representations) and s.61(12) (information on right to make representations and an appeal to the District Court).

Subsection (6)

This confers a discretion upon the Health Service Executive in the making of conditions in relation to the carrying on of a centre either at the time of registration or subsequently. The Health Service Executive may also stipulate other matters as it considers appropriate in light of its functions under this Part.

It is important to note that any conditions or other matters stipulated attach to the application which makes the registration contingent upon the satisfaction of those conditions or other matters. A centre which cannot be registered cannot lawfully operate as a children's residential centre.

The conditions likely to be imposed by the Health Service Executive are those provisions of S.I. No.397 of 1996, Child Care (Standards in Children's Residential Centres) Regulations 1996 which have not been complied with at the time of application for registration.

The Health Service Executive is not obliged to attach conditions universally applicable to all centres and may attach different conditions to different centres. Where a condition is attached to a registration, the Health Service Executive may amend or revoke that condition and must inform the registered proprietor of that centre, in writing, of the making, amending or revoking of that condition.

In addition the applicant or registered proprietor has a right to make representations of which he must be informed by the Health Service Executive (s.61(11) and (12)). In addition there is a right of appeal to the District Court against the decision of the Health Service Executive concerning a condition. The applicant or registered proprietor must be informed by the Health Service Executive of this right of appeal.

Subsection (7)

This provides that an application for registration be in the prescribed form or a form to like effect. The Schedule to S.I. No.397 of 1996, Child Care (Standards in Children's Residential Centres) Regulations 1996 contains the relevant form. Information on the following must be furnished: name and address of centre; aims, objectives and organisational structure of centre; proprietors of centre; person in charge; qualifications and employment record of person in charge; staffing; premises and details of accommodation for use by residents; education arrangements for residents; health and social care arrangements; insurance; other amenities; meals; and fire precaution arrangements. In addition to the application form, a report of a chartered engineer or suitably qualified architect with relevant experience in fire safety and management must be submitted stating that all the requirements of the statutory fire authority have been complied with.

Subsection (8)

In addition to the prescribed application form, the Health Service Executive may request an applicant or a registered proprietor to furnish such information as the Executive considers necessary for the purpose of its functions under this Part. The Schedule to S.I. No.397 of 1996, Child Care (Standards in Children's Residential Centres) Regulations 1996 (application form) identifies the type of information that may be requested under this provision. The information listed concerns: any brochure or advertisement to be used for the centre; plans of the interior design of the centre giving details of the dimensions of all rooms intended for residents use and also indicate owners/staff rooms; the name and address of the G.P./medical officer who will be responsible for the medical examination of residents; and a two-week menu plan for breakfast, lunch and dinner.

Additional information that may be requested relating to a certificate of planning permission for the centre and sample of job descriptions/contracts of staff and written statements to staff on Health and Safety at Work.

The furnishing of false or misleading information, whether requested by the Health Service Executive or otherwise furnished (in an application for registration) is an offence. The false information must be misleading as to a material particular. A material particular could be said to be such that the Health Service Executive would require satisfaction of before registering the centre. Any false or misleading information requested in the application form or those matters which the Health Service Executive must be satisfied of in S.I. No.397 of 1996, Child Care (Standards in Children's Residential Centres) Regulations 1996 could be considered a material particular.

A person who does furnish false or misleading information may avail of the defence provided that he was unaware that the material particular was false or misleading at the time the information was provided. The penalty on summary conviction for this offence is a fine not exceeding €1,269.74 or a term of imprisonment not exceeding 12 months or both (s.64).

Subsection (9)

This provides for a renewal of a registration of a centre and the procedure to be followed. The period of registration is three years from the date of registration (that date stated in the register on which registration is to commence) and the application to renew that registration must be made two months prior to the expiry of the registration. The application is made under s.61(3) which is in effect a first-time registration application to which the provisions of this Part apply (power of Health Service Executive to refuse, attachment of conditions and requests for information).

A renewal of a registration automatically occurs where the Health Service Executive does not notify the applicant of a refusal. The Health Service Executive must register the centre and in these circumstances the date of registration under this provision takes effect on the day following the expiry of the first registration.

Where there is notification of a refusal under this section, then the provisions of s.61(11) operate whereby the Health Service Executive is obliged to notify in writing the applicant of the proposed refusal and furnish the reasons for the refusal. Further, the applicant may, within 21 days of the notification proposing refusal, make representations in writing to the Health Service Executive which must consider those representations and notify the applicant of its decision and the reasons for it. The applicant may then appeal to the District Court.

Subsection (10)

This provides for the consequences and procedures to be followed where a registered children's residential centre commences to be carried on by a person other than a registered proprietor. This might arise where a registered proprietor is convicted of an offence under s.63(3) for failing or refusing to comply with a provision of the regulations (S.I. No.397 of 1996, Child Care (Standards in Children's Residential Centres) Regulations 1996) and is subsequently disqualified under s.63(4)(*a*) from carrying on a centre and another individual commences to carry on the centre.

Where this arises, the centre automatically ceases to be registered which renders the carrying on of the centre unlawful. The person must then apply within four weeks of the date on which the centre ceased to be registered to the Health Service Executive for registration of the centre. Where the Health Service Executive registers the centre, the date of registration is the day following the date of cessation. Provision is made for the period between cessation of registration and the date of registration to deem the centre registered under s.60 for that period. Any conditions that attached to the previous registration are deemed to attach to the registration (see s.62(4)(*b*)(ii)(II)).

Section 61(10)(*b*) makes it an offence to fail to apply for a registration where a previous registration has ceased. The penalty for such an offence is set out in s.64 where a person may be liable, on summary conviction, to a fine not exceeding €1,269.74 or to a term of imprisonment not exceeding 12 months or to both.

Subsection (11)

This obliges the Health Service Executive to notify the applicant or registered proprietor of a proposal and the reasons for it of the following: a refusal to register a children's residential centre; the removal of a children's residential centre from the register; attaching a condition to a registration of a centre; amending a condition to a registration of a centre; revoking a condition to a registration of a centre (see s.62(4)(*a*) on the status of centres on notification). The notification of the above must be accompanied by a statement adhering to the requirements of s.61(12) which requires the applicant or registered proprietor to be informed of the right to make representations to the Health Service Executive, within the time specified, in relation to a refusal to register and any conditions attaching thereto, and that an appeal lies to the District

Court against the decision of the Health Service Executive within the specified time.

Where a person has been notified under this subsection of a proposal, he may, within 21 days of receipt of notification, make representations in writing to the Health Service Executive. The applicant must be informed of the right to make such representations (see s.61(12)). On receipt of such representations the Health Service Executive is obliged to consider those representations before making a decision on the proposal. Where a decision is reached, the Health Service Executive must notify the applicant or registered proprietor of the decision and the reasons for it.

Subsection (12)

This obliges the Health Service Executive to furnish with a notification under s.61(11), a statement that the applicant or registered proprietor is entitled to make representations to the Health Service Executive within 21 days of receipt of that notification. The notification and statement as to representation relates to a proposal to refuse registration, attach, amend or revoke a condition of registration.

Where the Health Service Executive makes a decision on that proposal, that decision must be notified to the applicant or the registered proprietor with a statement informing them of the right to appeal to the District Court under s.62, within 21 days of receipt of the decision.

Subsection (13)

This makes it an offence to contravene a condition attaching to a registration. Both the registered proprietor and person in charge are liable on summary conviction to a fine not exceeding €1,269.74 or a term of imprisonment not exceeding 12 months or to both.

Appeals

62.—(1) A person, being the registered proprietor or, as the case may be, the person intending to be the registered proprietor, of a children's residential centre, may appeal to the District Court against a decision of [the Health Service Executive] to refuse to register the centre, to remove the centre from the register or to attach a condition, or to amend or revoke a condition attached, to the registration of the centre and such an appeal shall be brought within 21 days of the receipt by the person of the notification of the decision under *section 61* and that court may, as it thinks proper, confirm the decision or direct [the Health Service Executive], as may be appropriate, to register, or to restore the registration of, the centre, to withdraw the condition or the amendment to or revocation of a condition, to attach a specified condition to the registration or to make a specified amendment to a condition of the registration.

(2) The jurisdiction conferred on the District Court by this section shall be exercised by the justice of the District Court for the time being assigned to the district court district in which the centre concerned is situated.

(3) A decision of the District Court under this section on a question of fact shall be final.

(4) Where a notification of a decision specified in *subsection (1)* (other than a decision to refuse to register a centre which was not registered or deemed to be registered at the time of the relevant application for registration) is given under *section 61*, then—

    (*a*) during such period from such notification (not being less than 21 days) as the [Health Service Executive] considers reasonable and specifies in the notification, the centre shall be treated as if the decision had not been made and, if the decision was to refuse an application under *paragraph* (*a*) of *section 61(10)* for registration, be treated as if it had been registered and the registration had attached to it any conditions attached to the relevant registration that had ceased by virtue of *subparagraph* (i) of the said *paragraph* (*a*), and

(*b*) if an appeal against the decision is brought under this section, during—

    (i) the period from the end of the period aforesaid until the determination or withdrawal of the appeal or any appeal therefrom or from any such appeal, and

    (ii) such further period (if any) as the court concerned considers reasonable and specifies in its decision,

the centre shall—

    (I) be treated for the purposes of *section 61* as if the appeal had been upheld, and

    (II) if the appeal was against a decision of the [Health Service Executive] to refuse an application under *paragraph* (*a*) of *section 61(10)* for registration, be treated as if the registration had attached to it any conditions attached to the relevant registration that had ceased by virtue of *subparagraph* (i) of the said paragraph (*a*).

(5) The [Health Service Executive] shall be given notice of an appeal under this section and shall be entitled to appear, be heard and adduce evidence on the hearing of the appeal.

AMENDMENT

Amendments by s.75 and Schedule 7 of the Health Act 2004, No.42 of 2004, with effect from January 1, 2005 (S.I. No.887 of 2004).

DEFINITIONS

"centre": s.59.
"health board": s.2.
"registered proprietor": s.59.

COMMENCEMENT

Child Care Act, 1991 (Commencement) Order, 1996 (S.I. No. 399 of 1996) took effect as of December 18, 1996.

NOTE

This section provides for an appeal procedure to the District Court from a decision of the Health Service Executive. The decisions that may be appealed and the consequences of a district court decision on the matter is prescribed. In addition there is provision governing the status of children's residential centres in the period between the decision of the Health Service Executive and the determination of the district court appeal.

Subsection (1)
   This provides that the registered proprietor or person intending to be a registered proprietor may appeal against a decision of the Health Service Executive to the District Court, which is conferred with the jurisdiction to determine the appeal.
   The decisions that may be appealed are a refusal to register the centre, a removal of a centre from the register, the attaching of a condition to the registration and the amending or revoking of a condition to the registration of the centre.
   The appeal must be brought within 21 days of the date of notification of the Health Service Executive's decision and must be on notice to the Health Service Executive and served at least seven days prior to the hearing of the appeal. The appellant must also lodge with the district court clerk a copy of the Health Service Executive's decision or a copy of the notification under s.61(11)(*b*)(ii) (see Ord.84, r.32 of S.I. No.93 of 1997, District Court Rules 1997).
   The District Court may, as it thinks proper, determine the appeal in any one of the following ways: confirm the decision of the Health Service Executive; direct the Health Service Executive to register or restore registration of the centre; direct the withdrawal of the condition or the amendment or revocation of a condition. In addition, the District Court may also direct the attaching of specified conditions to the registration or make a specified amendment to a condition to the registration.

Subsection (2)
   This requires that the appeal be heard by a Judge of the District Court in the district court district in which the centre concerned is situated.

Subsection (3)
   This provides that a decision of the District Court on a question of fact shall be final and against which no appeal may lie.

Subsection (4)
   This provides for the status of a centre in the period after the Health Service Executive decision has been made and for the period between the expiry of the time within which to bring an appeal and the determination of that appeal. In effect the centre is deemed to be registered or a decision in relation to a condition thereto deemed to have been made during these periods.
   The period during which a centre is deemed to be registered arises when the Health Service Executive notifies its decision to the applicant or registered proprietor. From the time of notification of the decision, subs.4(*a*) deems that decision not to have been made and the centre is deemed to be registered, notwithstanding the decision to refuse registration. The relevant period during which this occurs commences from the time the notification is received until that time as considered reasonable by the Health Service Executive and specified in the notification. In any event the relevant period shall not be less than 21 days.
   The only exclusion to either the deeming of a decision having not been made or the deeming of a registration where there has been a refusal, is where under s.61(10) a centre may be deemed to be registered in the period between application for registration and the decision to register, where the application arises from a person carrying on a centre who is not the registered proprietor.
   Where there is an appeal to the District Court against a decision of the Health Service Executive, then between the expiry of the period stated in the notification and until the determination, withdrawal or appeal of the district court proceedings to the Circuit Court, the centre, during that period or such further period as considered reasonable and specified by the court (either District or Circuit), shall be treated as if the appeal

had been upheld (appeal against a refusal or a condition) and where the appeal concerns a refusal to register under s.61(10)(*a*) (an application to carrying on a centre by a person who is not the registered proprietor) any condition attaching to the registration, which automatically ceases, shall be deemed to attach.

Subsection (5)
   This provides that the Health Service Executive must be given notice of an appeal (see Ord.84, r.32 of S.I. No.93 of 1997, District Court Rules 1997). In addition the Health Service Executive has the right to appear, be heard and give evidence in any appeal.

Regulations in relation to children's residential centres

   63.—(1) The Minister shall, for the purpose of ensuring proper standards in relation to children's residential centres, including adequate and suitable accommodation, food and care for children while being maintained in centres, and the proper conduct of centres, make such regulations as he thinks appropriate in relation to centres.
   (2) Without prejudice to the generality of *subsection* (1), regulations under this section may—
   (*a*) prescribe requirements as to the maintenance, care and welfare of children while being maintained in centres,
   (*b*) prescribe requirements as to the numbers, qualifications and availability of members of the staffs of centres,
   (*c*) prescribe requirements as to the design, maintenance, repair, cleaning and cleanliness, ventilation, heating and lighting of centres,
   (*d*) prescribe requirements as to the accommodation (including the amount of space in bedrooms, the washing facilities and the sanitary conveniences) provided in centres,
   (*e*) prescribe requirements as to the food provided for children while being maintained in centres,
   (*f*) prescribe requirements as to the records to be kept in centres and for the examination and copying of any such records or of extracts therefrom by [employees of the Health Service Executive],
   (*g*) provide for the inspection of premises in which centres are being carried on or are proposed to be carried on or that are reasonably believed by [the Health Service Executive] to be premises in which a centre is being carried on and otherwise for the enforcement and execution of the regulations by [the Executive and its employees].
   (3)(*a*) Where, in relation to a centre, there is a failure or refusal to comply with a provision of the regulations, the registered proprietor and the person in charge of the centre shall be guilty of an offence.
   (*b*) A person who fails or refuses to comply with a provision of the regulations shall be guilty of an offence.
   (4)(*a*) Where a person is convicted of an offence under this section, the Circuit Court may, on the application of the [Health Service Executive], brought not more than six months after the conviction or, in the case of an appeal against the conviction, the final determination of it or of any further appeal (if it is a determination

affirming the conviction) or the withdrawal of any such appeal therefrom, by order declare that the person shall be disqualified during such period as may be specified in the order from carrying on, being in charge, or concerned with the management, of the centre to which the conviction related or, at the discretion of that Court, any centre.

(*b*) A person in respect of whom an order is made under this subsection shall not during the period specified in the order carry on, be in charge, or concerned with the management, of the centre specified in the order or, if the order so specifies, of any centre.

(*c*) A person who contravenes *paragraph* (*b*) shall be guilty of an offence.

(*d*) Notice of an application under this subsection shall be given to the person convicted of the offence concerned and he shall be entitled to appear, be heard and adduce evidence on the hearing of the application.

(*e*) The jurisdiction conferred on the Circuit Court by this subsection shall be exercised by the judge of the Circuit Court for the time being assigned to the circuit in which the premises concerned are situated.

(5) A person who wilfully obstructs or interferes with [the Health Service Executive or any of its employees] in the performance of functions under the regulations or who fails or refuses to comply with a requirement of the Health Service Executive or an officer of the Health Service Executive under such regulations shall be guilty of an offence.

AMENDMENT

Subsections (2), (4) and (5) amended by s.75 and Schedule 7 of the Health Act 2004, No.42 of 2004, with effect from January 1, 2005 (S.I. No.887 of 2004).

DEFINITIONS

"children's residential centre": s.59.
"health board": s.2.
"person in charge": art.3 of the Child Care (Standards in Children's Residential Centres) Regulations, 1996 (S.I. No. 397 of 1996).
"the Minister": s.2.
"registered proprietor": s.59.

COMMENCEMENT

Child Care Act, 1991 (Commencement) Order, 1996 (S.I. No. 399 of 1996) took effect as of December 18, 1996.

NOTE

This provides for the making of regulations governing standards in children's residential centres. The Minister for Health is obliged to make regulations which must require adequate and suitable accommodation, food and care for children while being maintained in centres and the proper conduct of centres. The regulations governing these requirements are S.I. No.259 of 1995, Child Care (Placement of Children in Residential Care) Regulations 1995 (S.I. No.259 of 1995) which imposes obligations upon the Health Service Executive to ensure that centres conform to those regulations and S.I. No.397 of 1996, Child Care (Standards in Children's Residential Centres) Regulations 1996, (S.I. No.397 of 1996) which impose upon the registered proprietor and person in charge the obligations specified in the regulations.

Subsection (2)

This lists seven general headings which regulations may prescribe. The first is a broad and general requirement to prescribe requirements as to the maintenance, care and welfare of children while being maintained in centres (see generally S.I. No.259 of 1995 and S.I. No.397 of 1996).

Secondly, regulation may prescribe requirements as to numbers, qualifications and availability of members of staff of centres (see art.6 of S.I. No.259 of 1995 and art.7 of S.I. No.397 of 1996).

Thirdly, regulations may prescribe standards as to the design, maintenance, repair, cleaning and cleanliness, ventilation, heating and lighting of centres (see art.7(*d*) and (*e*) of S.I. No.259 of 1995 and art.8(*d*) and (*e*) of S.I. No.397 of 1996).

Fourthly, regulations may prescribe requirements as to accommodation, including space in bedrooms, washing facilities and sanitary conveniences (see art.7(*a*), (*b*), (*c*) and (*f*) of S.I. No.259 of 1995 and art.8(*a*), (*b*), (*c*) and (*f*) of S.I. No.397 of 1996).

Fifthly, regulations may prescribe requirements as to the food provided while being maintained in centres. Article 11 of S.I. No.259 of 1995 and art.12 of S.I. No.397 of 1996 require food to be in quantities adequate to the needs of children, which is properly prepared, wholesome and nutritious, and involving an element of choice.

Food provided must also take account of any special dietary requirements. To this extent there must be suitable and sufficient catering equipment, crockery and cutlery.

There must be proper facilities for refrigeration and storage of food and a high standard of hygiene in storing and preparing food and in the disposal of domestic waste.

Sixthly, regulations may prescribe requirements for the keeping of records, and for the examination and copying of records or extracts therefrom by officers of the Health Service Executive (see arts 16 and 31(*b*) of S.I. No.259 of 1995 and arts 17 and 18(1)(*b*) of S.I. No.397 of 1996).

Seventhly, regulations may prescribe requirements for the inspection of premises in which centres are being carried on or are proposed to be carried on or premises in which the Health Service Executive reasonably believes that a centre is being carried on. Regulations may also prescribe for the enforcement and execution of the regulations by the appropriate Health Service Executive and their officials. Article 17 of S.I. No.259 of 1996 obliges the Health Service Executive to ensure that adequate arrangements are in place to enable an authorised person to enter and inspect the centre at all reasonable times and ensure that the centre is visited from time to time by an authorised person. Further, art.17(2) provides that, where, following an inspection, the Health Service Executive is of the opinion that the requirements of the regulations are not being complied with, it shall request the manager of the centre to take the necessary steps to ensure compliance with the regulations.

Article 31 of the regulations also authorises inspections by a person authorised on behalf of the Minister for Health, to examine the state and management of the centre and the treatment of children therein (see also s.63(3) on offences in relation to inspections and examinations).

Articles 18 and 19 oblige the registered proprietor of a centre to permit the entry and inspection of the centre by an authorised person and for the enforcement and execution of the regulations by the Health Service Executive.

Subsection (3)

This makes it an offence for a registered proprietor or the person in charge of a centre to fail or refuse to comply with the provisions of the regulations. The penalty for such an offence, on summary conviction, is a fine not exceeding €1,269.74 or a term of imprisonment not exceeding 12 months or both.

Subsection (4)

This provides for an additional penalty of disqualifying a person from carrying on, being in charge or concerned with the management of a centre. The application to disqualify must be brought by the Health Service Executive within six months of the person being convicted of an offence, or from an appeal against a conviction or final determination of a further appeal or withdrawal of an appeal. The application must be made to the Circuit Court which may declare the person disqualified in relation to the centre to which the conviction related or to any centre. Where an application to disqualify is made by the Health Service Executive, it must be on notice to the person convicted of the offence who has the right to appear, be heard and adduce evidence at the hearing to disqualify (see s.63(4)(*d*)).

Where an order is made by the Circuit Court disqualifying a person, that person is prohibited from carrying on, being in charge, or concerned with the management of the centre specified in the order or any centre. The Circuit Court may determine the duration of any disqualification.

Where a person carries on, is in charge of or concerned with the management of a centre in contravention of a disqualification, that person commits an offence, and on summary conviction, may be liable to a fine not exceeding €1,269.74 or a term of imprisonment not exceeding 12 months or both and may also be liable to further disqualification.

The Circuit Court is conferred with jurisdiction to hear and determine applications to disqualify persons. The application must be made to the Circuit Court in the circuit court district in which the premises are situated.

Subsection (5)

This makes it an offence for a person to wilfully obstruct or interfere with the Health Service Executive or officer of the Health Service Executive in the performance of functions under the regulations (inspections and examinations). It also makes it an offence to fail or refuse to comply with a requirement of the Health Service Executive or officer of the Health Service Executive under the regulations. The penalty on summary conviction may be a fine not exceeding €1,269.74 or a term of imprisonment not exceeding 12 months or both, with the possibility of a disqualification order.

Offences under *Part VIII*

64.—A person guilty of an offence under this Part shall be liable on summary conviction to a fine not exceeding €1,269.74 or to imprisonment for a term not exceeding 12 months or to both.

Commencement

Child Care Act, 1991 (Commencement) Order, 1996 (S.I. No. 399 of 1996) took effect as of December 18, 1996.

NOTE

This provides for the penalties to be imposed for offences under this Part. The penalty on summary conviction is a fine not exceeding €1,269.74 or a term of imprisonment not exceeding 12 months or both.

The offences which may be committed under Pt VIII are: carrying on or being in charge of a centre that is not registered in accordance with s.61 and not being a duly registered proprietor (s.60(3)); furnishing false or misleading information of a material particular in the application to register or by request of information by the Health Service Executive (s.61(7)(*b*)); failing to apply for registration where a centre is carried on by a person other than a registered proprietor (s.61(10)(*a*)(ii)); contravening a condition of registration (s.61(13)); failure or refusal to comply with a provision of regulations made under this Part (s.63(3)(*a*) and (*b*)); carrying on, being in charge or concerned with the management of a centre in contravention of a disqualification order (s.63(4)(*c*)); and wilful obstruction or interference with the Health Service Executive or the Health Service Executive officer in the performance of functions under the regulations or a failure or refusal to comply with a requirement of the Health Service Executive or officer of the Health Service Executive under the regulations (s.63(5)).

Discontinuance of centre

65.—(1) Where the registered proprietor of a children's residential centre intends to cease to carry on the centre, he shall give six months' notice in writing to the [Health Service Executive] and at the expiration of six months from the date of the notice (unless before that time the notice is withdrawn or the period of registration has expired) the centre shall cease to be registered under this Part.

(2) [The Health Service Executive] may, if it so thinks fit, accept a shorter period of notice for the purposes of *subsection (1)* and the provisions of that subsection shall apply with the necessary modifications.

[(3) A notice given to the Health Service Executive in accordance with *subsection (1)* before the amendment of that subsection by the Health Act 2004 shall be deemed to have been given to the Health Service Executive.]

AMENDMENT

Subsections (1) and (2) amended, and subs.(3) inserted, by s.75 and Schedule 7 of the Health Act 2004, No.42 of 2004, with effect from January 1, 2005 (S.I. No.887 of 2004).

DEFINITIONS
"centre": s.59.
"children's residential centre": s.59.
"health board": s.2.
"registered proprietor": s.59.

COMMENCEMENT

Child Care Act, 1991 (Commencement) Order, 1996 (S.I. No. 399 of 1996) took effect as of December 18, 1996.

Note

This provides for the procedure to be followed where a registered proprietor intends to cease carrying on a centre. The registered proprietor must give six months notice in writing of the intention to cease. The notice must be given to the Health Service Executive in the area in which the centre is situated. The Health Service Executive may accept a shorter period of notice, if it thinks fit (s.65(2)). On the expiry of the notice, the centre automatically ceases to be a registered children's centre. The notice may be withdrawn, which terminates the effect of the notice. Where a registration will lapse in advance of the expiry of a notice under this section, the centre will cease to be registered on the date on which the registration ceases and not on the date on which the notice expires.

Superannuation of certain staff

66.—[(1) An employee of a children's residential centre to which this section applies shall, for the purposes of *sections 23, 60(6)* and *61* of the Health Act 2004, be deemed to be employed by the Health Service Executive.]

(2) In this section, "employee" means a person employed by a children's residential centre who is the holder in a wholetime capacity of a position, the establishment, remuneration and conditions of service of which have been approved by the [Health Service Executive], with the consent of the Minister.

(3) This section applies to a children's residential centre which—

(a) is not directly operated or administered by [the Health Service Executive],

(b) is funded by [the Health Service Executive], and

(c) is specified by the Minister for the purpose of this section.

Amendment

Amendments by s.75 and Schedule 7 of the Health Act 2004, No.42 of 2004, with effect from January 1, 2005 (S.I. No.887 of 2004).

Definitions

"centre": s.59.
"children's residential centre": s.59.
"employee": s.66.
"health board": s.2.
"the Minister": s.2.

Commencement

Child Care Act, 1991 (Children's Residential Centres) (Superannuation) (No. 2) Order, 1992 (S.I. No. 125 of 1992) took effect as of June 1, 1992.

Note

The effect of this section is to provide a pension scheme for staff of children's residential centres. All employees of the centres listed in s.65(3) are deemed to be employees of the relevant Health Service Executive. An employee is defined as "a person employed by a children's residential centre who is the holder in a wholetime capacity of a position, the establishment, remuneration and conditions of service of which have been approved by the Health Service Executive for the area in which the centre is situated, with the consent of the Minister".

Subsection (3)
This sets out the children's residential centres to which the pension scheme applies. The centres are ones which are not directly operated or administered by the Health Service Executive, ones which are funded by the Health Service Executive and ones specified by the Minister for the purposes of this section.

This provision is given effect to by S.I. No.124 of 1992, Child Care Act 1991 (Children's Residential Centres) (Superannuation) Order 1992 and S.I. No.125 of 1992, Child Care Act 1991 (Children's Residential Centres) (Superannuation) (No.2) Order 1992.

Transitional provisions

67.—(1) On the commencement of this Part, every institution which, immediately before such commencement, was an industrial school certified in accordance with *Part IV* of the Children Act, 1908, functions in relation to which stood vested in the Minister, shall cease to be so certified and shall be deemed to be registered under this Part as a children's residential centre.

(2) On the commencement of this Part, every school which, immediately before such commencement, was a school approved (or deemed to be approved) for the purposes of *section 55* of the Health Act, 1953 shall be deemed to be registered under this Part as a children's residential centre.

DEFINITIONS

"children's residential centre": s.59.
"industrial school": s.44 of the Children Act, 1908.

COMMENCEMENT

Article 2 of the Child Care Act (Commencement) Order, 1996 (S.I. No. 399 of 1996) brought into effect section 67 on December 18, 1996.

NOTE

This provides for transitional measures for industrial schools under the Children Act 1908 which automatically cease to be so certified and are deemed to be registered children's residential centres for the purposes of Pt VIII of the Act.

Subsection (2)
This provides likewise for schools approved under s.55 of the Health Act 1953 to be deemed to be registered residential children's centres for Pt VIII.

PART IX

ADMINISTRATION

Regulations

68.—(1) The Minister may make regulations—

    (*a*) for any purpose in relation to which regulations are provided for by any of the provisions of this Act, and

    (*b*) for prescribing any matter or thing referred to in this Act as prescribed or to be prescribed.

(2) Every order and regulation made under any provision of an enactment repealed by this Act and in force immediately before such repeal shall continue in force under the corresponding provision, if any, of this Act, subject to such adaptations and modifications as the Minister may by regulations make to enable any such order or regulation to have effect in conformity with this Act.

(3) Every regulation made under this Act shall be laid before each House of the Oireachtas as soon as may be after it is made and, if a resolution annulling the regulation is passed by either House within the next 21 days on which that House has sat after the regulation is laid before it, the regulation shall be annulled accordingly but without prejudice to the validity of anything previously done thereunder.

DEFINITIONS

    "prescribed": s.2.

    "the Minister": s.2.

COMMENCEMENT

    Child Care Act, 1991 (Commencement) Order, 1995 (S.I. No. 258 of 1995) took effect as of October 31, 1995.

NOTE

    This confers upon the Minister for Health the authority to make regulations and the manner in which those regulations should be made.

    Regulations may be made for any provision of the Act and may prescribe any matter or thing referred to in the Act.

Subsection (2)

    This provides for the consequences to orders and regulations made under any provision of a statute which is in force immediately prior to the repeal of that provision by the Act. Any such order and regulation shall remain in force under the corresponding provision of the Act. Where such orders or regulations are carried over by this Act they are subject to any adaptation and modifications made by the Minister to enable those orders or regulations to have effect in conformity with the Act.

    Sections 48 and 67 of the Act are of relevance to this provision. The relevant repealed Statutory Instrument is S.I. No.67 of 1983, The Boarding Out of Children Regulations 1983.

Subsection (3)

This provides for the manner in which regulations are to be made under this Act. Every regulation made under this Act must be laid before both the Dáil and the Seanad as soon as may be after it is made. Once laid before each House of the Oireachtas, a resolution may be passed within 21 days, annulling that regulation. Such annulment does not affect the validity of anything previously done thereunder.

Powers of the Minister

69.—(1) The Minister may give general directions to [the Health Service Executive] in relation to the performance of the functions assigned to it by or under this Act and [the Executive] shall comply with any such direction.

(2) The Minister may cause to be inspected any service provided or premises maintained by [the Health Service Executive] under this Act.

(3) An inspection under this section shall be conducted by a person authorised in that behalf by the Minister (in this section referred to as an authorised person).

(4) An authorised person conducting an inspection under this section may—

(*a*) enter any premises maintained by [the Health Service Executive] under this Act and make such examination into the state and management of the premises and the treatment of children therein as he thinks fit, and

(*b*) examine such records and interview [employees of the Health Service Executive] as he thinks fit.

(5) The Minister may direct [the Health Service Executive] to supply him with such reports and statistics in relation to the performance of the functions assigned to it by or under this Act as he may require and [the Health Service Executive] shall comply with any such direction.

AMENDMENT

Amendments by s.75 and Schedule 7 of the Health Act 2004, No.42 of 2004, with effect from January 1, 2005 (S.I. No.887 of 2004).

DEFINITIONS

"functions": s.2.
"health board": s.2.
"the Minister": s.2.

COMMENCEMENT

Child Care Act, 1991 (Commencement) (No. 2) Order, 1992 (S.I. No. 264 of 1992) took effect as of October 1, 1992.

NOTE

This section confers upon the Minister for Health certain statutory powers. The Health and Children (Delegation of Ministerial Function) (No.2) Order (S.I. No.33 of 2000) delegated the Ministerial powers under the 1991 Act to the Minister of State at the Department of Health and Children. The Minister may give directions to the Health Service Executive in relation to the performance of the functions assigned to it by or under the Act. The Health Service Executive is obliged to comply with any such directions issued by the Minister. The Minister may inspect services and premises and appoint person to that effect.

Subsection (2)

This provides the Minister with the authority to inspect any service or premises maintained by the Health Service Executive.

Subsection (3)

This provides that any such inspection must be conducted by a person authorised in that behalf by the Minister.

Subsection (4)

This confers statutory powers of entry and examination on an authorised person.

Such a person may enter any premises maintained by the Health Service Executive under the Act and make examination into the state and management of the premises and the treatment of the children therein, as the person thinks fit. Further, an authorised person may examine records and interview members of staff of the Executive as he thinks fit.

The following make provision for inspections under this section: art.31 of S.I. No.259 of 1995, Child Care (Placement of Children in Residential Care) Regulations 1995; art.25 of S.I. No.260 of 1995, Child Care (Placement of Children in Foster Care) Regulations 1995; art.25 of S.I. No.261 of 1995, Child Care (Placement of Children with Relatives) Regulations 1995 and art.18 of S.I. No.397 of 1996, Child Care (Standards in Children's Residential Centres) Regulations 1996.

Subsection (5)

This empowers the Minister for Health to direct the Health Service Executive to supply the Minister with such reports and statistics concerning the performance of the Health Service Executive's functions which are assigned to it by or under the Act. Where the Health Service Executive receives such a direction, the Health Service Executive is obliged to comply with that direction.

Charges for certain services

70.—(1) In making available a service under *section 3, 4* or *56*, the [Health Service Executive] shall from time to time determine in each case whether such service shall be provided without charge or at such charge as it considers appropriate.

(2) In making a determination in accordance with *subsection (1)* [the Health Service Executive] shall comply with any general directions given by the Minister with the consent of the Minister for Finance.

(3) For the purposes of determining what charge, if any, should be made on any person for a service, [the Health Service Executive] may require that person to make a declaration in such form as it considers appropriate in relation to his means and may take such steps as it thinks fit to verify the declaration.

(4) Where a person is recorded by [the Health Service Executive] as entitled, because of specified circumstances, to a service without charge, he shall notify [the Executive] of any relevant change in those circumstances.

(5) Any charge which may be made by [the Health Service Executive] under

this Act may, in default of payment, be recovered as a simple contract debt in any court of competent jurisdiction from the person on whom the charge is made or, where the person has died, from his legal personal representative.

AMENDMENT

Amendments by s.75 and Schedule 7 of the Health Act 2004, No.42 of 2004, with effect from January 1, 2005 (S.I. No.887 of 2004).

DEFINITIONS

"health board": s.2.
"the Minister": s.2.

COMMENCEMENT

Child Care Act, 1991 (Commencement) Order, 1995 (S.I. No. 258 of 1995) took effect as of October 31, 1995.

NOTE

This enables the Health Service Executive to charge for certain services provided. They are obliged to determine whether a charge, if any, is to be levied and the means of assessing whether a person should pay for such services. A means of securing payment is also provided for.

Subsection (1)
This obliges the Health Service Executive to determine whether any charge should be levied for services under ss.3, 4 or 56. Where a charge is to be levied for services provided, the Health Service Executive must determine the amount. Section 3 confers upon the Health Service Executive a broad statutory function to promote the welfare of children who are not receiving adequate care and attention. Specific authority is conferred to provide child care and family support services and to maintain premises to this extent.

Section 4 authorises the Health Service Executive to take children into voluntary care and maintain children until such time as the welfare of the child so requires.

Section 56 relates to the provision of pre-school services by the Health Service Executive.

Subsection (2)
Whilst the Health Service Executive may determine whether to levy a charge and the amount for a service, this discretion is subject to any general direction given by the Minister for Health, with the consent of the Minister for Finance.

Subsection (3)
This provides that where the Health Service Executive levies a charge for a service provided against a person, the Health Service Executive may seek from that person a declaration as to his means. The Health Service Executive may take steps to verify any statement as to means. The Health Service Executive has a discretion in both seeking a declaration and verifying that declaration.

Subsection (4)
This imposes upon a person a duty to inform the Health Service Executive of any

change in circumstances where that change is relevant to the special circumstances leading the Health Service Executive to provide a service free of charge.

Subsection (5)

This provides a means by which the Health Service Executive may recover a charge on which a person has defaulted. The unpaid amount is stated to be a simple contract debt recoverable in proceedings brought in any competent court (either District or Circuit Court depending upon the amount due). The person liable to such proceedings is the person on whom the charge was made, or in the event of that person's death, his legal personal representatives.

Prosecution of offences

71.—(1) Summary proceedings for an offence under this Act may be brought and prosecuted by the [Health Service Executive] or by any other person.

(2) Notwithstanding *section 10(4)* of the Petty Sessions (Ireland) Act, 1851, summary proceedings for an offence under this Act may be instituted within 12 months from the date of the offence.

(3) Where an offence under this Act is committed by a body corporate or by a person purporting to act on behalf of a body corporate or an unincorporated body of persons and is proved to have been committed with the consent or approval of, or to have been attributable to any neglect on the part of, any person who, when the offence was committed, was director, member of the committee of management or other controlling authority of the body concerned, or the manager, secretary or other officer of the body, that person shall also be deemed to have committed the offence and may be proceeded against and punished accordingly.

AMENDMENT

Subsection (1) amended by s.75 and Schedule 7 of the Health Act 2004, No.42 of 2004, with effect from January 1, 2005 (S.I. No.887 of 2004).

DEFINITIONS

"area": s.2.
"health board": s.2.

COMMENCEMENT

Child Care Act, 1991 (Commencement) Order, 1995 (S.I. No. 258 of 1995) took effect as of October 31, 1995.

NOTE

This confers upon the Health Service Executive the authority to prosecute offences committed under the Act. The time limit within which a prosecution may be brought and the person or persons stated and deemed to be liable to prosecution are also specified.

Subsection (1)

This provides that the Health Service Executive for the area in which an offence under this Act is committed may prosecute the offender. In addition any other person may bring a prosecution.

Subsection (2)

This provides that the time limit for the institution of summary proceedings for offences under the Act is 12 months. Section 10(4) of the Petty Sessions (Ireland) Act 1851 ordinarily requires the prosecution of summary offences to be instituted within six months which is expressly stated not to apply.

Subsection (3)

This provides for the person or persons to be prosecuted in offences concerning corporate and unincorporated bodies. Where the offence is committed by a body corporate or an agent of a body corporate or unincorporated body of persons such will be liable to prosecution. In addition any person who is proved to have consented, approved or to whom any neglect is attributable in the commission of the offence is also liable to prosecution. Further any person who, at the time the offence was committed, was director, member of committee of management or other controlling authority of the body concerned, manager, secretary or other officer is deemed to have committed the offence.

Functions of chief executive officer

72.—Repealed by s.73 and Schedule 4 of the Health Act 2004, No.42 of 2004, with effect from January 1, 2005 (S.I. No.887 of 2004).

DEFINITIONS

"chief executive officer": s.72(3).
"functions": s.2.
"health board": s.2.
"the Minister": s.2.

COMMENCEMENT

Child Care Act, 1991 (Commencement) (No. 2) Order, 1992 (S.I. No. 264 of 1992) took effect as of October 1, 1992.

NOTE

This provides for a number of specified functions of the Health Service Executive to be functions of the chief executive officer of the Health Service Executive, which includes a person acting as deputy chief executive officer in accordance with s.13 of the Health Act 1970. Where a chief executive officer is temporarily unable to act, he may appoint any approved officer of the Executive to act as deputy for the period of the chief executive's incapacity. Where no deputy has been appointed the chairman or vice-chairman may appoint a deputy whose appointment may be terminated by the chairman, with the consent of the Minister. A deputy may perform all of the functions of a chief executive officer.

The functions specified to be functions of the chief executive officer are: a decision as to whether or not to provide a service or make facilities available to any particular person; a decision as to the making or recovery of a charge or the amount of any charge for a service provided in a particular case under ss.3, 4 or 56; a decision as to whether or not to receive a child into care under s.4; a decision as to the payment of a grant or allowance to a voluntary body or any other person; any decision as to legal proceedings in relation to the care and protection of a child; any decision as to a particular child in the care of the Health Service Executive or in relation to the provision of aftercare; any function in relation to the provision of pre-school services; any function in relation to the registration and regulation of children's residential services and any other functions as may be prescribed.

Subsection (2)
This provides that in the event of a query as to whether or not a particular function is a function of a chief executive officer such must be determined by the Minister for Health.

Expenses

73.—The expenses incurred by the Minister in the administration of this Act shall, to such extent as may be sanctioned by the Minister for Finance, be paid out of moneys provided by the Oireachtas.

DEFINITIONS

"the Minister": s.2.

COMMENCEMENT

Child Care Act, 1991 (Commencement) (No. 2) Order, 1992 (S.I. No. 264 of 1992) took effect as of October 1, 1992.

NOTE

This provides for the payment of expenses incurred in the administration of the Act to be paid out of moneys provided by the Oireachtas. This is subject to the sanction of the Minister for Finance.

PART X

MISCELLANEOUS AND SUPPLEMENTARY

Sale etc. of solvents

74.—(1) It shall be an offence for a person to sell, offer or make available a substance to a person under the age of eighteen years or to a person acting on behalf of that person if he knows or has reasonable cause to believe that the substance is, or its fumes are, likely to be inhaled by the person under the age of eighteen years for the purpose of causing intoxication.

(2) In proceedings against any person for an offence under *subsection (1)*, it shall be a defence for him to prove that at the time he sold, offered or made available the substance he was under the age of eighteen years and was acting otherwise than in the course of or furtherance of a business.

(3) In proceedings against any person for an offence under *subsection (1)* it shall be a defence for him to prove that he took reasonable steps to assure himself that the person to whom the substance was sold, offered or made available, or any person on whose behalf that person was acting, was not under the age of eighteen years.

(4) A person who is guilty of an offence under *subsection (1)* shall be liable

on summary conviction to a fine not exceeding €1,269.74 or to imprisonment for a term not exceeding 12 months or to both.

(5) Subject to *subsection* (6), a court by which a person is convicted of an offence under this section may order anything shown to the satisfaction of the court to relate to the offence to be forfeited and either destroyed or dealt with in such other manner as the court thinks fit.

(6) A court shall not order anything to be forfeited under this section unless an opportunity is given to any person appearing to the court to be the owner of or otherwise interested in it to show cause why the order should not be made.

(7) A member of the Garda Síochána may seize any substance which is in the possession of a child in any public place and which the member has reasonable cause to believe is being inhaled by that child in a manner likely to cause him to be intoxicated. Any substance so seized may be destroyed or otherwise disposed of in such a manner as a member of the Garda Síochána not below the rank of Superintendent may direct.

(8) This section is without prejudice to the provisions of the Misuse of Drugs Act, 1977 and 1984.

DEFINITIONS

"child": s.2 of the 1991 Act.

COMMENCEMENT

Child Care Act, 1991 (Commencement) Order, 1991 (S.I. No. 292 of 1991) took effect as of December 1, 1991.

NOTE

This provision was introduced as an attempt to curb solvent abuse. The section criminalises the sale and supply of solvents rather than the inhalation or consumption of substances by persons under the age of 18. The section provides for defences and the destruction of substances on conviction, subject to the right of the owner to make representation. There is also conferred upon the gardaí the right to seize substances in the possession of a child.

Subsection (1)

This creates the offence of selling, offering or making available a substance by a person who knows or has reasonable cause to believe that the substance or its fumes are likely to be inhaled by a person under the age of 18 for the purpose of causing intoxication. The person committing the offence must sell, offer or make the substances available to either a person under the age of 18 or to a person on behalf of that person.

The effect of this provision will make retailers of solvents inquire into the age of a person seeking to obtain solvents and, perhaps, the purpose for which the solvent is required. Where a retailer adopts such a policy, he may avail of the defence set out in s.74(2) and s.74(3). The offence can be committed by selling a substance to an individual over the age of 18 who is acting on behalf of a person under the age of 18.

As there are a number of factors to be established in a prosecution under this section, a successful conviction may be difficult to obtain and the primary purpose of the making of this offence is to deter and limit the supply of substances capable of abuse.

Subsection (2)

This provides a defence for a person prosecuted under s.74(1) where it can be proven that at the time of the offence that the person was under the age of 18 and was acting otherwise than in the course of or furtherance of a business.

Subsection (3)

This provides for a defence for a person prosecuted under s.74(1). Where a person can prove that he took reasonable steps to assure himself that the person to whom the substance was sold, offered or made available, or any person on whose behalf that person was acting, was not under the age of 18 years.

The defence only operates in relation to the age of the person acquiring the substances and the degree to which the person has assured himself that the individual is not under the age of 18 years.

Subsection (4)

This provides for the penalties on summary conviction for an offence under this section. A fine not exceeding €1,269.74 or a term of imprisonment or both may be imposed. The Health Service Executive or any other person may bring a prosecution.

Subsection (5)

In addition to the imposition of a fine on conviction, the court may order the forfeiture and destruction or dealing with in a manner as the court thinks fit, of anything shown to the satisfaction of the court that relates to the offence.

This would include the substance which is the subject matter of the offence and any other thing relating to the commission of the offence, such as supplies of the substance. This power of forfeiture and destruction is subject to s.74(6), which obliges a court to give an opportunity to the person appearing to be the owner of the thing to be forfeited to show cause why the order may not be made.

Subsection (6)

An order for the forfeiture and destruction or other dealing with of a thing relating to the offence cannot be made until the court has afforded the owner or any person interested in the thing an opportunity to show cause why the order should not be made.

Subsection (7)

This confers upon a member of the gardaí the authority to seize and destroy or otherwise dispose of a substance which the member reasonably believes is being inhaled.

There are a number of constituent elements to be fulfilled for the exercise of this power. The person in possession of the substance must be a child, that is someone under the age of 18 years. The possession by the child must be in a public place. The power cannot be exercised where a child is in possession of a substance on private property (e.g. front garden, doorway of a private residence). The child must be inhaling the substance at the time or the member of the gardaí has reasonable cause to believe this. Finally the inhalation must be in a manner likely to cause the child to be intoxicated. Where these circumstances arise, a member of the gardaí may seize the substance.

Once seized the substance may only be destroyed or otherwise disposed of on the direction of a Superintendent.

Subsection (8)

This provides that s.74 is without prejudice to the Misuse of Drugs Acts 1977 and 1984.

Amendment of section 17 of the School Attendance Act, 1926

75.—Section 17 of the School Attendance Act, 1926 (which deals with the failure of a parent to comply with the Act) is hereby amended by the substitution for *paragraph* (*b*) of *subsection* (*4*) of the following:—

"(*b*) having heard the health board for the area in which he is resident, make a care order committing him to the care of that board and in such case the provisions of *Part IV* of the *Child Care Act, 1991* shall apply as if the order were an order made thereunder.".

DEFINITIONS

"health board": s.2 of the 1991 Act.

COMMENCEMENT

Child Care Act, 1991 (Commencement) Order, 1995 (S.I. No. 258 of 1995) took effect as of October 31, 1995.

NOTE

This amends s.17(4)(*b*) of the School Attendance Act 1926 which is substituted by the provision of this section. Section 17 of the School Attendance Act 1926 concerns the failure or neglect of a parent to cause his child to attend school and the consequences of a failure to abide by any warning issued in respect of that failure or neglect. Section 17(4) of the School Attendance Act 1926 concerns proceedings against a parent, where that parent satisfies the court that all reasonable efforts have been made to make the child attend school or where the parent is convicted of a second or subsequent offence under the section, the court could, under s.17(4)(*b*), commit the child to the care of a relative or other fit person under Pt II of the Children Act 1908. The power to make this order is repealed.

The court may now, under the amended provision, make a care order committing the child to the care of the Health Service Executive for the area in which the child is resident. The effect of an order under this section is to have the same effect as if it were an order made under Pt IV. Before a court makes an order under this section, it must first hear the Health Service Executive concerned.

An order to commit a child to the care of the Health Service Executive under s.75 must be in the form prescribed and served upon the parent of the child (see Ord.84, r.33 of S.I. No.93 of 1997, District (Child Care) Rules 1997).

Amendment of section 15 of the Guardianship of Infants Act, 1964

76.—Section 15 of the Guardianship of Infants Act, 1964 (which gives power to the court to order repayment of costs of bringing up an infant) is hereby amended by the insertion in *paragraph* (*b*) after the words "assistance has been provided for the infant by a health authority under section 55 of the Health Act, 1953," of the words "or that at any time the infant has been maintained in the care of the Health Service Executive under section 4 of the *Child Care Act, 1991*".

DEFINITIONS

"health board": s.2 of the 1991 Act.

COMMENCEMENT

Child Care Act, 1991 (Commencement) Order, 1995 (S.I. No. 258 of 1995) took effect as of October 31, 1995.

NOTE

Section 76 amends s.15 of the Guardianship of Infants Act 1964 by the insertion of the words set out in this section. The effect of this is to enable a court to order the payment to the Health Service Executive of the whole or such portion as the court considers reasonable, of the cost of bringing up or providing assistance for the infant (child), having regard to all the circumstances of the case, including, in particular, the means of the parent.

An order directing payment by a parent is at the discretion of the court and can only be made in an application by a parent seeking the production of a child by the Health Service Executive. In this regard the amendment specifies the care the Health Service Executive has provided for a child under s.4, which is the voluntary placing of a child in the care of the Health Service Executive.

Amendment of section 16 of the Guardianship of Infants Act, 1964

77.—Section 16 of the Guardianship of Infants Act, 1964 (which requires the court in making an order for the delivery of an infant to its parent to have regard to the conduct of the parent) is hereby amended by the insertion in *paragraph (b)* after the words "or to be provided with assistance by a health authority under section 55 of the Health Act, 1953" of the words "or to be maintained in the care of the Health Service Executive under *section 4* of the *Child Care Act, 1991*".

DEFINITIONS

"health board": s.2 of the 1991 Act.

COMMENCEMENT

Child Care Act, 1991 (Commencement) Order, 1995 (S.I. No. 258 of 1995) took effect as of October 31, 1995.

NOTE

This section amends s.16 of the Guardianship of Infants Act 1964 which provides for a court to refuse to deliver up a child to a parent who has allowed one of the provisions of s.16 to happen to the child, unless the parent has satisfied the court that he is a fit person to have custody of the infant. To the existing list of circumstances that a parent may allow happen to a child, which are, abandoning or deserting an infant and allowing a child to be brought up by another person at that person's expense or allowing a child to be provided with assistance by a health authority under s.55 of the Health Act 1953, is added: or to be maintained in the care of the Health Service Executive under s.4 of the Child Care Act 1991. Where a parent has allowed any of the above circumstances to arise, for such a length of time and under such circumstances as to satisfy the court that the parent was unmindful of his parental duties, the court may not make an order delivering the child to a parent. The parent must satisfy the court that he is a fit parent to have custody.

Maintenance—saver in relation to members of Defence Forces

78.—(1) Section 98 of the Defence Act, 1954 (which provides for deductions from pay of members of the Permanent Defence Force and reservists called out on permanent service in respect of court orders under sections 75, 82 or 99 of the Children Act, 1908) shall apply in like manner to an order made under *section 18*.

(2) Section 107 of the Defence Act, 1954 (which provides that court orders made under the aforementioned sections against a member of the Permanent Defence Force or a reservist during any period when he is called out on permanent service shall not be enforceable by imprisonment) shall apply in like manner in the case of an order made under *section 18*.

COMMENCEMENT

Child Care Act, 1991 (Commencement) Order, 1995 (S.I. No. 258 of 1995) took effect as of October 31, 1995.

NOTE

This section makes applicable s.98 of the Defence Act 1954 to s.18 of the 1991 Act. Section 98 of the Defence Act provides for the deductions from pay of the members of the Permanent Defence Force and reservists called out on permanent service in relation to orders made under ss.75, 82 or 99 of the Children Act 1908. These provisions of the Children Act 1908 concern contributions by parents for children in the care of the Health Service Executive as ordered by a court. Section 18(7) of the 1991 Act authorises a court to order a parent to pay a weekly or other periodic sum to the Health Service Executive towards the cost of maintaining the child.

Subsection (2)

This makes applicable s.107 of the Defence Act 1954, to an order under s.18 to contribute to the cost of maintaining a child in the care of the Health Service Executive. Section 107 of the Defence Act 1954 precludes the imprisonment of a member of the Permanent Defence Force or reservist called out on permanent service for failing to comply with an order to contribute.

Repeals

79.—The enactments specified in the *Schedule* are hereby repealed to the extent specified in the *third column*.

COMMENCEMENT

Article 3 of the Child Care Act, 1991 (Commencement) Order, 1995 (S.I. No. 258 of 1995) repeals the whole of the Prevention of Cruelty to Children Act 1904. The Children Act 1908, sections 20 to 25, sections 34, 36 and 38(1), section 58(1), (5), (6),

(7) and (8), section 59, section 74(11), sections 118, 122 and 126. The whole of the Children (Employment Abroad) Act 1913. Section 10(1) of the Children Act 1941. Sections 55 and 56 of the Health Act 1953.

NOTE

Section 79 sets out a schedule of enactments which are repealed. Article 3 of S.I. No.123 of 1992 Child Care Act 1991 (Commencement) Order 1993 repeals s.65(2) of the Health Act 1953 as of June 1, 1992.

Section 79   SCHEDULE

ENACTMENTS REPEALED

Session and Chapter or Number and Year	Short Title	Extent of Repeal
4 Edw. 7, c. 15	Prevention of Cruelty to Children Act 1904.	The whole Act.
8 Edw. 7, c. 67	Children Act 1908.	Part 1, Sections 13 and 15, Sections 20 to 26, Sections 34, 36 and 38(1), Section 58(1), (5), (6), (7) and (8), Section 59, Section 74(11), Sections 118, 119, 122 and 126.
3 & 4 Geo. 5, c. 7	Children (Employment Abroad) Act 1913.	The whole Act.
No.15 of 1934	Children Act 1934	The whole Act.
No.12 of 1941	Children Act 1941	Section 10(1).
No.25 of 1952	Adoption Act 1952	Section 31(2).
No.26 of 1953	Health Act 1953	Sections 55, 56, 57 and 65(2).
No.28 of 1957	Children (Amendment) Act 1957	Sections 2, 3 and 10.
No.2 of 1964	Adoption Act 1964	Section 10.

CHILDREN ACT 2001

(No. 24 of 2001)

PART 2

FAMILY WELFARE CONFERENCES

Convening of family welfare conference

7.—(1) Where—
   (a) [the Health Service Executive] receives a direction from the Children Court under *section 77* to convene a family welfare conference in respect of a child, or
   (b) it appears [to the Health Service Executive that a child may require] special care or protection which the child is unlikely to receive unless a court makes an order in respect of him or her under *Part IVA* (inserted by this Act) of the Act of 1991,

[the Health Service Executive shall] appoint a person (in this Part referred to as a "coordinator") to convene on its behalf a family welfare conference in respect of the child.

(2) The coordinator shall act as chairperson of a family welfare conference.

(3) [The Health Service Executive] may direct that a family welfare conference shall consider such matters in relation to the child as [the Health Service Executive] considers appropriate.

AMENDMENT

Subsections (1) and (3) amended by s.75 and Schedule 7 of the Health Act 2004, No.42 of 2004, with effect from January 1, 2005 (S.I. No.887 of 2004).

Functions of conference

8.—(1) A family welfare conference shall—

(*a*) decide if a child in respect of whom the conference is being convened is in need of special care or protection which the child is unlikely to receive unless an order is made in respect of him or her under *Part IVA* (inserted by this Act) of the Act of 1991,

(*b*) if it decides that the child is in such need, recommend to the [Health Service Executive] that it should apply for an order under that Part, and

(*c*) if it does not so decide, make such recommendations to [Health Service Executive] in relation to the care or protection of the child as the conference considers necessary, including, where appropriate, a recommendation that the [Health Service Executive] should apply for a care order or a supervision order under the Act of 1991 in respect of the child.

(2) Any recommendations made by a family welfare conference shall be agreed unanimously by those present at the conference, unless the disagreement of any person present is regarded by the coordinator as unreasonable, in which case the coordinator may dispense with that person's agreement.

(3) Where any such recommendations are not agreed unanimously (disregarding any disagreement mentioned in *subsection (2)*), the matter shall be referred to the [Health Service Executive] for determination.

AMENDMENT

Subsections (1) and (3) amended by s.75 and Schedule 7 of the Health Act 2004, No.42 of 2004, with effect from January 1, 2005 (S.I. No.887 of 2004).

Persons entitled to attend conference

9.—(1) The following persons shall be entitled to attend a family welfare conference—

(*a*) the child in respect of whom the conference is being convened,

(*b*) the parents or guardian of the child,

(*c*) any guardian ad litem appointed for the child,

(*d*) such other relatives of the child as may be determined by the coordinator, after consultation with the child and the child's parents or guardian,

[(*e*) an employee or employees of the Health Service Executive;],

(*f*) any other person who, in the opinion of the coordinator, after consultation with the child and his or her parents or guardian, would make a positive contribution to the conference because of the person's knowledge of the child or the child's family or because of his or her particular expertise.

(2) If, before or during a family welfare conference, the coordinator is of opinion that the presence or continued presence of any person is not in the best interests of the conference or the child, the coordinator may exclude that person from participation or further participation in the conference.

(3) The coordinator shall take all reasonable steps to ensure that notice of the time, date and place of a family welfare conference is given to every person who is entitled to attend.

(4) Failure to notify any person entitled to attend a family welfare conference, or failure of any such person to attend it, shall not invalidate its proceedings.

AMENDMENT

Paragraph (1)(*e*) substituted by s.75 and Schedule 7 of the Health Act 2004, No.42 of 2004, with effect from January 1, 2005 (S.I. No.887 of 2004).

Procedure at conference

10.—(1) Subject to the provisions of this Part or any regulations under section 15, a family welfare conference may regulate its procedure in such manner as it thinks fit.

(2) Subject to any direction of the Children Court pursuant to *section 77*, a family welfare conference may be adjourned to a time and place to be determined by it.

(3) The coordinator of a family welfare conference shall ensure, as far as practicable, that any information and advice required by the conference to carry out its functions are made available to it.

Administrative services

11.—[The Health Service Executive] shall provide, or arrange for the provision of such administrative services as may be necessary to enable a family welfare conference to discharge its functions.

AMENDMENT

Amended by s.75 and Schedule 7 of the Health Act 2004, No.42 of 2004, with effect from January 1, 2005 (S.I. No.887 of 2004).

Notification of recommendations of conference

12.—The coordinator of a family welfare conference shall notify the following persons or bodies in writing of any recommendations of the conference:
  (*a*) the child in respect of whom the conference was convened,
  (*b*) the parents or guardian of the child,
  (*c*) any guardian ad litem appointed for the child,
  (*d*) any other persons who attended the conference,
  [(*e*) the Health Service Executive;],
  (*f*) if the child was referred to the [Health Service Executive] health board by another body, that body, and
  (*g*) any other body or persons who should, in the coordinator's opinion, be so notified.

AMENDMENT

Paragraph (*e*) substituted and paragraph (*f*) amended by s.75 and Schedule 7 of the Health Act 2004, No.42 of 2004, with effect from January 1, 2005 (S.I. No.887 of 2004).

Action by [Health Service Executive] on recommendations

13.—(1) On receipt of the recommendations of a family welfare conference, the [the Health Service Executive] may—

- (*a*) apply for an order under *Part IVA* (inserted by this Act) of the Act of 1991,
- (*b*) apply for a care order or a supervision order under that Act, or
- (*c*) provide any service or assistance for the child or his or her family as it considers appropriate, having regard to the recommendations of the conference.

(2) Where a family welfare conference has been convened following a direction of the Children Court under *section 77*, the [Health Service Executive] shall communicate with that Court in accordance with *subsection (2)* of that section.

AMENDMENT

Amended by s.75 and Schedule 7 of the Health Act 2004, No.42 of 2004, with effect from January 1, 2005 (S.I. No.887 of 2004).

Privilege

14.—(1) No evidence shall be admissible in any court of any information, statement or admission disclosed or made in the course of a family welfare conference.

(2) *Subsection (1)* does not apply to a record of decisions or recommendations of a family welfare conference.

(3) *Section 51* shall apply, with the necessary modifications, in relation to publication of proceedings at a family welfare conference and the protection of the identity of a child in respect of whom such a conference is being held.

Regulations

15.—The Minister for Health and Children may make regulations prescribing any or all of the following matters:

- (*a*) the arrangements for convening a family welfare conference and the appointment and role of the coordinator,
- (*b*) subject to *section 9*, the categories of persons who shall be entitled to attend such a conference and the conditions under which a person or category of persons may so attend, and
- (*c*) the arrangements for notifying any other body or person of any recommendations of such a conference,

or for the purposes of enabling any provision of this Part to have full effect and for its due administration.

[Transitional provisions relating to Health Act 2004

[15A.—(1) In this section, a reference to a provision of this Act is to that provision as it was before it was amended by the Health Act 2004.

(2) Where a family welfare conference convened under *section 7* on behalf of the Health Service Executive has not discharged its functions before the establishment day of the Health Service Executive, the conference shall be deemed to have been convened on behalf of the Executive.

(3) Where a direction given by the Health Service Executive under *section 7(3)* to a family welfare conference is not complied with before the establishment day of the Health Service Executive, the direction shall be deemed to have been given to the Executive.

(4) Where a recommendation has been made or a matter has been referred to the Health Service Executive by a family welfare conference under *section 8* and all matters relating to or arising from the conference proceedings relating to the child concerned have not been concluded under this Act or the Child Care Act 1991 before the establishment day of the Health Service Executive, the recommendation shall be deemed for the purposes of this Act and the Child Care Act 1991 to have been made or the matter referred to the Executive.]

Amendment

Section 15A inserted by s.75 and Schedule 7 of the Health Act 2004, No.42 of 2004, with effect from January 1, 2005 (S.I. No.887 of 2004).

Amendment of sections 17(2) and 59 of Act of 1991

267.—(1) The Act of 1991 is hereby amended—
  (*a*) in *paragraphs* (*a*) and (*b*) of *section 17(2)* (period in care of health board under interim care order), by the substitution of "twenty-eight days" for "eight days", and
  (*b*) in *section 59* (definitions for purposes of Part VIII), by the deletion of *paragraph* (*c*) from the definition of "children's residential centre".

(2) References in *Part V* (Jurisdiction and Procedure) of the Act of 1991 to *Part IV* of that Act shall be construed as including references to *Parts IVA* and *IVB* (inserted by *section 16*) thereof.

Index